Pandemic, Disruption and Adjustment in Higher Education

Comparative and International Education

A DIVERSITY OF VOICES

Series Editors

Allan Pitman (*University of Western Ontario, Canada*)
Miguel A. Pereyra (*University of Granada, Spain*)
Suzanne Majhanovich (*University of Western Ontario, Canada*)

Editorial Board

Ali Abdi (*University of Alberta, Canada*)
Clementina Acedo (*Webster University Geneva, Switzerland*)
Mark Bray (*University of Hong Kong, China*)
Christina Fox (*University of Wollongong, Australia*)
Steven Klees (*University of Maryland, USA*)
Nagwa Megahed (*Ain Shams University, Egypt*)
Crain Soudien (*University of Cape Town, South Africa*)
David Turner (*University of Glamorgan, England*)
Medardo Tapia Uribe (*Universidad Nacional Autónoma de Mexico*)

VOLUME 53

The titles published in this series are listed at *brill.com/caie*

Pandemic, Disruption and Adjustment in Higher Education

Edited by

Susana Gonçalves and Suzanne Majhanovich

BRILL

LEIDEN | BOSTON

Cover illustration: Photograph by Susana Gonçalves

All chapters in this book have undergone peer review.

The Library of Congress Cataloging-in-Publication Data is available online at https://catalog.loc.gov

Typeface for the Latin, Greek, and Cyrillic scripts: "Brill". See and download: brill.com/brill-typeface.

ISSN 2214-9880
ISBN 978-90-04-51265-8 (paperback)
ISBN 978-90-04-51266-5 (hardback)
ISBN 978-90-04-51267-2 (e-book)

Copyright 2022 by Koninklijke Brill NV, Leiden, The Netherlands.
Koninklijke Brill NV incorporates the imprints Brill, Brill Nijhoff, Brill Hotei, Brill Schöningh, Brill Fink, Brill mentis, Vandenhoeck & Ruprecht, Böhlau Verlag and V&R Unipress.
All rights reserved. No part of this publication may be reproduced, translated, stored in a retrieval system, or transmitted in any form or by any means, electronic, mechanical, photocopying, recording or otherwise, without prior written permission from the publisher. Requests for re-use and/or translations must be addressed to Koninklijke Brill NV via brill.com or copyright.com.

This book is printed on acid-free paper and produced in a sustainable manner.

Contents

Foreword VII
   Allan Pitman
List of Figures and Tables X
Notes on Contributors XII

1 Introduction: Pandemic, Disruption and Adjustment in Higher Education 1
   Susana Gonçalves and Suzanne Majhanovich

PART 1
New Modes of Teaching

2 Ramifications of COVID-19 for Higher Education Systems and Institutions 15
   Pete Leihy, Brigid Freeman, Ian Teo and Dong Kwang Kim

3 Transformation of Universities during the COVID-19 Pandemic: Digitalization, New Formats, "Re-education of Educators" 31
   Vadim Kozlov, Elena Levina and Tatiana Tregubova

4 Thoughts on Higher Education for Sustainable Development (HESD) amid the Pandemic 46
   Weimin Delcroix-Tang

5 Digitalization of Higher Education in Turkey and COVID-19 59
   Nilüfer Pembecioğlu

6 Switching to Online Teaching within a Teacher Training Programme during the COVID-19 Pandemic 85
   Dana Crăciun and Monica Oprescu

7 The Pandemic and the End of the Lecture 100
   Pete Woodcock

8 Facing Adversity at the University: A Case Study to Reflect on Pedagogical Challenges in Times of Pandemic Risk 112
   Aurora Ricci and Elena Luppi

PART 2
Teaching from Home: Teachers' Wellbeing

9   'Overall It Was OK': COVID-19 and the Wellbeing of University
    Teachers   131
    Susan Beltman, Rachel Sheffield and Tina Hascher

10 Rethinking Academic Teaching at and beyond the Pandemic   147
    Marta Ilardo and Morena Cuconato

11 Higher Education Academics' Perspectives: Working from Home during
    COVID-19   157
    Rashmi Watson, Upasana Singh and Chenicheri Sid Nair

12 Reconnecting Teaching Discourse in Higher Education: Establishing and
    Remodeling Interfaces   171
    Beatrix Kreß

13 Afterword   180
    Suzanne Majhanovich and Allan Pitman

    Index   187

Foreword

Allan Pitman

In trying to make sense of the ways in which the 2020 SARS-CoV2 (COVID-19 pandemic and the political responses to it had impact on university faculty members, a group of scholars contributing to this collection have taken multiple approaches to study the problem, both from a range of geographic locations and at different levels of institutional analysis, while maintaining a focus on the changed professional lives of academics involved in teaching. Thus, the volume consists of some work that looks at systemic issues while other writers concentrate on the local and institutional and personal levels. We then have the central question: How has the sudden disruption of the existing routines of university life played out in the professional lives of university faculty members? This concern has then been broken into two parts: one related to teaching methods and the transition of much teaching to an on-line modality, the second on the loss of presence on campus as campuses were closed to in-person contacts between faculty, their students and each other with the consequences for their wellbeing.

A crisis has effects at multiple levels throughout societies and their institutions, at the macro-, meso- and micro-levels. Such crises may be triggered by any number of causes: economic disruption, social upheaval, international political tensions and a myriad of other forms. The advent of the SARS-CoV2 (COVID-19) pandemic of 2020 and later provides an excellent context for considering the strengths and fragilities of institutions as they adapt and are transformed by major disruptions to their modes of operation and organizational and financial structures when crisis occurs.

Universities have been hit heavily by the emergence of the virus and by the political and health policy responses to it. The pandemic has triggered a set of crises across every aspect of society, internationally as well as within nations.

Organizations can be viewed from two interconnected positions. First, there is the organizational, administrative dimension; second, the work conducted within the organization has its own distinct features, strengths and vulnerabilities.

The crisis has had varied effects on universities in different national settings. Throughout the Western world, the prevalence of neoliberal economic and political policies has tied universities more tightly than ever into the local and international trade and employment policies of governments, with the concomitant dependence of these institutions on revenue generation other than that obtained through government funding. Increasingly, the shift of post-secondary knowledge and training into the economic and trade sector has seen universities in these countries dependent for much of their operating costs on the on-campus presence of international students (see, for example, Pitman, 2022). On the other hand, in other parts of the world this has not been the major problem: rather, a lack of resources (at the institutional and personal levels) is more of a driving problem in dealing with the loss of on-campus interactions.

The arrival of the impacts of the 2020 pandemic brought all of these into focus, but not for the first time. The "Asian Flu" economic crisis of 1997, for example, which originated in Thailand and spread through the Pacific region (International Monetary Fund, 2012), had major effects on the Australian university system, dependent as many of its universities and specific departments were on the sale of degree programs and courses to students from southeast Asia. Particularly affected then were Business Schools around the world due to a sharp drop in demand. Massive declines were seen in foreign enrolments in Engineering and Technology, particularly in Information Technology departments, which had ballooned in the previous years as sources of student fee income. The outcome was the near-bankruptcy of some universities and the closure of a number of Departments with the termination of tenured faculty members.

Now as then, at the institutional level, budgets were hard hit, with many universities and colleges dependent for up to a third of their student body being full-fee paying foreign undergraduate and graduate students. This has precipitated reassessments of the short- and long-term viability of individual Departments and programs, and in many cases has led to significant cuts in faculty and support staffing.

The point to be emphasized here is the complex play between uniqueness and the to-be-expected nature of the current situation created by responses to the COVID pandemic in universities. While organizationally universities are vulnerable to disruption to their working models, the COVID situation is unique in its closure of in-person on-campus activities for an extended period and the necessity to shift teaching to remote learning models.

Historically, the role of universities has been in the education of those entering a range of the professions and for the study of the disciplines of knowledge. Over time and in interaction with the technologies of the day, the work associated with fulfilling this mandate has evolved, while maintaining certain characteristic features. These features are of both a knowledge transmission and social interaction form: lectures, seminars and other on-campus and near-campus activities such as student clubs, fraternities etc. are significant among these. In a sense, the university has been expected to provide to students a development beyond the learning within the lecture hall and texts, to include a rather more general growth of the whole individual – closer to the northern European notions of Bildung than a straightforward degree qualification. The effect of the growing reliance on international students has varied greatly between universities, ranging from the intensification of on-line and other remote learning models and of making very little adjustment away from traditional lecture – seminar models.

The context in which faculty now work has become one in which the future is less certain and workload stresses have increased. The focus of this book is on the teaching role rather than that of research activity. Here, the increase in workload involves new or enhanced skill development associated with teaching at a distance, in development of on-line materials and in real-time on-line presentations and interactions with students.

For many academics, the pandemic has led to a severing of the day-to-day in-person interactions with fellow faculty and with students. This has constituted both a loss of one significant form of intellectual discourse and also to a weakening of internal institutional interpersonal relationships.

With respect to the shift to on-line provision of coursework, the pandemic can be seen as having accelerated a process which was occurring already as the online technologies were being integrated into complementary roles with in-person contacts in the years prior to 2020. In this regard, some institutions were better prepared than others to be able to assist faculty as they were forced to translate their courses from structures based on in-person or mixed mode delivery to wholly on-line.

It is still too soon to draw conclusions about the significance and permanence of the changes that have taken place, or to the long-term effects on the stress levels and conflicts in how faculty members understand their roles in academia. Central to this concern is how they see their relationships with their students and with each other.

References

International Monetary Fund. (2012). *Asian Flu: Financial crisis in the Pacific*.
https://www.imf.org/external/pubs/ft/history/2012/pdf/c11.pdf

Pitman, A. (2022). The World Trade Organization and the entrepreneurial university: The global competition for students. In D. Turner, Y. Hüseyin, & S. Hüsrevşahi (Eds.), *The role of international organizations in education*. Brill.

Figures and Tables

Figures

2.1 Positioning the higher education in emergencies domains within an emergency management framework. 19

4.1 The whole-institution approach (from UNESCO, 2017, p. 53). 49

5.1 Distribution of the HE students in Turkey (2019–2020). 73

6.1 Comic created by students during the CAI course. 91

6.2 Pre-service teachers' responses regarding the use of technology. 92

6.3 Preservice teachers' competences formed during completing the initial teacher training programme. 95

8.1 Phases of the learning and teaching innovation process (from Luppi et al., 2021). 114

8.2 The CIPP model of evaluation (from Stufflebeam, 1983). 117

9.1 Andrew's wellbeing plot line. 137

9.2 Jennifer's wellbeing plot line. 138

9.3 Peter's wellbeing plot line. 140

9.4 Sia's wellbeing plot line. 140

11.1 Themes emerging from challenges associated with the forced WFH scenario. 163

11.2 Benefits in working from home. 165

12.1 Silhouette adult, male and female (from Krumm & Jenkins, 2001; open source http://heteroglossia.net/Home.2.0.html). 176

12.2 Two language portraits, one with migration background (left); one "monolingual" portrait (right) (adapted from Krumm & Jenkins, 2001). 177

Tables

2.1 Defining higher education in emergencies domains. 17

5.1 Distance education agenda in the COVID-19 period. 63

6.1 Competences formed after the teacher training programme (1 totally disagree – 5 totally agree). 94

8.1 Distribution of participants by class enrolment. 119

8.2 Input variables: Paired t-test comparing the face to face and emergency distance learning. 120

8.3 Process variables: Paired t-test comparing the face to face and emergency distance learning. 121

FIGURES AND TABLES

8.4 Product variables: Paired t-test comparing the face to face and emergency distance learning. 122

9.1 Timeline for university and research activities. 133

9.2 Workplace-related challenges, frequency and example. 136

9.3 Nominated successes, frequency and example. 136

9.4 Strategies, resources, frequency and example. 137

11.1 Challenges faced by academics. 162

11.2 Sustainability of work at home. 166

11.3 Communication tools used (with students & staff). 167

Notes on Contributors

Susan Beltman

is Associate Professor and has taught and developed units relating to educational psychology and mentoring. She researches in the areas of wellbeing, resilience and mentoring in various education settings. She has been part of nationally and internationally funded projects and published widely in the area of teacher resilience. Susan was one of the developers of the fully online BRiTE modules designed to develop preservice teachers' capacity for resilience which now have over 12,000 users.

Dana Crăciun

is Senior Lecturer in the Teacher Training Department at the West University of Timişoara, Romania. She has received her BSC in Physics (1988) and in Mathematics (2004), her MSC in Theoretical Physics (2003) and her PhD in Physics (2010) at the West University of Timişoara. She has been teaching courses in ICT, Didactics of Physics in the pre-service teacher training programme. Her research interests are also in the field of Science Education, Bioinformatics, as well as different aspects of e-Learning and Computer Assisted Instruction applied in Natural Sciences and Humanities. She has participated in educational projects and has co-authored 13 books and more than 40 ISI papers.

Morena Cuconato

is Associate Professor at the University of Bologna since 2002 and since 1996 a member of the international research group EGRIS (European Group for Integrated Social Research). She has been researching in several EU-funded research projects on young people's transition from youth to adulthood with a special focus on second-generation young people. Her main research areas are youth education, youth policy and welfare, intercultural education and migration literature. Her recent international publications include "Doing transition in Education" (edited with A. Walther) of the *International Journal of Qualitative Studies in Education* (Routledge, Taylor and Francis group, 2015). In 2017 she published *Pedagogia e letteratura della migrazione. Sguardi sulla scrittura che cura e resiste* [Pedagogy and Migration Literature. The healing and resisting power of writing] (Carocci).

Weimin Delcroix-Tang

(née Weimin Tang) holds a PhD in English from the University of Oxford, UK, as well as Masters degrees in Women's Studies, English and Sinology from the

University of Oxford, UK, and University of Trier, Germany. Currently she is the dean of the School of Foreign Languages, director of the Language and Culture Research Center at the University of Sanya, and Deputy Director of the Hainan Association of Comparative Literature and World Literature, China. Apart from her expertise in areas of literary and cultural studies where she has published widely, she directs and evaluates curriculum design, teaching practice and teacher training as the deputy director of the Hainan Provincial Advisory Board on Foreign Language Teaching in Higher Education.

Brigid Freeman

is academic fellow with the Australia India Institute at the University of Melbourne, with research interests in higher education, policy, governance and comparative education.

Susana Gonçalves

(PhD, Psychology) is a Professor at the Polytechnic of Coimbra. She is a researcher at NIEFI, the Research Unit for Education, Training and Intervention (Escola Superior de Educação de Coimbra) and she teaches Psychology and Intercultural Education and a range of topics in the field of cultural studies. She is a member of the Children's Identity and Citizenship in Europe Association, where she has served as Secretary General from September 2007 to September 2019. She has been Director of the Centre for the Study and Advancement of Pedagogy in Higher Education (CINEP) from 2011 till 2021. Her main research interests are art in education, citizenship and Higher Education. Among other publications, she co-edited with Suzanne Majhanovich the books *Art in Diverse Social Settings* (Emerald, 2021) and *Art and Intercultural Dialogue* (Sense, 2016), and with M.A. Carpenter the books *The Challenges of Diversity and Intercultural Encounters* (Routledge, 2013) and *Intercultural Policies and Education* (Peter Lang, 2011). She is also a visual artist and a photographer.

Tina Hascher

is a professor of Education Science at the University of Bern, Switzerland. Her research interests lie in emotions and motivation in school, wellbeing and health education as well as teacher education. She graduated from studies in Psycholinguistics, Psychology and Special Education at the LM-University in Munich, Germany. Her PhD studies were completed at the Max-Planck-Institute for Psychological Research in Munich and her Habilitation (post-doc studies, Habilitation thesis: "Well-being in school") at the University of Fribourg, Switzerland. She is the recipient of multiple research grants and has over 200 publications.

Marta Ilardo

holds a PhD in educational sciences, research fellow at the Department of Education Studies "Giovanni Maria Bertin", University of Bologna. Her interests have focused on Hannah Arendt's thought in education and the themes that investigate the relationship between violence, power and educational contexts/spaces. She conducts research on issues relating to teaching-learning process in Higher Education Institutions; childhood and philosophy (philosophical practices with children and critical thinking); youth participation practices in formal and non-formal contexts of education.

Dong Kwang Kim

is a professor at Okayama University's Institute of Global Human Resource Development and teaches Global Studies.

Vadim Kozlov

is Director of the Institute of Pedagogy, Psychology and Social Problems (Kazan, Russia), a Candidate of Historical Sciences, and Associate Professor. He is a Member of the Scientific Council of the Russian Academy of Sciences on complex problems of ethnicity and interethnic relations, a Member of the Council under the President of the Tatarstan Republic on interethnic and interfaith relations. He has been teaching at Kazan Federal University for 20 years. The focus of his scientific interests is the issues of inter-ethnic and interreligious interaction, ethnic conflicts, migration, and ethnic minorities. He is the author of more than 10 monographs, including: *Ethnology* (2017), *Positive Interethnic Relations and the Prevention of Intolerance: The Experience of Tatarstan in the All-Russian Context* (2016), *Diaspora and Migrant Communities in the Republic of Tatarstan: Ethnosociological Essays* (2016). He participated in a great number of international and all-Russian conferences as the Chair of organizational committee, as a presenter, as an expert and a member of the international consortium in social-educational projects.

Beatrix Kreß

is a linguist and full professor for intercultural communication at Hildesheim University. She studied Slavic languages and literature and wrote her PhD about conflict communication in Russian and Czech. She teaches intercultural communication, applied linguistics and German as a foreign language. Research interests are oral and written forms of intercultural communication, political and media communication and theoretical and empirical aspects of pragmatics.

Pete Leihy

teaches at Universidad Andres Beilo, Chile where he researches higher education and society and is co-editing a forthcoming special issue of Quality Assurance in Education covering higher education in Spanish- and Portuguese-speaking countries.

Elena Levina

is Doctor of Pedagogical Sciences, Head of the Department "Cognitive Pedagogy and Digitalization of Education" of the Institute of Pedagogy, Psychology and Social Problems, Editor-in-chief of the *Kazan Pedagogical Journal*. She is Head of the project of the Ministry of Science and Higher Education of the Russian Federation "The problem of modern methodology for studying the formation and development of human beings in the era of digitalization". She teaches the disciplines Higher education management, Quality management in education, and others. Research interests are concentrated in the field of higher education methodology in the era of digitalization, the development of data mining methods, and the development of cognitive management in higher education. Some publications include *Qualimetric Methods of Diagnosing Educational Activities* (2011); *Mechanisms for Managing the Development of Educational Systems* (2015); *Innovative Systems for Managing the Development of Higher Education* (2018); *Cognitive Management for Educational Organizations of Higher Education* (2019).

Elena Luppi

(PhD) is Associate Professor in Educational Research at the University of Bologna – Department of Education. She is currently Rector's Delegate for Innovation in Teaching and Learning at the University of Bologna and has been Rector's Delegate for Gender Equality. She carries out Evidence Based Research and Action Research on Design, Assessment and Evaluation in Education. She is expert in Lifelong Learning – especially Education of the Elderly, Intergenerationality, Elderly Care – and in Gender issues, tackling these topics with an interdisciplinary perspective. She is the author of books and articles concerning these subjects. She is the Italian representative for the University of Bologna in WiTEC (the European Association for Women in Science, Engineering and Technology). She lectures in "Theories and Methods of Planning and Evaluation" and "Methodology of Educational Research".

Suzanne Majhanovich

is Professor Emerita/Adjunct Research Professor at the Faculty of Education, University of Western Ontario in London, Ontario, Canada. She is the past

Chair of the wcces Standing Committee for Publications and the former editor of the journal Canadian and International Education. With Allan Pitman, she co-edits of the Brill series *A Diversity of Voices*. She was guest editor of four special issues of the International Review of Education related to presentations from wcces Congresses in Havana, Sarajevo, Istanbul, and Buenos Aires. Her research interests include first and second language acquisition, esl teaching in international contexts, globalization, education restructuring, decentralization and privatization of education. She is the author of numerous articles and books, including a special issue of the *International Review of Education*, co-edited with Marie-Christine Deyrich, entitled "Language Learning to Support Active Social Inclusion: Issues and Challenges for Lifelong Learning" (2017). Most recently she co-edited with Susana Gonçalves *Art in Diverse Social Settings* (Emerald, 2021).

Chenicheri Sid Nair

is currently the Executive Dean at the Victorian Institute of Technology, Australia. His primary role looks at the quality of Learning, Teaching and the Student Experience. Prior to this he was the Executive Director of the Tertiary Education Commission, Mauritius responsible for the formulation and execution of strategies, policies and procedures in the higher education sector in Mauritius. Before taking up the role at tec, Mauritius, he was Professor of Higher Education Development at The University of Western Australia. His research work lies in the areas of quality of teaching and learning, classroom and school environments, and the implementation of improvements from stakeholder feedback.

Monica Oprescu

is Senior Lecturer in the Teacher Training Department at the West University of Timişoara, Romania. Her teaching and research interests are in the fields of English Didactics, clil/Content and Language Integrated Learning, Cultural Identities, Literary Studies, Interdisciplinary Approaches in the training of future teachers. She received her PhD at the West University of Timişoara and is enrolled for a second one at the University of Vienna. She has been involved in educational projects, being institutional coordinator for the West University of Timişoara of cice (Children's Identity and Citizenship in Europe). She has published teaching guides, translations, chapters in volumes and articles extensively in journals (e.g., *Journal of Educational Studies & Psychology, Romanian Journal of English Studies*).

Nilüfer Pembecioğlu

is an academic of the Istanbul University Faculty in the Communication Radio Television Cinema Department. Professor Pembecioğlu has many articles on a national and international basis regarding education, communication, journalism, peace education and peace journalism, new media, children, women and advertising fields. Specialized in Children & Media Issues and Media Literacy, her academic interests also cover Social Discrimination and Exclusion, Cyber Bullying, Systemic Family Therapy, Film Therapy and she has served as consultant for various institutions and organizations. She is a film director having 8 feature documentary films. Out of the film workshops she organizes with children, she has around 30 short films and 8 animations. Coordinating many national and international academic projects and she works more with disadvantaged groups such as refugees, gifted, deaf and handicapped children. She also has 15 books, many book chapters, academic papers as well as international research projects.

Allan Pitman

is Professor Emeritus in the Education Faculty at the University of Western Ontario. He holds degrees from the University of Melbourne, Latrobe University and the University of Wisconsin-Madison. He has held tenured positions at Deakin University in Australia and at the University of Western Ontario, and was a Research Consultant in the Wisconsin Center for Education Research. He is a former President of the Comparative and International Education Society of Canada and was awarded its David Wilson Award for his contribution to comparative and international education. He has been Secretary of the Higher Education Research Society of Australia. His principal research interests are mathematics education and society, the changing nature of the university and the nature of professional practice.

Aurora Ricci

(PhD) is Research Fellow in the field of Educational Research (M-PED04) at the University of Bologna (Department of Education) on the research project "The promotion of quality in university teaching". She carries out Evidence Based Research and Action Research on Design, Assessment and Evaluation in Education (Higher Education and Vocational Education and Training). In particular, she is an expert in Soft Skills (developing innovative pedagogical methodology and self-assessment and evaluation tools) with a multidisciplinary perspective (soft skills for guidance and soft skills for safety). Furthermore, she is involved as a gender issues expert in the Horizon2020 Project "H-Work". She lectures in "Educational research" and "Soft skills to be effective at work".

Rachel Sheffield

is Associate Professor and researches and publishes in science, STEM education and professional identity. She is currently exploring the transversal competencies and their role in STEM. Rachel has won several Faculty, University and National awards for Teaching Excellence, and was awarded an Executive Endeavour Fellowship in 2016. She is also the Chair of the prestigious Curtin Academy for excellence in Learning and Teaching. Her research and grants in India, Indonesia and Malaysia support pre-service teachers and primary students to develop expertise in STEM content and 21st century skills.

Upasana Singh

is a senior lecturer in the Discipline of Information Systems and Technology at the University of KwaZulu Natal, Westville Campus, in Durban South Africa. She lectures on a wide-range of IT-related subjects and she has a keen interest in Educational Technologies. In 2019 she completed her Fellowship in "Teaching Advancement in Universities" (TAU), from the CHE. Her primary area of research is Digital Teaching and Learning in Higher Education.

Ian Teo

works as a researcher in the Centre of Education Policy and Practice, which is located in the Australian Council for Educational Research.

Tatiana Tregubova

is Doctor of Pedagogical Sciences, professor, and leading researcher of the Institute of Pedagogy, Psychology and Social Problems, Director of the Center for international cooperation and academic mobility. Successfully engaged in fundraising activities, she coordinates the participation of the Institute in international projects and programmes: "TEMPUS-IV," "ERASMUS+", "FULBRIGHT," etc. Her research agenda concerns tertiary professional education for teachers as well as social-pedagogical services for students, women's issues and issues of diversity in educational settings. She has published more than 300 books, journal articles, and textbooks on professional education and social work, development of students' social activity. Among them are: *Models of Competencies in the Conditions of Globalization and Integration of Education* (2015), *Theory and Practice of Multicultural Education* (2017); *Teachers' Professional Development in the Process of Workers' Training for Worldskills Championships' Participation* (2019); *Professional Development of Teachers: Conceptual Ideas and Benchmarking of Best Practices* (2020).

Rashmi Watson

(Assessment Lead, Medical Education Unit) has been recognised for university teaching and for her leadership skills and knowledge of university programs and is called upon regularly to provide senior-level support. In recent years, she has strengthened her expertise in leadership and culture development and provides facilitation and strategic consultancy using strengths-based approaches such as Appreciative Inquiry, coaching and psychometric behaviour analysis to support organisations in their journey towards greater staff culture and continuous development and learning.

Pete Woodcock

teaches politics at the University of Huddersfield in the United Kingdom and specialises in political theory and the impact of technology on politics. He has published several papers on using technology to support teaching and learning in higher education, and is interested in how educators can use student's informal education to help grapple with key political concepts. His book *Political Theory: A Beginner's Guide* was published by Polity in 2020.

CHAPTER 1

Introduction: Pandemic, Disruption and Adjustment in Higher Education

Susana Gonçalves and Suzanne Majhanovich

The campus can be seen as an ecosystem where students acquire information and develop knowledge and skills, character and worldviews together. Students learn from teachers and from multimedia learning resources, from devices, labs and classrooms as well as from their peers in formal and informal contexts. The university promotes not only the acquisition of up-to-date and grounded professional information and terminology, but also deontology, human relations, tacit knowledge, intellectual tools, modes of doing and living styles. Besides that, the campus also promotes values, expectations and desires for the future. It is a social hub and as such, it works as a laboratory of life that generates emotions, sensations, beliefs and guesses. Being a community in itself, with its own dynamic culture, the campus is not only made of ground, buildings and equipment, it is a network of souls, dreams and expectations.

One of the first dimensions of the university functioning to have been corrupted by the coronavirus pandemic because of the lockdown and forced distance learning was the socioecological fabric of the university. Due to the COVID-19 pandemic, many students were prevented from living the full academic experience, as emergency remote teaching became the rule worldwide. The academic years 2019–2020 and 2020–21 signal the advent of a profound change in Higher Education and the time that made us realize that the way courses work may be changed – and perhaps has to be changed – in order to accommodate any threads and challenges in the near future.

While some authors (e.g. Harrikari, Romakkaniemi, Tiitinen & Ovaskainen, 2021) claim this pandemic is a black swan event (Taleb, 2010) others avoid such a classification (McGillivray, 2020) as this pandemic was expectable somewhere in our times and it is not an outlier (pandemics are common and have happened all over documented history). The fact is that the global lockdown and the associated pervasive fear provided an impulse for creative solutions and the world kept on going. Some of those solutions will remain in the near future as they seem to work well – not only because they solve problems, but they solve them in a sustainable way.

© KONINKLIJKE BRILL NV, LEIDEN, 2022 | DOI:10.1163/9789004512672_001

Remote emergency teaching generated enormous online dynamism of both faculty and students. It caused the improvement of videoconferencing systems (Zoom, Teams, JITSI, Google Meets, etc.), it fostered the development of digital competence of academics, online assessment and plagiarism control programs appeared, encouraged reform of teaching methods and programs to better adjust to computer-mediated teaching, and a lot of training sessions, workshops and webinars in the area of educational technology were offered. Ultimately, people survived this digital flood of academic life and Institutions resisted, adjusted and adapted to the new circumstances. Many innovative experiences took place in the online classrooms. Within the scope of SOTL numerous studies where developed that elucidate the perspectives of students and clarify the special features and dimensions of remote teaching in general and especially emergency remote teaching. The international sharing of pedagogical experiences has generated a database of information and extensive knowledge of online teaching and the best responses to forced social distance. This collective learning movement accompanied the movement in science R&D at the service of public health (as we have seen, within a year several companies developed vaccines, hopefully effective to vaccinate the population and fight COVID-19 efficiently). Various sectors of society and the economy have been altered in an unprecedented crisis, but the results glorify human resilience and creativity, and the power of collective union.

In great crises great opportunities arise. Economic, social, security, environmental or other crises, including the personal crises that individuals experience throughout their lives, although they can leave traumas and scars, are also turning points that allow the creation of new adaptive tools, new skills, new understandings of reality and maturing of points of view. Crises always lead to a kind of practical wisdom. We also know that in the first moments of security or abundance after serious crises such as war, famine, environmental devastation or pandemics, there is an excessive need to return to a previous normal life and this manifests itself with an exaggeration of socializing, consumption, dissipation and some irresponsibility concerning the future. It is a moment of antithesis that precedes the synthesis, maturation and beginning of a new paradigm. Now, what will be the synthesis for society in general and for higher education in particular? What paradigm is being drawn?

What form will the new normal take in Higher Education? For sure academic resilience grew and, in rigour, this is not a true revolution or dawn of novel things. It is just accentuating trends that had already been on stage. Here are some of them:
- On the one hand, the revaluation of the practical interest of science and greater transparency and consumption of science communication (therein a role/opportunity for the media and for universities).

INTRODUCTION

– On the other hand, the rise of individualism and the empire of the "I" that abounds in young people increases in tone with the demand for everyone to be heard with a personal voice, to self-broadcast, and the appreciation of success in individual online commercial ventures (e.g. Instagram, Tik Tok, ETSY as places of business), the fostering of personal brands and ideological assertion. This individualism can result in a self-centered post-constructivist tendency to accept that everything is worth it as long as "I", the individual believes in it and desires it.
– At the same time, there is greater volatility of the concepts in the so-called late modernity or liquid society (Bauman, 2000) – nothing is seen as being for life, everything is replaceable, and recyclable – the *Ikea model* spills over into all areas of life.
– The largest technological and digital support in the world of work and the immediate, universal and complex access to learning from complex technical and theoretical topics to everyday knowledge that allow DIY (acronym for *Do It Yourself*) and the transformation of people without formal qualifications into specialists in various fields and arts. In social networks, teachers of various arts abound who teach, often with very high pedagogical quality and technical rigor, the knowledge, ideas and techniques that were once reserved for the domain of the school and formal learning spaces.
– Accelerated change in social values and even ethical and moral values. Notions of privacy and intimacy are diluted in favor of social visibility and charisma present in social networks; the triumph of vanity and arrogance and the cult of alpha people (owners and social status, wealth, fame or influence) seem to emerge in association with authoritarian forms of leadership and populist movements. At the same time, and this is one of the great paradoxes of our time, we are also witnessing innovative forms of social and environmental activism and change in consumption habits, in certain groups of young people and socio-political quadrants associated with green ideologies and volunteering movements who call for social justice.

Higher education institutions will have to deal with these paradoxes and contingencies. Is it to be expected that this new reality will make young people less receptive to monotonous classes, away from their direct – and more demanding – interests of entertainment, success or individualization? Just think of the global success of some star professors from major North American universities (e.g. Jordan B Peterson in psychology or Michael Sandel in law and philosophy), whose lectures and videotaped lectures account for many thousands (or even millions) of views on YouTube, to ask ourselves which classes, teaching styles and teacher profiles will be best positioned to attract young university students in the near future.

The hedonism that has characterized the new generations makes us think that these students will increasingly prefer classes that provide them with immediate satisfaction, including some aspect of entertainment, to traditional learning contexts that were slower, more focused on reading, methodical experiments or lecturing. The difficulty in overcoming frustration and boredom has always characterized young people, but current generations have gotten used to immediate gratification and easy access to information and being more visual (one of the consequences of the digital age, where the image almost surpassed writing as the source of information) also more easily reject reading stimuli, lengthy lectures or topics without immediate relevance. This is a pressing challenge for teaching at all levels.

We could then conjecture that distance learning, blended learning and other hybrid teaching models, with their admirable possibilities (self-paced learning, greater individualization of learning experiences, gamification, student-centered learning, flipped classrooms, etc.) would be the suitable model for new generations (cf. Pelletier et al., 2021). Emergency remote teaching that characterized the main form of teaching-learning since the beginning of the pandemic has become a laboratory for countless experiments and tests of this conjecture. All over the world, innovative computer-mediated teaching strategies have been developed and digital technological tools at the service of education have proliferated in an unimaginable way.

This book presents some of the experiences and reflections arising from this very unique period in the history of humanity, institutions and education. In other works (see Gonçalves & Majhanovich, 2021a, 2021b) we have already discussed the results of several teaching trials worldwide, both from the point of view of students and teachers. In this manuscript we are focused on how innovative higher education institutions have coped and adapted to the new reality, as well as on the very special topic of the personal and professional wellbeing of teachers when working from home.

When we consider the actions taken by universities and colleges worldwide to preserve themselves in a highly destabilized situation caused by the pandemic that resulted in lockdowns, closure and disruption of all programs, we can see that the short and simple response was for them to resort to technology and move everything online. However, depending on the degree of prior development of the necessary technology to provide a workable alternative program, the transition did not play out equally across institutions and countries. Furthermore, simply putting all lectures and content online was an insufficient solution to address the complexity of programs, especially those requiring hands-on experiments or practicum placements in particular fields. How could research be carried out at a distance? Totally new approaches had to be developed to find ways to provide programs that allowed for interaction and active participation of the staff and students. Other factors had to be taken into account such as financial and funding considerations; fees for courses; maintenance of university buildings and residences; staffing considerations; managing examinations and records. In current times when many universities depend to a great deal on international students as a large part of their student body, how were they to cope in a time of restricted travel? The following chapters in Part 1, "New Modes of Teaching", outline various facets of the new reality that higher education institutes have had to deal with.

The first chapter, "Ramifications of COVID-19 for Higher Education Systems and Institutions" by Leihy, Freeman, Teo and Kim addresses the issues that arose during the pandemic from the perspective of an emergency management framework, considering how HE facilities in both developed and developing nations positioned themselves in terms of preparedness, prevention and mitigation, response and recovery. The authors identify nine areas that are impacted under an emergency: geopolitics and jurisdictions; system regulation; financing; infrastructure; teaching and learning; research and research training; pathways and portals; governance and leadership; and human resources. As they discuss each issue, they compare responses from educational systems in industrialized, highly developed countries such as Australia, Japan, the United Kingdom and the United States with those from developing economies – Chile, India and South Africa. They conclude that the COVID-19 emergency has been a catalyst for change that has demanded that stakeholders develop alternative and innovative ways of dealing with the conditions that arose because of the emergency situation in order to survive and persevere. The lessons learned from COVID-19 should provide guidelines on how to face future crises that will inevitably arise.

Kozlov, Levina and Tregubova in their chapter "Transformation of Universities during the COVID-19 Pandemic: Digitalization, New Formats, 'Re-education of Educators'" note that the Coronavirus has disrupted all aspects of society including even normally sustainable systems like education. They aim to show how the place of the university in civic society during this emergency situation has been rethought and transformed. They stress the importance of university teachers in making the "new normal" work and note the need for appropriate training of these people who will be responsible for implementing the "third mission" of the university which will involve social participation, intergenerational components, health conservation and cultural diversity among others. Digitalization has provided a means to realize the new way of fulfilling the university mission using imaginative and innovative ways to permit intercommunication. Surveys of university teachers and students yielded important information as to the efficacy and success of the digitalized formats. The authors note that the crisis situation has actually had the positive effect of forcing universities to address longstanding problems and indeed strengthen the universities' role within the development of the world order all the while respecting the integrity of what education and the humanities have to offer in the development of civil society.

The chapter by Delcroix-Tang, "Thoughts on Higher Education for Sustainable Development (HESD) amid the Pandemic" asserts that education in general and higher education in particular were perhaps the worst affected areas during the COVID-19 pandemic. The disruption caused by delay of programs or outright closure, and the unfortunate situation of stranded students away from their place of study either at home or abroad was mitigated by online education which most universities hastened to offer as an alternative means to ensure course continuity. However, quality of online teaching and outcomes of student learning emerged as major challenges. Delcroix-Tang maintains that higher education is crucial to the achievement of Sustainable Development Goals but under the conditions of the pandemic, it became well-nigh impossible for higher education institutions struggling for their own existence to attain. Delcroix-Tang presents the case of Sanya University in China to show the transformational shift the university programs underwent to enable the university to meet Sustainable Development Goals. The necessary transformation involved an integrated educational approach, as well as an innovative educational and research approach along with a student-centered quality system. The success of the transformational changes led the author to conclude that the university needs to view the measures taken in the long term rather than just as a stopgap in order to be prepared for a future in which the pandemic is still present, or for future crises.

Nilufür Pembecioğlu in her chapter "Digitalization of Higher Education in Turkey and COVID-19" reports on the way Turkey has transitioned to digital education as a result of the restraints posed by the pandemic situation. She reviews the news coverage over the past several years on the transformations and notes that education has been restructured, functionalized and repositioned as a consequence of the pandemic. She detects through the media reports that educational ideals have changed. The majority of reports reflect a positive response to the new modalities and ways of providing educational programs. In addition, because of the changes, more participatory education, digital education and inclusive education now permeate all levels of the system.

As the pandemic took hold in 2020, across the world higher education institutions quickly closed their campuses and switched their programs from face

INTRODUCTION

to face to online. Depending on the nature of the educational program, different challenges arose in the transformation of delivery methods. In "Switching to Online Teaching within a Teacher Training Programme during the COVID-19 Pandemic", Crăcium and Oprescu provide a case study from the West University of Timişoara in Romania on how a teacher education program was adapted for the unusual pandemic conditions. They discuss the ways in which the program designers sought to make communication between students and instructors accessible and how to encourage student engagement; which elements of the program could be delivered asynchronously and where students should be instructed synchronously as well as how program assessment had to be adapted. The program also had to include training for instructors to facilitate the new means of instruction. Surveys with staff and students who participated in the online program were conducted to uncover their perceptions regarding the efficacy of the program and which elements of technology they found most useful and accessible. They also tried to measure pedagogical competences formed by the preservice teachers through the digital resources. The data gathered from the questionnaires will help course designers to improve online teaching activity in future as no doubt beyond the pandemic times, some parts of the program will continue to be offered digitally online.

In "The Pandemic and the End of the Lecture" Pete Woodcock provides a think piece in which he speculates on what will happen to the lecture after the pandemic is past and students return to onsite university classes. He notes that some have suggested that the changes in university courses brought about by the pandemic where virtually everything has been moved to an online distance teaching mode will result in a radical change in the way universities operate in future. Woodcock contends that when classes return to campus lecture halls, the education students receive will largely revert to the way it was before the pandemic. He asserts that the lecture is a quintessential element of university life that cannot be replicated online. However, new techniques that have been learned from the online experience to encourage more interaction between lecturer and class may remain. In this way, COVID-19 has contributed to a certain transformation of delivery of content in educational settings. Whatever happens once COVID-19 is behind us, more questions remain: what do students think about online lectures? How should the institutional management respond to potential changes in the ways higher education is experienced? How should academics position themselves post-pandemic?

When the pandemic was declared, universities everywhere made the decision to close their campuses and move all courses to on-line learning. Although many universities already offered some of their courses in on-line versions and had some experience with how to set up the platforms for this type of learning, others had little experience and lacked the technological infrastructure for this massive transformation. In addition, some programs that required hands-on practicums and learning through hands-on practice were ill suited for a basic change to offering lectures on-line. In the chapter by Ricci and Luppi, "Facing Adversity at the University: A Case Study to Reflect on Pedagogical Challenges in Times of Pandemic Risk" the authors outline a case study of how teaching and learning practices changed at the School of Veterinary Medicine of the University of Bologna. They note that the University of Bologna as of March 2020 had transferred 100% or their courses online using Microsoft Teams as the platform. This translated into 3,667 lectures, 215,880 examinations and 10,069 graduations online in the semester. They stressed that internships were not interrupted however although they were carried on remotely. A survey was set up for the School of Veterinary Medicine to compare in class (pre-epidemic) with emergency distance learning. The results indicate that students understood that this was an emergency situation and so managed to maintain their motivation to learn, their self-efficacy and coping skills. Although satisfaction with the teaching practices proved to be medium to low, still the students were by and large happy with the quality of their learning. The authors conclude that in future universities will continue to use a mixture of teaching strategies including face-to face, distance and blended learning. They also see that universities may use the virtual learning environment to promote teaching and learning innovation.

In this first part of the book we have seen case study examples of the ways universities transformed programs during the pandemic so that they could sustain learning and research while adhering to the rules imposed by the pandemic involving closure of campuses, an end to in person learning and development of varieties of distance learning to accommodate the needs of the disciplines. The first chapter also offered a kind of template of factors to be considered during an emergency. These chapters show that despite the considerable challenges thrown up by the pandemic, universities remained resilient and developed innovative ways to permit them to continue their mission of education. In the next part we turn to the situation of the actors in this situation and how instructors managed their well-being during unprecedented times.

The world has been dealing with the pandemic for over a year now. How many times have people dared to hope that the end was in sight when yet another outbreak of COVID-19 occurred forcing yet another lockdown and preventing hoped-for reunions with family, friends and colleagues? It is no wonder that so many feel psychologically fragile and suffer from stress and anxiety. Teachers in higher education are no exception. Teaching is a social activity and so much depends on the interactions between teacher and students, and physical presence in the classroom environment. All this has changed because of the pandemic with universities closed down and courses being offered through distance education in virtual, digital spaces. Although course designers have done their best to create possibilities in the digital classroom that will in some way replicate an actual physical classroom and allow for the best practices of a regular class, it is not quite the same. Teachers and students still feel isolated; teachers complain about added workload necessary to make the online programs work; it is exhausting to spend so many hours in front of a screen or participating in endless Zoom meetings; teachers grow to resent being on call 24/7 for students who expect immediate feedback from posted work; many instructors required extensive training to gain the necessary knowledge to work in the digital environment. There is also the uncertainty of whether individuals' employment will continue, since online programs may not require the same number of instructors but may just rely on one expert to deliver the perfect lectures. There is no doubt that universities in the developed world that had grown to depend on the money brought in by international students suffered financial losses when they had to shut down their campuses. Even when programs were offered through a distance online mode, enrolment still fell resulting in some sections of courses or even parts of programs being cancelled altogether. This, of course resulted in staff layoffs, a source of great stress to instructors whose teaching positions became precarious. In this part of the book, we present several chapters addressing teachers' wellbeing while working from home.

In the first chapter in this part, "'Overall It Was OK': COVID-19 and the Wellbeing of University Teachers", Beltman, Sheffield and Hascher report on a study carried out in Western Australia on the wellbeing of instructors during the pandemic. The study arose because of earlier reports from the UK and Australia showing that 75% of university teachers claimed that working from home had negatively affected their psychological health. In this study the authors addressed the questions "How do university teachers appraise their wellbeing? What aspects of their working conditions do university teachers appraise as challenging? And what resources and strategies do university teachers draw upon to support their wellbeing? The research instruments consisted of a short online survey (pulse check) administered every two weeks over six weeks, followed by online interviews to capture the participants' perceptions of their wellbeing while working from home during the pandemic. They began with 27 participants to complete the "pulse checks" although the number declined over the weeks of the study. Four participants agreed to be interviewed. The researchers graphed a plot line representing the degree of well being of participants. In general, their sense of wellbeing rose and fell over the time of the study but typically declined as time went on. In some cases, as instructors became more confident in using the new technologies in their teaching, the sense of wellbeing improved. Their findings concerning the challenges instructors faced as well as the resources and strategies they called upon to help them through the difficult situation will be helpful for institutions seeking to find ways to support their teaching staff under such emergency situations.

The next chapter by Ilardo and Cuconato, "Rethinking Academic Teaching at and beyond the Pandemic" provides a short commentary on skills and reflective practices that higher education instructors need to develop to be able to meet the particular challenges that arose during the COVID-19 pandemic. They discuss how the role of HE teachers has changed in the knowledge society with the need to transform themselves from transmitters of knowledge to facilitators who involve the students' active participation in the learning process and also attempt through a variety of techniques to take into account the learning needs, interests, aspirations and cultural backgrounds of their students. When the pandemic forced universities to move all courses to the online format, that presented a new challenge to instructors if they were to continue the more inclusive ways of teaching. That meant that the design of the online modules had to ensure high levels of student-instructor interactions. They conclude that any technology used in future teaching situations must acknowledge the changes in teaching approaches to create the kind of learning environment that supports students in drawing their own conclusions and in developing critical thinking skills.

The chapter by Watson, Singh and Nair, "Higher Education Academics' Perspectives: Working from Home during COVID-19" provides another study from Australia, this time involving twelve universities with responses from 71 academics. The study focused on how instructors were coping while working from home during the pandemic. The study involved the collection of both qualitative and quantitative data. The researchers sought to sound the opinions of academic staff on the use of technology pre and post pandemic as well as specifically inquiring about arrangements made for working from home during the pandemic such as sustainability, challenges and future preparedness. Their findings uncovered issues related to the wellbeing of the participants while working from home alone, trying to carry on with their normal teaching and research programs. These included Pandemic anxiety, communication with colleagues, internet access with students and social isolation. Although the majority claimed that it would be possible to work from home indefinitely, most affirmed that should their institutions continue to use blended learning approaches post pandemic, instructors and students will require ongoing support from the institution to achieve any success in such programs.

Effective teaching should not involve solely the transmission of knowledge from the expert (teacher) to the learner; interactive participation enhances the learning experience. And yet when the pandemic struck, and universities were forced to place their courses online, there was the danger that the transmission mode of teaching would predominate. However, those tasked with transferring courses to online mode, creatively sought to include elements that would make the online experience an interactive one to enhance learning involvement. The last chapter in this part, "Reconnecting Teaching Discourse in Higher Education: Establishing and Remodelling Interfaces" by Beatrix Kreß offers an example of some adaptive teaching practices in the online environment that could improve the dynamics and interaction of collaborative and autonomous learning processes. She notes that even before the pandemic struck, universities were already fairly comfortable with different teaching modalities like mobile learning, and distance learning. This enabled an instructor to create a learning situation online that allowed for multiple perspectives, argumentation and a dialogue thus engendering a fruitful debate. She gives the example of an activity from her seminar on "Language and migration" that permitted students to express their point of view and receive feedback. Although the remote teaching scenario cannot replace the benefits of face-to-face classes, with some imaginative adaptations, it can provide a profitable learning experience supporting classroom discourse, and in some cases even some advantages to the learner that would not be possible in regular classrooms.

Over the past few decades where the influence of neoliberalism has brought about great changes to higher education institutions, making them leaner, meaner, business-oriented enterprises and threatening their traditional mission for engaging students in a liberal education, the entire higher education endeavour has become fragile; in some cases, its very survival is at stake. The continuity of long held values for education is no longer a certainty and change in purpose is assured. The COVID-19 pandemic has been a signal event that has brought many of the existential issues higher education is facing to the fore. The question now is what higher education will be like in a post-pandemic world. Fernando León Garcia, President of CETYS University (Centro de Enseñanza Técnica y Superior) in Mexico and incoming president of the International Association of University Presidents (IAUP) was interviewed on his opinions of what to expect post-pandemic (Sharma, 2021). He views recovery, transformation, innovation and inclusion as four key words describing what higher education institutions will have to face. Recovery implies economic recovery as the financial impact on universities during the pandemic has been great. He believes HE institutions need to start now to embrace transformation even while still battling the effects of the pandemic. He acknowledges that new innovative models for education delivery are needed and they will incorporate technology. However, the alternate delivery modes do not necessarily mean only through technology as many are sceptical about technology as the only way to meet the educational challenges. The response to the pandemic by universities has seen many innovative and transformative solutions to sustain higher education. The chapters in this book provide an overview of some of those responses as formulated by institutions and academics all over the world. While no one can declare we are home free, there is hope for a positive outcome for universities. We salute those who have worked to sustain higher education, surely, one of the most worthwhile endeavours.

References

Bauman, Z. (2000). *Liquid modernity*. Polity.

Gonçalves, S., & Majhanovich, S. (2021a). *Ensino Superior em Transição: Estudantes Online* [*Higher education in transition: Students online*]. CINEP/IPC.

Gonçalves, S., & Majhanovich, S. (2021b). *Pandemic and remote teaching in higher education*. CINEP/IPC.

Harrikari, T., Romakkaniemi, M., Tiitinen, L., & Ovaskainen, S. (2021, March 29). Pandemic and social work: Exploring Finnish social workers' Experiences through a SWOT analysis. *The British Journal of Social Work*, bcab052. https://doi.org/10.1093/bjsw/bcab052

McGillivray, G. (2020, April 30). Coronavirus is significant, but is it a true black swan event? *The Conversation*. https://theconversation.com/coronavirus-is-significant-but-is-it-a-true-black-swan-event-136675

Pelletier, K., Brown, M., Brooks, D. C., McCormack, M., Reeves, J., Arbino, N., Bozkurt, A., Crawford, S., Czerniewicz, L., Gibson, R., Linder, K., Mason, J., & Mondelli, V. (2021). *2021 EDUCAUSE horizon report, teaching and learning edition*. Educause. https://library.educause.edu/-/media/files/library/2021/4/2021hrteachinglearning.pdf?la=en&hash=C9DEC12398593F297CC634409DFF4B8C5A60B36E

Sharma, Y. (2021, June 19). IAUP: Leading universities into a post-pandemic world. *University World News*. https://www.universityworldnews.com/post.php?story=20210618153932412

Taleb, N. N. (2010). *The black swan: The impact of the highly improbable* (2nd ed.). Random House Trade Paperbacks.

PART 1

New Modes of Teaching

∵

CHAPTER 2

Ramifications of COVID-19 for Higher Education Systems and Institutions

Pete Leihy, Brigid Freeman, Ian Teo and Dong Kwang Kim

Abstract

The COVID-19 pandemic has destabilised higher education systems globally, nationally and locally. At present, while long-term ramifications of this emergency are unclear, early and ongoing responses have sought to avert COVID-induced institutional collapse.

Higher education systems are seeking to return to business-as-usual, while developing disruption-resilient responses by embracing rapid decision-making, technology-enabled learning, and flexible student admissions. At the same time, they are reimagining internationalization. This chapter provides a diagnostic lens through which to view how higher education systems and institutions have responded to the COVID-19 pandemic in industrialised (Australia, Japan, the United Kingdom, and the United States) and developing (Chile, India and South Africa) economies.

The study also examines how higher education stakeholders might better prepare for future crisis situations. In particular, a range of diagnostic indicators is proposed and evidenced to highlight how stakeholders might monitor institutional and sector-wide vulnerabilities and gaps in coverage at pre-crisis and post-crisis stages. The analysis closes with a presentation and discussion of indicators spanning system geopolitics and jurisdictions, system regulation, teaching and learning, research, pathways, governance and leadership, infrastructure, human resources and financing.

1 Outbreaks, Offshoots and Ramifications

The COVID-19 pandemic would serve as a catalyst both for change in the conditions of higher education and for active repositioning of public policy and institutions to exploit or simply withstand these new conditions. To project lasting ramifications is speculation that must be traced back to what we already know. Any prospect of a more stable environment calls on observation and analysis of vulnerabilities, inequalities and interdependencies that the pandemic has brought to bear. For learning communities, evidence and lack of emergency preparedness, response and recovery can be mined to prevent and mitigate future disruptions.

Great is the temptation either to long for things as they were and brisk trade in business as usual or to congratulate ourselves on forging new normals, or both, but in reality the monitoring and evaluation of what happened and why will remain a key and contested problematic. COVID-19 and its instantiations – outbreaks – occur and mutate in never entirely predictable ways as offshoots of ongoing effects. As these offshoots swell and harden into ramifications, we can begin to speculate how to accommodate and even exploit them. At the very least, they should help us prepare for future emergencies. If rolling alarm does not persist or return through a sufficiently challenging wave or mutation of coronavirus, it could be through something else. Here, a framing of broad components of higher education leads into a discussion focusing on the descriptions and positionings of various countries. We focus particularly on the 'industrialised' higher education of the United States, Japan, the United Kingdom, and Australia, and as yet 'developing' India, South Africa and Chile.

2 Conceptual Frameworks

This chapter introduces a diagnostic instrument for addressing education in emergencies (EiE), informed by a separate review of the higher education literature.

While the concept of EiE originates in the maintenance of education within man-made conflicts or natural disasters, it can also be applied to situations involving pandemics such as the COVID-19 crisis and its wide-ranging ramifications (UNESCO, n.d.).

Accordingly, the proposed instrument comprises nine generalisable domains for guiding government and institutional action and reactions to this and other EiE situations.

The indicators exemplify key elements of the domains, rather than serving as exhaustive or definitive catalogues. Table 2.1 outlines the domains, and corresponding domain definitions and indicators.

Emergency dynamics fall within the management framework proposed by the Australian Institute of Disaster Resilience (2020): Prevention and mitigation, Preparedness, Response, and Recovery (PPRR). Prevention involves eliminating and minimising risks and shocks. Preparedness is ensuring the availability of resources, services, and policies to support community response and recovery. Typically, preparations should be commensurate with the risk of emergencies, as anticipated by the auditing and testing of policies and

TABLE 2.1   Defining higher education in emergencies domains

Domains	Definition	Indicators
Geopolitics and jurisdictions	This domain covers national and supranational geographical and political pressures, and overall higher education systems	– Geopolitics – National jurisdiction and borders – Higher education system (institutions, faculty and staff, students, academic calendar)
System regulation	This domain focuses on the regulatory framework governing higher education institutions' academic and corporate practices, academic programs, student participation, accountability, competition and collaboration	– Academic practices and programs (teaching and assessment, curriculum and qualifications) – Corporate practices (finances, human resources, other contracts) – International mobility (international student and faculty visas) – Accountability – Competition and collaboration (domestic and international)
Financing	This domain focuses on the financial position of higher education institutions and student finances	– HEI revenue – HEI expenditure – HEI losses – Student finances
Infrastruture	This domain refers to infrastructure, assets, technology, and channels owned or managed by higher education institutions.	– Higher education infrastructure (teaching, research, accommodation, events, retail, sports) – Cultural institutions (galleries, libraries, archives, museums) – Technology – Traditional and new teaching and communication channels (distance and social media)
Teaching and learning	This domain refers to all aspects involved in the preparation, delivery, and assessment of teaching and learning including academic practices and programs, teaching resources, and academic and student support	– Academic practices and programs (teaching and assessment, curriculum and qualifications) – Resources – Professional development – Academic support
Research and research training	This domain refers to all aspects involved in research (including emergency-related), science communication, collaborations, publication outputs, repositories and ethics, as well as research training	– Research – Research training

(*cont.*)

TABLE 2.1   Defining higher education in emergencies domains (*cont.*)

Domains	Definition	Indicators
Pathways and portals in and out	This domain refers to formal pathways into and between higher education programs for local and international students across all levels of undergraduate and postgraduate study. It also includes transitions out of higher education to employment	– Senior secondary school examinations – Language tests – Higher education entrance examinations – Admissions (national and international, recognition of prior learning, mature entry) – Transition to employment
Governance and leadership	This domain refers to the governance and leadership of higher education institutions, including governance structures, instruments and processes, emergency planning and decision-making, risk, quality and internal reporting, and record-keeping	– Governance structures, instruments and processes – Executive management and leadership – Emergency planning – Emergency decision-making – Risk management – Quality assurance – Communications – Record keeping
Human resources	This domain refers to the employment and management of institutional faculty and professional staff. This includes employment contracts, staffing profiles and workload models, and practices enabling career progression	– Contracts of employment (permanent, fixed, casual) – Conditions of employment – Staffing profile – Faculty workload models

processes. Response as an emergency unfolds provides relief of negative impacts and the coordination of support, including post-emergency information and warnings, risk assessments, containing threats, situation reporting, assessing damage, incidents leading to investigations, and lessons learnt/ debriefing. Recovery is often protracted action seeking to sustain relief within and for communities, environments, and contexts. Importantly, the process of recovering can be grounded prior to emergencies, and is guided by six principles: understanding the context, recognising complexity, community-led approaches, holistic coordination, communicating effectively, and recognising and building capacity (Australian Institute of Disaster Resilience, 2020).

Conceptually then, these domains inform higher education policymakers and actors, and cut across the four emergency management phases and rolling ramifications. It is not necessary for policymakers to identify or consciously

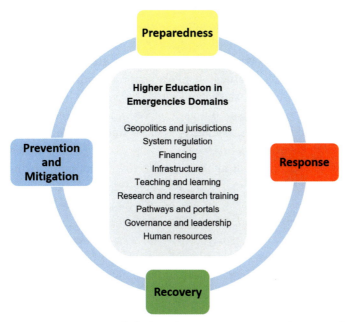

FIGURE 2.1 Positioning the higher education in emergencies domains within an emergency management framework

begin at a specific phase when first using this diagnostic tool; they form a cyclical checklist of modes of action and resilience. Figure 2.1 combines the Higher Education in Emergencies Domains within the aforementioned emergency management framework.

3 Exploring the Domains

3.1 *Geopolitics and Jurisdictions*

Geopolitics is twentieth-century thinking from when the world was under the clear and present danger of competitive imperialism and tenuous diplomatic equilibrium (Reich, 1904). Now urgency gathers around a 'new Cold War', with an uneasy accent on metaphorical war; the United States and China are the obvious opposing ringleaders this time (Kaplan, 2019). One contextual aspect of the twentieth century Cold War resonates with our times: different conceptions of unlocking human potential and enjoyment and the general fear that particular commitments are arrayed in adversarial blocs. East vs West once more, with South as proxy battleground and trophy room.

Intuitively we talk of industrialised and developing countries. Higher education at least in wealthy countries is meaningfully industrialised and developed to the extent that it can provide opportunities for inclusivity and empowerment. The United States, Japan, United Kingdom and Australia have different systems of opportunity and engagement in global science, and historical inequities certainly mark them, but the level of elaboration is industrial. India, South Africa and Chile have enthusiastic and rapidly expanding higher education systems, but any universalistic purchase on learning and generalised global science activity remains under development as injustices and investments remain far from adequately addressed.

We witness certain countries touting their vaccine development programs and manufacturing capabilities, therapeutics and population health trackers, as if their knowledge bases and research programs were champion warriors of national prowess and global benevolence. As different countries have cast aspersions on one another's emergency responses, with the World Health Organization struggling to sponsor meaningful cooperation based on sometimes scattershot data, the grandeur of geopolitics is also the scramble for coherence within national jurisdictions.

On the one hand, those countries most developed at the end of the last century have struggled to make sense of responses not only in China but in other global powers such as Russia and Iran. World health reporting protocols permit such opaqueness that medium-term planning of the human circulation of traditional higher education in wealthy open societies is fraught in EiE circumstances. Some advanced economies have used federal sub-jurisdictions not only to contain cases but to test differential measures, while avoiding a sense of blanket coverage and so conspicuously non-consultative action. Australian institutions lobbying for 'corridors' to allow international students from less infected regions, or outbreaks spreading following attempts to reconvene face-to-face classes in British and US universities exemplify such experiments. For Japan, COVID-19 is less a shock than a piquant reminder of the qualitative change to ageing populations – still-good job prospects provide respite with the higher education system administering credentials, but overall pressure on youth remains.

Developing countries are often noted as dependent on technologies arising in other places. Yet, India, South Africa and Chile are all practised in lean public health drives to make up for limited coverage of cutting-edge clinical care, and the coronavirus has allowed governments to present home-grown responses and gestures of pursuing what works that is dually globalist and nationalist. India, whose Hindu nationalist government's 'world teacher' (Vishwa Guru) postures as an internal discourse is especially compatible with the prominence of orientalist associations between simplicity, holistic human health and empowering educational access (Rao, 2020). The situation of South Africa as an iconic regional leader – in higher education, imposingly – rests, awkwardly, on having come through the anti-democratic Apartheid regime rather than the more ostensibly populist caprices of post-colonial elites (Chisholm, 2012; Lee, 2017). In the cult of youth that looks to poorer, warmer countries to develop, the big-picture damage control responses of developing countries may indeed be a moderating force on the individualistic horizons in wealthier countries' interventions.

3.2   System Regulation

Burton Clark, who more or less invented weighted comparison of whole national higher education systems, repeatedly began discussions of the notion with disclaimers over any deceptive tightness in 'the murky term system' (1983, 1987). The regulation of national systems is certainly one mediating factor in the coordination of emergency responses to the vulnerabilities and opportunities exposed and exacerbated by secular events such as COVID-19.

How countries regulate higher education systems, cross-border mobility and financial matters reflects levels of state control and institutional autonomy, competition and the framing of choice, as well as collegial and hierarchical traditions. While regulators in industrialised economies are routinely concerned with education exportability and transnational cooperation, COVID-19 has had direct contingent effects on student and faculty visa conditions. Modes and costs of study are more negotiable, although how regulators will be able to exercise oversight, strengthen the in-country premium (that is, spending time and money in the degree-granting economy) and student experience is unclear. In some countries, visa and international collaboration agreement vetting will become more onerous as matters of national security and intellectual property are highlighted.

Industrialised countries have attended to their international education industries. UK and Australian migration regulators relaxed international student visa conditions (mode of delivery, hours of work for health science students and post-study work rights), while higher education regulators extended routine administrative reporting requirements and emphasised academic standards regarding teaching, assessment and academic integrity (Australian Government, 2021; TEQSA, 2021). The UK tightened risk allowances for short-term education and training provision, a sector where unscrupulous practices are historically present (Office for Students, 2021). As international student hosts, these countries have welcomed China's interim measure recognising foreign qualifications obtained through online learning (Department of Education, Skills and Employment, 2020). In Japan, application, renewal and processing periods for international student visas and residence cards were extended (Kyodo, 2020); the US government would attempt to deploy the student visa requirement of face-to-face attendance to pressure institutional reopening (Kumar, 2020).

In developing countries, growing participation has been stretching regulatory capacities. The Indian government mandated that faculty, non-teaching staff and students download the COVID-tracking app, against privacy concerns (Garg et al., 2020), higher education authorities have relaxed regulations regarding student attendance, face-to-face and remote teaching, and extended examination timeframes and the 2020–2021 academic calendar (University Grants Commission, 2021). Chile's public subsidy of poorer students' fees has brought troubled private institutions into closer conversance with the state (CNN, 2020), while the social justice agenda in South Africa increasingly complicates strategic institutional autonomy.

3.3   *Financing*

Financing also falls largely under the notion of national systems, at least in the sense of a particular society's rules and norms for resourcing higher education. A general lack of EiE readiness is evident in the financial ramifications of the coronavirus pandemic. While institutional leadership and initiatives have much to do with operational finance levels and apportionment, ultimately the rules of engagement are subject to budgetary and legal frameworks. During the COVID-19 pandemic, as national borders closed, institutions shifted learning online, and faculty and staff worked from home, revenue streams and expenditure demands were immediately impacted. Student numbers fell and commencing and continuing students protested paying full fees for compromised experiences; in the UK, a petition for relief was rejected by parliament (UK Government and Parliament, 2020).

At a societal level, far from deferred, issues of social justice were amplified as governments sought to balance support for fiscal stimulus, well-endowed medical research, more recruitment-oriented institutions, as well as job generation. In those developed systems with crucial international student populations, the boosterish notion of higher education as an export was met with especially acute problems for another key ingredient of the prospectus; regardless of whatever formal guarantees to the contrary, many students fund their living and often their tuition fees on the basis of work alongside their studies. Suddenly insistent subsistence and healthcare needs of international students had clearly not been factored into international education strategies.

One compounding financial impact falls upon the normally strategic and ancillary budgeting function itself. Far from risk aversion, divestment and underinvestment in the resources that attract and sustain academic communities become risks in themselves. While there is a general lack of clarity with regard to future revenues and COVID-safe expenditures, the issue is clouded by uncertainty inherent in cuts, especially of personnel, and speculation around future conditions. While financial markets have boomed throughout the emergency, institutional health rests on disparate government and student contributions, white knight philanthropy, institutional endowments and reserves, and access to borrowing.

Some industrialised countries have seen limited state commitment to shore up higher education teaching and research as an economic sector in itself; at the same time emergency relief is by definition soft money and may compromise longer planning that finds itself misaligned. In the UK in particular, commentators welcomed new low interest loans (crucial for less wealthy students) and grants being brought forward after raising the spectre of the outright financial failure of the many heavily indebted institutions. The redoubled Must Fall and Black Lives Matter movements served as a backdrop to inherited inequalities and the front-line exposure of poorer communities to the virus itself, becoming especially pressing issues in the US, UK and South Africa.

3.4 *Architectural and Technical Infrastructure*

The physical infrastructure of higher education has as much presence in the public imagination as it does utility for academic communities. In some systems, building styles of temporally decreasing construction and maintenance costs denote whole waves of intellectual tradition. Now, with campuses facing possibly permanently altered physical attendance regimes, it remains to be seen whether government and private donors will continue to look to the sensation of permanence offered by construction drives.

Many institutions around the world benefit from land holdings, anchortenant presences within their host municipalities and charitable status within taxation regimes. Financial positions have been parlayed into consolidated commercial student housing projects demanded especially by non-local students, whose demand may abate. Investment in facilities is one of the most publicly visible aspects of higher education; historically, there is outsized promotional value in the discrete transaction of sponsoring new building for supporters including government (and often indeed tax exemptions). In that sense, to upsize is to right-size; a swagger undoubtedly against the foreseeable grain. Insofar as institutions themselves are able to prove capacities in operating online, they may undermine their historical birthright to construction funds.

While to some extent life sciences laboratories would be kept open and busy by the sustained health emergency, other academic interfaces have been shuttered and perhaps pushed further towards virtual platforms. These include teaching spaces, but also libraries and archives, and public-facing cultural enrichment such as galleries and museums. Australian and British advocates advance the terms GLAM sector and purple economy respectively, tying these to digital humanities and scientific literacy initiatives (Hardy & di Gravio, 2020). In the US, UK, Australia and Japan, institutions suffered significant lost revenue from conferences, events and facility hire, as well as campus retail outlets. With so many costs sunk in existing physical plant and capital development projects, everywhere, economisation and modifications for COVID-safe reopening has been a major challenge.

3.5 Teaching and Learning

The organisation of teaching and learning traditionally are the first inputs in tessellating out academic calendars. In many ways the preciousness of higher education hangs on the proximity paradox that it is better to commit to a residential experience than to fit it more rationally around all the other things people have to do. Thus, when the pandemic hit, it has been difficult to tell whether there was little preparation for force majeure conditions, or rather studied reticence and ambivalence – commercially understandable – towards scalable platforms.

In the context of more online activity, learning and teaching have if anything been brought closer together. While widespread connectivity and subscription cost issues have been resolved in some places better than others, copious data tracing the forced experiments in online modalities report some positive effects on attendance, shared class participation and perceived legitimacy. This has not, however, been the case in all jurisdictions, for all institutions nor all student cohorts. Everywhere, higher education institutions have contemplated questions of academic integrity, reputation management, privacy and technical issues associated with synchronous and asynchronous online teaching, progressive assessment and examinations. By removing the commuting function that was a clear inequality in time commitments, efficiencies have emerged and prompted considerable re-evaluation of instructional methods (Ranga, 2020). Whether an online-heavy blended hybrid will assert itself as the new normal or even gold standard is far from a foregone conclusion, but here higher education institutions have certainly broken from the old business as usual.

Qualitative differences of information and intimacy in online as opposed to in-person settings are notable. Mass online open courses (MOOCs), platforms, communication channels, resource repositories, technologies and standardised materials have developed quickly. Many institutions have sought to consolidate supposed local and international authority in priority fields, and enhance student engagement. Obvious features of more intensively digitised learning include higher profile pushing of academic support resources, and more sophisticated promotion and monitoring of academic integrity. In Japan, amelioration of physical isolation is informed by research on social withdrawal (hikikomori) (Kato et al., 2020).

In India, Chile and South Africa in particular, uneven accessibility of online technologies is a significant weakness; however, connectivity challenges have been observed in industrialised economies such as Australia (World Population Review, 2021). India may be iconic for its technological revolution powered from centres such as Bengaluru, but vast sections of the country use this connectivity for social media (WhatsApp, Facebook), while lacking adequate internet and indeed electrical connectivity and data affordability for online learning (Azeez, 2020). Alternative learning channels enjoy longstanding popularity – correspondence education, television, radio, videos and populated tablets. In any case, the world's poorest faced COVID-19 even more than usual preoccupied by food supplies as barriers to distribution arrived.

3.6   *Research and Research Training*

The reassuring inclusion of research in academic activity has been a key feature of the massification of higher learning in many but not all countries; the generation and assay of knowledge appears self-evident sustenance for up-to-date teaching. At the same time, while the coronavirus pandemic has resulted in a proliferation of research and publications, this has not necessarily yielded an obvious surge in research quality. Indeed, the state of exception may have exacerbated some of through-the-motions elements of producing research not so much for its own sake as heavily patterned by reporting requirements and inducements. While in all fields the charms and drawbacks of not being on campus are noted – with vast torrents of research material produced, and perhaps doomed to be less closely read than ever as publication outlets buckle – the self-evident imperatives that fundamental, applied and social sciences address the emergency (and EiE upskilling) are particularly intense. In many ways the pandemic recalls the Manhattan Project or the Sputnik shock that foreshadowed grand articulated science programs (Geiger, 2008); new mileage for technocracy may well correspond to ongoing propaganda to keep disaster in the public consciousness.

In some countries, certain academic institutions have been in the news, starting with the Wuhan Institute of Virology, and soon others researching coronavirus diagnostics, therapeutics and vaccines. University/Big Pharma partnerships are prominent, including the University of Oxford/AstraZeneca, Pfizer/BioNTech and Osaka University/AnGes/Takara Bio (see World Health

Organization, 2021). Prominent research infrastructures and resources have also been deployed, including Japan's supercomputer Fugaku and RIKEN institution, the South African Medical Research Council and India's All India Institute of Medical Science. Much data projection has run into the politicisation of medical statistics; the US Johns Hopkins University (Center for Systems Science and Engineering) and the University of Washington (Institute for Health Metrics and Evaluation) would become brokers of the intermittent quality of epidemiological data emitted from national and state health authorities.

The more winners are speculated upon in advance, the more they are set up to fail. An extreme example is the UK government's decision to selectively parade leading academic institutions such as Imperial College and various research centres within Oxford as bizarrely inverted Bletchley Parks – in the very opposite of top secrecy, they were called upon to deliver hope to match appetites for Blitz spirit boosterism. Scientists put enough pressure on themselves chasing down epiphanies without a phoney war on emergencies, and the integration of responsiveness to emergencies has much to learn from such theatrics.

3.7   *Pathways and Portals in and Out*

The design of pathways in and out and passageways through courses of study captures the enthusiasm, agency, aspirations and needs of students. As with previous recessions, the pandemic has worsened projections and certainly heightened anxiety over the prospects of graduates. In highly developed systems, potential employment skills are now both compartmentalised in instrumentalist (industry-ready) ways, and pondered over longer time scales, embracing the possibility of serial career structures. In some developing systems, although there are recognised problems in the occupationalist formulations of undergraduate courses, any employability drive may find resistance as a direct attack on the existing offerings. In many countries, trainees in health professions were pressed into active service, in some cases for accelerated credentials or favourable student visa conditions.

Many countries have been revising modes, timeframes and substance of secondary leaving examinations, entrance examinations, aptitude tests and higher education admissions. Notable examples include the UK's cavalcade of fixes to accommodate cancelled A-level and GCSE examinations, alterations to Japan and India's high-stakes entry examinations and complications for reforms for Chile's equivalent. Some aspiring international students have faced difficulties accessing English language tests required for visa processing. Higher education systems and individual institutions in several countries are also reviewing foundation programs, and remote teaching prior learning credit

structures with a view to facilitating qualified entry into undergraduate programs. COVID-19 may define the pivot point, but the reforms have long been
ruminated; narratives of better future readiness through all levels of education
gather steam (Kidman & Chang, 2020).

3.8   Governance and Leadership

In the context of this global crisis, institutions have initiated emergency governance and leadership functions, a double-edged sword of ready promulgation
and blind spots. Many governments and institutions had previously developed
crisis, contingency or emergency planning, and the pandemic would test the
robustness and generalisability of such models and protocols.

Institutions, to varying extents, have relied on such plans to invoke emergency decision-making powers, and to accommodate rapidly transformed
governance and leadership practices including prohibited physical proximity
and shuttered offices, at least for some period of lockdown. Institutions have
also extended or introduced technology-enabled communication channels for
executive management, key leadership teams and institutional and academic
governance bodies. At the same time, institutions have modified governance
documentation (e.g., regulations, institutional policies) to the extent necessary to effect emergency powers and delegations, and transform practices. This
includes governance of key academic practices (e.g., assessment, admissions,
mode of study) as well as administrative matters (e.g., travel, privacy).

Variability in steerage within industrialised and developing economies, and
within individual jurisdictions is notable. The gamut of responses reflects general crisis-preparedness and access to technical solutions, but also contrasting
and deep-seated legal foundations, levels of autonomy and modes of direction
of institutions, as well as their strategies and missions.

3.9   Human Resources

The shedding of casual, contract and permanent personnel to satisfy pro-
jected losses when hard times hit belies any benign intent in the term 'human
resources'. Many higher education communities were generally receptive to
concessions on previous conditions, but more adversarial relations came into
being as harsh cuts took shape. In some industrialised economies, flexibilities
invoked furlough schemes (a well-known feature of US higher education's
vacillations), drawing on national and state subsidies (Bauman, 2021; Bodin,
2020). Australia's entrenched carousels of fixed-termed contracts based on soft
research monies and gendered work/life imbalances (Broadbent et al., 2017),
and highly casualised labour respondent to fluctuating student numbers,
would face near-blanket non-renewal, while hiring in general was largely frozen

(Universities Australia, 2021). In developing and industrial higher education systems alike, academic and professional support staff scrambled to reinvent components of instruction and assessment online. In some places, large teams of maintenance and security staff weighed heavy on shattered operating models, while outsourced elements were cut back with quiet aplomb.

Purpose-constructed surveying of staff, combined with longitudinal studies adjusted to force majeure conditions, have provided a wealth of information on responses to new working conditions. These shed light on the anthropocentric nature of higher education processes, including such features as patterned unpaid labour conditions (e.g., greater care loads taken on by women within extended families (Wenham et al., 2020)).

4 Looking Forward

With higher education often understood in terms of concepts such as brain drain and knowledge hubs, COVID-19 offers the levelling sensation that no society is smart or put-upon enough to shrug off any emergency that humans and the planet exchange. For higher education, preparing for an emergency cannot simply be understood in terms of core and non-core ventures, nor prevention and mitigation prioritised wholly along such lines; the enterprise has so much to do with supporting trust, curiosity and experiment within and between societies. In responses to this emergency, we have seen inventive alternatives to restrictions on the physical togetherness that has traditionally fomented higher learning. If recovery is a matter of building things back, the great strides in the circulation of information – as well as capacities of critical and empathetic judgment of priorities – will form virtual components of building back better, with their own vulnerabilities to manage. Ultimately, we are all higher education's stakeholders, and just as competition drives innovation, mutuality is the enjoyment of human diversity and potential.

References

Australian Government. (2021). *COVID-19 and the border: Student visa.* https://covid19.homeaffairs.gov.au/student-visa

Australian Institute of Disaster Resilience. (2020). *National emergency risk assessment guidelines.* https://www.aidr.org.au/media/7600/aidr_handbookcollection_nerag_2020-02-05_v10.pdf

Azeez, A. (2020, May). Higher education during COVID and thereafter: Considerations for India and the developing world. *Social Science Space*.

Bauman, D. (2021, February 5). A brutal tally: Higher Ed lost 650,000 jobs last year. *The Chronicle of Higher Education*. https://www.chronicle.com/article/a-brutal-tally-higher-ed-lost-650-000-jobs-last-year?cid2=gen_login_refresh&cid=gen_sign_in

Bodin, M. (2020, July 30). University redundancies, furloughs and pay cuts might loom amid the pandemic, survey finds. *Nature*. https://www.nature.com/articles/d41586-020-02265-w

Broadbent, K., Strachan, G., & May, R. (2017). Academic staff on insecure contracts and the interplay of gender in Australian universities. In K. Broadbent, G. Strachan, & G. Healy (Eds.), *Gender and the professions* (pp. 39–54). Routledge.

Chisholm, L. (2012). Apartheid education legacies and new directions in post-apartheid South Africa. *Storia delle Donne, 8*, 81–103.

Clark, B. (1983). *The higher education system*. University of California Press.

Clark, B. (Ed.). (1987). *The academic profession: National, disciplinary, and institutional settings*. University of California Press.

CNN. (2020, June 26). *Mineduc abre proceso de apelación para acceder a gratuidad, becas y créditos* [*Ministry of Education opens appeals process to access fee-free study, scholarships and credit*]. https://www.cnnchile.com/pais/proceso-apelacion-gratuidad-becas-creditos_20200626/

Department of Education, Skills and Employment. (2020). *Formal advice on degree verification for Chinese international students – online learning due to COVID-19*. https://internationaleducation.gov.au/international-network/china/PolicyUpdates-China/Pages/Formal-advice-on-degree-verification-for-Chinese-international-students---online-learning-due-to-COVID-19.aspx

Garg, S., Bhatnagar, N., & Gangadharan, N. (2020). A case for participatory disease surveillance of the COVID-19 pandemic in India. *JMIR Public Health and Surveillance, 6*(2), e18795.

Geiger, R. (2008). *Research and relevant knowledge: American research universities since World War II*. Transaction Publishers.

Hardy, A., & di Gravio, G. (2020). Engaging tertiary students with university archival collections and digitisation processes. In J. Atkinson (Ed.), *Technology, change and the academic library* (pp. 131–142). Chandos Publishing.

Kaplan, R. (2019). A new Cold War has begun. *Foreign Policy, 7*.

Kato, T., Sartorius, N., & Shinfuku, N. (2020). Forced social isolation due to COVID-19 and consequent mental health problems: Lessons from hikikomori. *Psychiatry and Clinical Neurosciences*. https://doi.org/10.1111/pcn.13112

Kidman, G., & Chang, C. H. (2020). What does "crisis" education look like? *International Research in Geographical and Environmental Education, 29*(2), 107–111.

Kumar, A. (2020, July 11). Education interrupted. Years lost. Students face 'cruelty' of new visa policy. *National Geographic.* https://www.nationalgeographic.com/history/article/education-interrupted-years-lost-students-face-new-visa-policy

Kyodo. (2020, August 22). Japan to ease entry restrictions for foreign students. *Kyodo News.* https://english.kyodonews.net/news/2020/08/0781ed7f22bf-japan-to-ease-entry-restrictions-for-foreign-students.html

Lee, J. (2017). Neo-nationalism in higher education: Case of South Africa. *Studies in Higher Education, 42*(5), 869–886.

Office for Students. (2021). *Provider guide to coronavirus.* https://www.officeforstudents.org.uk/advice-and-guidance/coronavirus/provider-guide-to-coronavirus/regulatory-requirements/

Ranga, J. (2020). Online engagement of commuter students in a general chemistry course during COVID-19. *Journal of Chemical Education, 97*(9), 2866–2870.

Rao, K. V. (2020). Virtual education: A viable first choice in post COVID era. *University News, 58*, 16.

Reich, E. (1904). *The foundations of modern Europe.* Bell and Sons.

Tertiary Education Quality Standards Agency. (2021). *Online learning good practice.* https://www.teqsa.gov.au/online-learning-good-practice

UK Government and Parliament. (2020). *Rejected petition: Lower university fees for September 2020.* https://petition.parliament.uk/petitions/334283

UNESCO. (n.d.). *Education in emergencies.* https://en.unesco.org/themes/education-emergencies

Universities Australia. (2021, February 3). *17,000 uni jobs lost to COVID-19.* https://www.universitiesaustralia.edu.au/media-item/17000-uni-jobs-lost-to-covid-19/

University Grants Commission. (2021). *Notices@UGC.* https://www.ugc.ac.in/ugc_notices.aspx

Wenham, C., Smith, J., & Morgan, R. (2020). COVID-19: The gendered impacts of the outbreak. *The Lancet, 395*(10227), 846–848.

World Health Organization. (2021). *Draft landscape and tracker of COVID-19 candidate vacines.* https://www.who.int/publications/m/item/draft-landscape-of-covid-19-candidate-vaccines

World Population Review. (2021). *Internet speeds by country 2021.* https://worldpopulationreview.com/country-rankings/internet-speeds-by-country

CHAPTER 3

Transformation of Universities during the COVID-19 Pandemic

Digitalization, New Formats, "Re-education of Educators"

Vadim Kozlov, Elena Levina and Tatiana Tregubova

Abstract

The COVID-19 pandemic has significantly changed the lives of people around the world. Influencing each person, the coronavirus has violated all socio-economic relations, breaking seemingly stable life models. The most sustainable social institution in times of any change is the education system which needs to be capable of successfully facing any social transformations.

This chapter will offer insights that may be helpful for rethinking the place of the university in a civic society during the pandemic. The expansion of university teachers' functions in the formative ideology "New normal" from the point of view of human-oriented priorities of higher education is justified and explained. The importance of university teachers in the implementation of the "third mission of the university" (social participation, intergenerational component, health conservation, cultural diversity, etc.) is revealed. Since the success of the university in the new operational format depends to a great extent on the qualification of teachers, universities hastily and without sparing resources organized teachers' retraining programs; in fact, a total system of "re-education of educators" has unfolded.

Interpreting the results of surveys of university teachers and students in Russia in the light of the COVID-19 pandemic, the authors point out the relevance of digital formats, software products and the implementation of learning technologies in the university setting. Moreover, a network of intermediate forms of virtual involvement of "clients" in university education has arisen: webinars for the public and the local community, consultations with firms and public organizations, etc.

In the opinion of the authors, COVID-19, having served as a catalyst for many transformations in higher education, made it possible to solve overdue problems and strengthen the role of universities in the development of the world order of regions and countries where the university acts as a stronghold of society, offering the highest good – education and the humanities.

© KONINKLIJKE BRILL NV, LEIDEN, 2022 | DOI:10.1163/9789004512672_003

1 Modern Universities: Change is Imperative

Higher education is facing unprecedented challenges from perception of its relevance to coping with the COVID-19 pandemic. This chapter looks at the common problems faced by higher education providers and the university role in meeting students' educational needs in the era of globalization, digitalization and the COVID-19 pandemic.

The task of increasing the social significance of the educational system dictates the need for systemic innovations, forming strategies, and tactical directions for the development of its subsystems. The challenges to higher education have radically transformed its mission (development of the intellectual potential of the nation), vision (integration of science, education and innovation) and format (expansion of the subjectivity of educational institutions of higher education). The emergence of new conditions, opportunities and needs (financial; regulatory; scientific and technical; organizational; informational; motivational; the need to move higher education on line, etc.) predetermines the search for new forms of higher education development, shaping the present and future of the state in socio-economic, scientific and technological contexts (Dudija, 2019; Economist Intelligence Unit, 2015; Firat, 2016). The unique multidimensional role of higher education lies in its mutual relevance with society as a system that simultaneously ensures integrity, reproduction, and development.

The era of globalization has a very vivid impact on higher education in all countries of the world, and in this regard, Russia is by no means an exception. Moreover, we are talking not only and not so much about the obvious consequences of the processes of globalization: among them – the predominance of permanent changes over the state of stability; a kind of reduction in geographical spaces; new types of interaction of local and global practices; virtualization of many spheres of life; hybridization of cultural phenomena (Tregubova et al., 2020). We are talking about changing the innermost paradigm of the university as an educational establishment, that is, about the emergence of new patterns, norms, challenges, and motivations in higher professional schools.

Quite recently, many educational experts described the situation of the modern university in the context of globalization: "Globalization is perhaps the most fundamental challenge faced by the university in its long history, and more serious than the challenges, posed to the medieval university by the era of humanism, a scientific revolution, or a revolutionary Europe ..." (Verbitsky, 2019, pp. 4–5).

The university could live as a special institution and a productive idea in the era of higher education (even mass higher education), but will it survive during the transition to global continuing education, which will become the work of many, and many different structures, organizations and institutions? As such, universities have found it difficult to adapt to the demands of the emerging age of globalization (Ainoutdinova, Tregubova & Khuziakhmetov, 2017).

During the last decades, another global challenge has faced higher education – total digitalization of education.

The era of digitalization has become an integral part of the natural continuation of mass informatization, computerization and automation. It has also enlarged the integral capacities of informational and communicative, mobile technologies, and global information resources.

Taking into consideration the whole triad of education (teaching, upbringing, development), digitalization causes a variety of humanitarian, didactic, and even ideological problems. At the moment, it is treated from the standpoint of problems and threats, prospects and potential, calls and risks to pedagogical research in the sphere of digitalization, that possesses a debatable character. Their generalization allowed us to outline several points of view (Levina, 2019; Andryukhina et al., 2020; Morakanyane et al., 2017).

The "optimistic and technological" position of researchers is based on the actual lack of changes, and is substantiated by transformation of habitual technologies when a "paper-based format" is replaced by a digital format, and we can see digitization of textbooks, lectures, educational and methodical complexes, formats of representation of teaching material are changed, and the range of forms, methods and means of teaching are enlarged.

Indeed, to some extent, each of the trends of digitalization, mentioned above, causes rather habitual possibilities of education by introducing a variety of ways to exchange information; manipulated information technologies and platforms for teaching; new abilities for collection and analysis of information; consolidation of educational resources for collaborative work on remote subjects; formation of professional network communities, and so on. It is obvious that the above-mentioned technologies will be updated, enlarged, and become more and more available for educational purposes. The negative aspect is in the overflow and glut of educational space with educational materials, a part of which just duplicates each other not only because of informational openness, but also due to the lack of time for the pedagogical development of authors.

The second position is the opposite of the first position – "technological pessimism", when authors consider that implementation of digital, information and communication technologies in education considerably exceeds their technological potential. As a rule, this postulate is proved by the fact of transformation of a teacher's role in the modern educational process, leveling it to a role of the tutor – the supervisor (the supporter) or the navigator in the variety of educational resources, technologies and means of teaching, surrounding students.

The fears of the followers of this position are clear: first, consideration of the teacher not only as a source of educational information demands a new (high) "format of the personality" of the teacher and his (her) system of knowledge, teaching methods and technologies, implying high level of professional requirements to the teacher, which is quite difficult to achieve; secondly, the essence of the Russian education system (teaching, upbringing, development) is partially lost – in the digital world the upbringing potential really "drops out", the level of socialization is lowered in comparison with the process of group teaching within the educational organization.

According to the opinion of the authors, such a position is not only premature, but is also insufficiently proved. So, for example, some attempts of foreign higher education organizations to transform the system of higher education exclusively into the distance learning format, without the presence of a real teacher (but not a tutor), resulted in poor quality of education and low demand for graduates in the labor market, while teaching online was regarded as a main form of education. However, the received experience expanded the parameters and possibilities of the educational process, having shown its potential in supplementing the standard educational process (self-guided learning, inclusive education, consultations, network interactions, etc.). It is much more useful, with the help of technological capacities which are available nowadays, to create a multidimensional system with various formats of Teaching & Learning, and provide a real (but not declared) individual orientation of Teaching & Learning.

The third direction of pedagogical research in the sphere of digitalization is connected, apparently, the obvious duty of an educational system – directly with teaching, and we may call it "overcoming pedagogical barriers". Multiple publications on nominally "innovative" ways of performing educational activity, implementation of technical and technological means in educational process fill the informational space of pedagogy for the last 10 years, creating a layer for "new digital" educational opportunities, up to formation of new methodologies (though all these items are the same, educational resources with use of ICT which entered education in the last 15 years are limited). The problem of this direction, in our opinion, is revealed in digital "inequality". What is considered by people who are older than 30 years as an obligatory skill and digital literacy, for youth – it is a norm of life, and it does not require any effort, so, there is no gap, and no subject for pedagogical activity, especially in the system of higher education. It is indicatively represented even in "pedagogical slang" where we see terms like: "digital natives" and "digital immigrants", and, as a rule, the more advanced age of "the digital immigrant", the more difficulties it causes with instilling the teachers with digital literacy and its positioning in their profession (Levina, 2019; Barak, 2018; Allwood, 2017).

At the same time, certainly, the teacher has a profound subject knowledge which needs to be transferred to the student. This issue, seeking a balance between perception and transfer of knowledge and skills, is one of the paradoxes of modern education. The situation has also become more complicated by the fact that in the system of Russian education due to the social and economic situation over the last decades of the last century, there is a rather deep age gap in education nowadays – there are few educators aged 40–50 years, who could perform this transition without serious consequences, and become a "buffer" between generations.

Consequently, it turns out that the most serious problem of the Russian education system is not teaching the youth, but educating the teacher in digital literacy, immersion of the teacher into this (digital) environment, and the development of the teacher's digital competences. The importance of this problem is very high and implies a need for urgent and serious changes in the system of additional professional education, developing teachers' skills for the purpose of connection of their subject knowledge with the digital realities of the time. The directions of research mentioned above which are nominally called "technological optimism", "technological pessimism" and "overcoming pedagogical barriers" consider digitalization as a condition for the existence of education systems, i.e. the condition for setting new parameters, possibilities and requirements, influencing an educational activity.

Since the success of the university depends to a great extent on the quality of teachers, the universities hastily and without sparing money have organized teacher training programmes in all the above mentioned areas. The total "re-education of educators" theme is starting to unfold. It calls upon the opening of new centers for teaching methods, centers of educational technologies, centers for technical support for education, etc. This is an imperative associated with the transformation of the university into a modern corporation. Moreover, the leading universities seek to capture the market for these services on a national and even international scale (Maslennikova et al., 2017).

2 New Challenges Caused by the COVID-19 Pandemic of 2020

The COVID-19 pandemic of 2020 has highlighted new challenges and opportunities. With social-distancing being enforced around the world, most academic institutions have been forced into continuing their educational provision online. COVID-19 has significantly changed the lives of people around the world. Influencing each person, the coronavirus has violated all socio-economic relations, breaking seemingly stable life models (UNESCO, 2020). The most sustainable social institution in times of any change is the education system; it must always grapple with any social transformations successfully (UNESCO-IESALC, 2020).

However, there are many issues this sudden move has highlighted:

a.   Technology is not always accessible easily or cheaply to teachers and students;
b.   Both students and teachers must be taught how to use the technology to learn and teach.
c.   The teacher must understand how to translate pedagogy online with the same level of effectiveness as face-to-face.

On March 13, 2020, more than 60 countries around the world announced the closure of schools and universities and the use of distance learning modalities (UNESCO, 2020). In light of this situation caused by the virus and of the consequent need to adopt preventive policies of social distancing, universities and colleges were soon identified as high-risk environments, as frequented by thousands of students, in close contact with each other, often crowded in cluttered classrooms which, in the presence of contagious asymptomatic patients, would have constituted a strong element of danger and uncertainty.

The transition from face-to-face to remote teaching has been an emergency measure designed to allow for the implementation of social distancing aimed at averting the danger of epidemic outbreaks in higher educational establishments.

The naturally evolving digitalization of education has progressed dramatically during the COVID 2019 pandemic. The effects of digitalization have certainly played a critical role in expanding the boundaries and opportunities of educational process, showing its potential to complement the traditional educational process "face to face". Forced, into an emergency mode, teachers and universities launched educational processes, ensuring the continuity of learning, clearly, with some loss of quality. It was impossible otherwise: the issues of digitalization are still insufficiently substantiated methodologically, methodically, didactically and psychologically.

And now, we, the pedagogical community, have the opportunity to comprehend what happened, to identify new opportunities and gaps of a pedagogical experiment that is unique in time, mass and speed of implementation (Arora & Srinivasan, 2020; Darr & Hipkins, 2020; Vydrevich et al., 2020).

As the delivery of higher education as we knew it is replaced in light of the COVID-19 pandemic by distance learning, it is absolutely vital that higher education providers review the way in which they are doing things: should completely new ways of doing things be considered, or can old ways be combined to create new pathways? It is hoped that these questions can act as 'conversation starters' for new approaches to higher education.

3 IPPSP Research on Teachers

Our institute, The Institute of Pedagogy, Psychology and Social Problems (IPPSP), is the Kazan branch of the Russian Academy of Education, that is the supreme scientific and coordinating body for research in the socio-educational field and educational technology in the Russian Federation.

The Institute was founded in 1976, and as a research institute is being integrated with the Kazan Academy of Social Education, that is a private higher education institution, and builds together with it a scientific-educational complex. As a Research Institute, during 2020, we have conducted several research projects embracing the period of the COVID-19 pandemic.

Based on the empirical approach, we interviewed teachers from the humanities disciplines working at the Kazan universities, namely, Kazan (Volga region) Federal University (KFU), Kazan National Research Technological University, and Kazan Academy of Social Education (ASE). We aimed to identify teachers' attitudes and needs in the changing conditions enhanced by the necessity to use information and communication technologies (ICT) during the COVID-19 pandemic. The total number of teachers surveyed was 62, aged from 25 to 60 years. The survey was conducted by distributing individual questionnaires issued to each participant. Participation in the study was voluntary and confidential, and this survey does not pretend to show any in-depth scientific data; it was just an attempt to collect primary information to confirm our hypotheses.

The data-driven analysis of the results of the survey proved that participants (62 teachers from the humanities disciplines from three high-ranking Russian universities) could be divided almost equally into three groups as follows: (1) those who fully support ICT integration into educational settings and possess positive attitudes toward distance learning (DL) (42%); (2) those who oppose ICT and show negative attitudes toward ICT and DL (34%); (3) those who generally possess positive attitudes towards ICT, but feel scared when it comes to DL and ICT integration into educational process due to various reasons (24%). The questionnaire contained 30 questions in four sections. Both open-ended and closed-ended questions (as fixed alternative, multiple choice and matrix questions, the latter offering identical response options arranged one after the other, as: Strongly satisfied; Satisfied; Neutral; Unsatisfied; Strongly unsatisfied) were used during the survey. The first section covered standard questions concerning age, gender, educational level and access to ICT at home. The second section consisted of fixed alternative questions regarding teachers' private use of ICT outside their profession; their perceived self-efficacy in using ICT and how and how often ICT is used for private purposes. In the third section, fixed-alternative questions about teachers' use of ICT in classroom practice were formulated as were questions about their self-efficacy in using ICT in classroom practice and how and how often they had made use of ICT-based technologies there. Finally, questions about teachers' attitudes to ICT use in education were asked. These questions contained fixed queries and the respondents were asked to agree or disagree with a series of statements. The respondents also had an opportunity to add responses in their own words in a number of open-ended questions after each of the sequences in the questionnaire. The results of our empirical research confirmed that the majority of teachers realize the absolute need for ICT integration into higher education as a driver for its successful on-line reform (82%); admit that ICT has totally changed the way teachers work in the classroom (77%); agree that ICT facilitates student learning modes and styles (75%); favor ICT in education since it contributes to cooperation between colleagues (68%). Some teachers believe that a true professionalism of their students is only achievable in multidisciplinary settings where ICT promotes subject integration and makes students' work more active, experiential and problem-based (64%); increases students' awareness of the range of possibilities of ICT for their future profession (59%), increases students' readiness for their future career (57%) and serves as an important factor in preparing students for active social and public life (53%). Teachers also admit that ICT might make teaching and learning enjoyable and more attractive to their students (12%), and, as a result, increase students' motivation and learning outcomes (15%).

The survey also showed that at least four factors – confidence, good command of ICT and knowledge, gender, and age – should be taken into account when measuring teachers' attitudes toward DL. Though age and gender do not have a direct influence on confidence, knowledge or attitudes toward ICT, they sometimes obstruct and limit the free use of technology in the academic environment of the university that prevent them from organizing e-learning.

The teaching profession in Russia is female-dominated (86%), especially in the humanities sphere. In our case, from 62 participants of the experiment only 12 respondents were male teachers (19%), while 50 respondents were female teachers (81%). Though gender is regarded in this study as one of the difficulties in using ICT, no direct relationships between gender and teachers' attitudes toward ICT were statistically proven. At the same time, the results revealed some evident differences between male and female teachers in using ICT; two-thirds (65%) of male teachers had regularly accessed the Internet at their workplace and at home, whereas only 34% of female teachers had attempted to do so. The results show that almost 100% of male teachers had habitually used computers in their teaching, whereas only 50% of female teachers had taught using computers and other ICT tools and resources. Also, 60% of male teachers had attended ICT training courses, while only 17% of female teachers had attended any ICT training courses before the COVID-19 pandemic.

Age and experience were the next factors whose effect on teachers' attitudes toward distance learning we aimed to measure and compare during our research. It should be noted that the selection of teachers was conducted based on the cluster sampling method; the teachers were then virtually divided according to their age into the following groups: of 23–30, 31–40, 41–50, and 51 and above. The results indicate that there is no significant difference in using ICT between different groups of teachers according to their age or experience. Where the younger teachers (23–30, 31–40) demonstrate keen curiosity in various ICT tools including such novelties as new high-tech brands of smartphones, tablets, laptops, etc. for everyday use, their more mature colleagues (41–50, 51 and above) show more interest in ICT-based technologies, methods and resources for educational purposes. Most of the teachers though recognized the need to enhance their ICT knowledge (86%) and widen their training up to "continuity" (76%), including further regular upgrading of ICT literacy via lifelong learning in order to enlarge their ICT competencies (Ainoutdinova, 2017). While we found that teachers of all age groups demonstrated much better computer behavior and skills than in the former years, the share of teachers who stated that they had a good command of computers and the Internet could negatively correlate with age. About 77% of the teachers who are 25 years or younger stated that they have a good command of the use of the Internet, compared to 25% of the teachers who are 51 years or older.

Our research also helped to clarify new and updated roles any technically competent teacher is expected to perform or demonstrate in the ICT-mediated learning environment of the university, for example a tutor (we will address this matter below), a guide; integrator of media; researcher; designer of complex learning scenarios; collaborator with other colleagues; mediator; orchestrator of technology, learners, and curriculum; evaluator and learner. In addition, our research demonstrated that much attention should be paid to theoretical and practical details of technical training of modern teachers and educators to enhance and upgrade their ICT-literacy and ICT-competencies. It would be better if their training could be organized, managed and controlled.

4 THE TUTOR as a New Instructional Position in Online Education

In the findings of Russian researchers (Ainutdinova et al., 2017; Maslennikova et al., 2017; Levina, 2019), it is stated that although the tutoring position is relatively new, the activity of a tutor is at an advanced position; while a tutor coordinates, supervises, guides, and stimulates human potential, a tutor develops not only professional competencies, but also specific features of a pedagogue, that make him/her unique and outstanding as a specialist. It should be stressed that the demand for implementation for the support of a tutor is caused by the need to enhance the efficiency of teachers' work and the quality of higher education by improving the teaching and learning processes in order to satisfy high-quality international standards of obtaining higher education.

Moreover, in the modern Russian pedagogical sciences, the tutor's support is treated as a pedagogical activity related to the individualization of education, aimed at determination and development of educational motives and interests of the learner, search for educational resources for the creation of individual educational programmers based on the educational reflection of a learner.

To address the theoretical gap regarding the responsibilities and the general role of tutors in higher schools with online teaching, the work on enhancing support from the tutor continues. One of the major problems appearing while introducing the tutor's support in the students' development is psychological and methodological unpreparedness (unavailability) of pedagogues for the new social role in the educational environment of a university or college.

It should be stressed that a tutor is not a "translator" of knowledge and he (she) doesn't take part in the organization of the educational process. The main tasks of a tutor are to promote pedagogues' interest in self-development and to create such an environment, where additional resources for the creation and realization of one's individual educational path would be of use. It is especially very important now under the conditions of the COVID-19 pandemic.

Having analyzed the process of implementation of the tutor's practice in the educational process in modern Russian universities and colleges, it should be pointed out that currently there is an ongoing process of the establishment of the tutor as a completely new pedagogical position, aimed at individualization of education, understanding the uniqueness of the individual's personality, and realizing his/her creative potential. Each of the existing educational practices provides the condition to establish the culture of choice, enhancing skills of research and design of one's teaching and learning.

5   IPPSP Research on Students

Research on students aims to analyze the impact that the introduction of online teaching in the courses of the Kazan federal university (KFU) and the Academy of social education (ASE), previously delivered in traditional formats, has had not only on using of ICT learning methods, but also on representations of the students' roles.

Five open-ended questions were administered to a sample of 80 students (35 males and 45 females), attending bachelor degree courses in Law and Psychology, in all cases engaged in following online lessons:

1.   What are the positive aspects of taking the lessons online?
2.   What are the downsides?
3.   Do you think that online lessons allow teachers to improve the effectiveness of their teaching? How and why?
4.   Do you think that online lessons limit and penalize the teaching possibilities of teachers? How and why?
5.   Overall, are you satisfied? Do you prefer this modality or the traditional form of face-to-face lessons? (Zannoni, 2020)

The research was conducted five weeks after the start of the distance courses, when the efforts of domestic isolation began to be strongly felt and an initial assessment of the approach to online teaching could be made.

For many students, online lessons during the days of quarantine were fixed moments in the daily routine that allowed them not only to keep busy, but also to distract themselves from the darkest, most fearful and anguished thoughts related to the epidemic. In the interminable days spent at home, the lessons have helped to keep the mind busy in a profitable way, removing the temptations to go outside despite the prohibitions and risk factors. Student D. (KFU) wrote "The online lectures allowed me to occupy my day and find the routine that was lost. I am pleased to be able to maintain contact with others and above all with the people with whom I have been most connected, without interrupting relationships". Student V. (ASE): "Surely the online courses allow me to maintain the idea of normality and allow me to interface with other people in addition to my family members with whom I am at home all day".

The online courses made it possible to limit the feeling of caesura with the life that one led before quarantine, facilitating the maintenance of contact with one's reality as a university student and with an idea of normality in which it is still possible to keep the mind active. They offered moments of sharing, intellectual sociability and interaction, contrasting loneliness, conversing through chat and video interventions.

The domestic fruition of the lessons would allow students to sit more comfortably on a home sofa or at a desk, having everything at hand, remaining in pajamas or in any case in a casual outfit, without the further commitment to dress in an appropriate style; it would allow students to have breakfast with roommates or family members while watching the teacher on the video, go to the bathroom at any time, sleep more, even cook, or do anything else. Quite different would be the memories of classrooms crammed beyond the safety rules and hasty movement from one room to another in university buildings, with inevitable delays in starting times and unfinished learning programs. Punctuality and compliance with timetables, more guaranteed in online lessons, would increase effectiveness, concentration and profit in studies.

"It is more comfortable to follow the lessons from home without having to move, and when everything works correctly, you can follow without interruptions and background buzz" (Student G. (KFU)). For some students, the online teaching methods make it possible to be subject to fewer distractions. In the university classrooms the possibilities of distraction would be numerous: vibrating telephones, chatting among classmates, confusion, buzz, background noises, people who enter after class has begun, others who do not follow, interruptions, waste of time. Such opportunities for distraction would compromise the attention thresholds of students and make it more difficult for teachers to conduct the lesson. The online environment would cancel these risks, avoiding the problem of discipline and silence management in the classroom.

Since the teaching material is shared by the teacher directly on the platform, the slides would be better seen (because they are closer, on the screen), the audio recordings of the lesson would be of better quality and all the material would be available on the personal computer. Overcoming certain physical limitations would make it possible not to waste precious time; moreover, the Microsoft Teams and Zoom platform would be quite intuitive and easy to use.

The online mode would make it more difficult, in some cases impossible, for appropriate and practical activities, the illustration of clinical cases and the laboratory and group exercises, and would not suit those disciplines that, such as psychology, pedagogy and statistics, need more discussion and interaction. When it comes down to reading slides, the lessons would be boring; moreover, very often professors would be inclined to speak faster than they would in the classroom and to take fewer breaks, even between lessons, making classes more difficult to follow.

In contrast to what has been said in reference to a good number of respondents, some students admit that they feel inhibited in making interventions and asking questions during face-to-face lessons: out of shyness, out of discomfort in speaking in front of many people, out of shame, out of fear of interrupting or asking an appropriate or inappropriate question. Conversely, online platforms would allow them to interact more frequently and effectively, eliminating inhibitions and emotional blocks, also thanks to the use of written chat instead of oral intervention.

Overall, online courses are considered a good solution, probably the only possible one, to deal with this in an appropriate way during the emergency without interrupting teaching activities. Some students (21%) prefer them even regardless of the emergency, considering them more effective especially in relation to their character and personality traits and personal needs. There are also students (34%) who hope for a return to face-to-face lessons, seeing them as preferable as they would lend themselves to fewer distractions, would favor social relations and human contact, and would be more complete and formative.

Finally, there are those (31%) who find positive and negative aspects both in the online mode and in the face-to-face one, and hope, in future to see the introduction of a mixed approach, which includes both, in order to facilitate commuters and enhance the different disciplines, addressing them with more tools and strategies.

6   Conclusions

Interpreting the results of all the research conducted in the light of the COVID-19 pandemic, the authors suggest the relevance of digital formats, software products and the implementation of learning technologies in the university setting. No doubt, COVID-19, having served as a catalyst for many transformations in higher education, made it possible to solve overdue problems and strengthen the role of universities in the development of the world order of regions and countries where the university acts as a stronghold of society, offering the highest good – education and the humanities.

References

Ainoutdinova, I. N. (2017). Prospects for popularization and implementation of distance learning of foreign languages at Russian universities. *Kazan Pedagogical Journal, 2*(121), 26–31.

Ainutdinova, I. N., Tregubova, T. M., & Khuziakhmetov, A. N. (2017). Advantages and disadvantages of distance education for university students in Russia. *Modern Journal of Language Teaching Methods, 7*(9/2), 72–86. https://mjltm.org/browse.php?mag_id=38&slc_lang=en&sid=1

Allwood, J. (2017). Is digitalization dehumanization? *Dystopic Traits of Digitalization. Proceedings, 1*(3), 259. https/doi.org/10.3390/is4si-2017-04120

Andryukhina, L. M., Lomovtseva, N. V., & Sadovnikov, N. O. (2020). Kontsepty tsifrovoy didaktiki kak osnovaniya proyektirovaniya operezhayushchego obrazovaniya pedagogov professional'nogo obucheniya [Concepts of digital didactics as the basis of design of advanced education of teachers of professional training]. *Vocational Education and the Labour Market, 1*, 30–43. [in Russian] http/doi.org/10.24411/2307-4264-2020-10103

Arora, A. K., & Srinivasan, R. (2020). Impact of Pandemic COVID-19 on the teaching – learning process. A study of higher education teachers. *Prabandhan: Indian Journal of Management, 13*(4), 43. http/doi.org/10.17010/pijom/2020/v13i4/151825

Barak, M. (2018). Are digital natives open to change? Examining flexible thinking and resistance to change. *Computers & Education, 121*(1), 115–123. https://www.learntechlib.org/p/201748/

Darr, C., & Hipkins, R. (2020). Opportunities to reframe moderation practices in the wake of the COVID-19 pandemic. *Set: Research Information for Teachers.* https://doi.org/10.18296/set.0172

Dudija, N. (2019). Digital transformation: Is gonna be culture shock? In *Proceedings of the 1st international conference on psychology.* http://dx.doi.org/10.5220/0009447602690275

Economist Intelligence Unit. (2015). Driving the skills agenda: Preparing students for the future. *The Economist*, 3–4. https://eiuperspectives.economist.com/sites/default/files/Drivingtheskillsagenda.pdf

Firat, M. (2016). Measuring the e-learning autonomy of distance education students. *Open Praxis, 8*(3), 191–201. https://doi.org/10.5944/openpraxis.8.3.310

Levina, E. Y. (2019). Tsifrovizatsiya – usloviye ili epokha razvitiya sistemy vysshego obrazovaniya? [Digitalization – condition or era of development of higher education system?]. *Kazan Pedagogical Journal, 5*, 8–14. [in Russian] https/doi.org/10.34772/KPJ.2019.136.5.001

Maslennikova, V. S., Tregubova, T. M., Khuziakhmetov, A. N., & Nasibullov, R. R. (2017). The problem of innovative development of the modern professional education In Russia. *The European Proceedings of Social & Behavioral Sciences, 3*, 508–517. https/doi.org/10.15405/epsbs.2017.08.02.59

Morakanyane, R., Grace, A., & O'Reilly, P. (2017). Conceptualizing digital transformation in business organizations: A systematic review of literature. In A. Pucihar (Ed.), *Digital transformation – From connecting things to transforming our lives.* University of Maribor Press. https/doi.org/10.18690/978-961-286-043-1.30

Tregubova, T. M., Shibankova, L. A., & Kats, A. S. (2020). Conceptual framework for teachers' professional development design in the era of digitalization. In I. Gafurov & R. Valeeva (Eds.), *VI international forum on teacher education* (ARPHA Proceedings, Vol. 3, pp. 2595–2608). https://doi.org/10.3897/ap.2.e2595

UNESCO. (2020). *COVID-19 crisis and curriculum: Sustaining quality outcomes in the context of remote learning.* Issue note No. 4.2. COVID-19 Education Response. Education Sector. https://unesdoc.unesco.org/ark:/48223/pf0000373273

UNESCO-IESALC. (2019). *COVID-19 and higher education: Today and tomorrow.* http://www.iesalc.unesco.org/en/wp-content/uploads/2020/04/COVID-19-EN-090420-2.pdf

Verbitsky, A. A. (2019). Tsifrovoye obucheniye: problemy, riski i perspektivy [Digital learning: Problems, risks and prospects]. *Homo Cyberus, 1*(6). [in Russian] http://journal.homocyberus.ru/Verbitskiy_AA_1_2019

Vydrevich, M. B., & Pervukhina, I. V. (2020). The role of the COVID-19 pandemic in the development of remote education in Universities in Russia. In *Proceedings of the Research Technologies of Pandemic Coronavirus Impact (RTCOV)* (Advances in Social Science, Education and Humanities Research, Vol. 486, pp. 344–349). https://doi.org/10.2991/assehr.k.201105.062

Zannoni, F. (2020). The irruption of the distance teaching in Italian universities during the COVID-19 pandemic. In *Development of man in the era of digitalization* (Conference proceedings) (pp. 135–140).

CHAPTER 4

Thoughts on Higher Education for Sustainable Development (HESD) amid the Pandemic

Weimin Delcroix-Tang

Abstract

With the COVID-19 pandemic sweeping around the world, one much, if not the worst, affected area is higher education, indeed, education in general.

Universities either delayed or halted the spring semester in 2020, while millions of international students were stranded at home or abroad, and some higher education institutions were forced to shut down or face closure permanently. For those fortunate enough to proceed with online education, teaching quality and student learning outcomes presented a big challenge. Education, especially higher education, plays an indispensable crucial role in achieving sustainable development goals (SDGs). How then, against the backdrop of the pandemic, can higher education institutions (HEIs) strive to be the enabler of sustainable development while struggling for their own survival and development?

This chapter takes a look at the practices at the University of Sanya (USY) in China and intends to exemplify the necessary transformative shift in higher education for sustainable development (HESD) from mainly three aspects, namely, an integrated educational approach, an innovative educational and research approach, and a student-centered quality system, hoping to generate more ideas and share good practices for implementing HESD. Finally, the chapter suggests that long-term measures should be taken to meet the challenges for HESD in the unprecedented situation of having to live with the pandemic currently and in the future.

1 Introduction

Ever since the two world wars, nothing has exerted such a massive impact on education around the world more than the COVID-19 pandemic. As of April 1, 2020, UNESCO (n.d.) reported that about 1.47 billion learners equivalent to 84.3% of the total enrolled learners at all levels of learning in 173 countries were affected by the shutdown of schools and universities (Global monitoring). While billions of students and teachers had to face challenges of online

© KONINKLIJKE BRILL NV, LEIDEN, 2022 | DOI:10.1163/9789004512672_004

teaching and learning, many educational institutions were either closed down permanently or struggling on the verge of closure due to enormous loss of revenue. According to online reports, many small, tuition-dependent tertiary institutions in the U.S. closed down forever in the middle of the pandemic and experts in higher education have assessed that about 20% of colleges and universities faced severe market risk (Zemsky, 2020, as cited in Schermele, 2020, para. 5). In the U.K., 13 universities face complete shutdown and up to £19 billion loss has been incurred in higher education (Burns, 2020, para. 6). Despite an investment pledge of 2.6 billion by the British government (Education and Training Update, 2020, title page), which is indeed a drop in the bucket, the severe lack of funding, exacerbated by the general economic downturn, has pushed higher education to take self-rescue measures, such as cutting spending, reducing personnel costs, enticing international students with scholarships and discounted study fees. However, the "austerity" measures, in addition to the blended on- and offline teaching amid the pandemic, have raised concerns as to how HE can live up to its role of becoming an enabler of sustainable development goals and how to maintain teaching and learning qualities with regard to HESD.

Scholars around the world working in the field of HE as well as organizations, such as the UN and many independent academic research groups, have been much drawn to the concerns raised above, setting goals and tackling rising problems related to higher education for sustainable development. This chapter, set against the backdrop of the COVID-19 pandemic, which caused unprecedented human health and economic crises putting a strain on education in general, will take a close look at one Chinese university, the University of Sanya (USY), to share thoughts, limited though they are, on applicable approaches aimed at contributing to integrating the awareness of SDGs into HE and achieving sustainable development of teaching and learning quality in HE.

2 Interaction: HE and Sustainable Development

The UNESCO report on the SDGs for Education 2030 agenda clearly emphasizes the importance of education with regards to SDGs. "Education is both a goal in itself and a means for attaining all the other SDGs. It is not only an integral part of sustainable development, but also a key enabler for it. That is why education represents an essential strategy in the pursuit of the SDGs" (UNESCO, 2017, p. 1). In line with the UNESCO 2030 agenda, a report compiled by a Norwegian working group headed by Solve Sæbø (NMBU) aiming at promoting a common public space for knowledge sharing and mutual learning among universities, reiterates the "three pillars" of sustainable development set forth in the United Nations 2005 World Summit Outcome, namely, "economic viability, social equity and environmental protection" (SDG – Quality, 2020, p. 4; UN, 2005, p. 12). One crucial aspect of the important role of education is to make such major SDGs be recognized by the future change-makers who are vital agents for the achievement of sustainable development. How then can SDGs be integrated into HE so as to contribute to the new vision and practice of HESD?

In the first place, a fundamental change in HE has become an urgent necessity, as "more than ever, education has a responsibility to be in gear with 21st century challenges and aspirations, and foster the right types of values and skills" (UNESCO, 2017, p. 7). The change aims at fostering the development of sustainability competencies, including the knowledge, skills, values and attitudes crucial for the achievement of sustainable development. In this respect, the traditional way of teaching and learning has to be reformed to enable "a holistic and transformational education that addresses learning content and outcomes, pedagogy and the learning environment" (UNESCO, 2017, p. 7). This suggests that the traditional "single-discipline-based model" (Scott, 2014, p. 231) has to be scrutinized and replaced by an interdisciplinary, open-minded, learner-centered and integrated approach, encouraging the cultivation of critical thinking, creativity, innovation, and a new world view indispensable for change-makers for social, economic and environmental sustainability. As stated in the UNESCO 2030 agenda,

> Thus, ESD [education for sustainable development] not only integrates contents such as climate change, poverty and sustainable consumption into the curriculum; it also creates interactive, learner-centred teaching and learning settings. What ESD requires is a shift from teaching to learning. It asks for an action-oriented, transformative pedagogy, which supports self-directed learning, participation and collaboration, problem-orientation, inter- and transdisciplinarity and the linking of formal and informal learning. Only such pedagogical approaches make possible the development of the key competencies needed for promoting sustainable development. (UNESCO, 2017, p. 7)

Such a transformative shift aims to bring about the learning outcomes that enable individuals to tackle challenges in facilitating the achievement of SDGs. Secondly, the holistic approach of HE also involves a so-called "whole-institution approach" as suggested in the UNESCO 2030 agenda (UNESCO, 2017, p. 53).

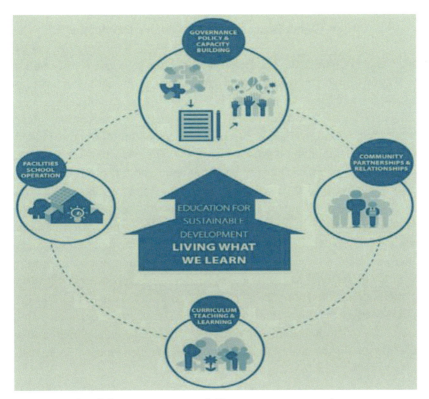

FIGURE 4.1   The whole-institution approach (from UNESCO, 2017, p. 53)

As shown in Figure 4.1, such a comprehensive approach aims at mobilizing all aspects of the HEI to "allow educators and learners to integrate sustainability principles into their daily practices and facilitate capacity-building, competency development and value education in a comprehensive manner" (UNESCO, 2017, p. 53).

Thirdly, if education lies at the heart of global efforts for achieving SDGs, then quality education provides the foundation for initiating change at both individual and societal levels. For HESD, the transformational shift in terms of teaching content and approach aiming at fostering sustainability competencies of future change-makers still requires compatible quality development and management. It is particularly important to sustain and enhance teaching and learning quality amid the difficult situation of the pandemic which poses enormous challenges for most HEIs and education in general around the world. Innovation, institutional policies, and development of quality criteria constitute, among others, some of the crucial aspects in sustaining teaching and learning quality for HESD.

3 Case Study: Higher Education for Sustainable Development at USY

The University of Sanya (USY) is the earliest and largest private HEI located in Sanya City on China's tropical island of Hainan. It is also one of the fastest developing and most competitive private universities in China. Established in 2005, USY has 21 colleges covering 64 subjects and specialties and accommodates a student population of over 20,000. In line with education for the three pillars of sustainable development (UNESCO, 2015, p. 12), the USY with its motto, "The purpose of entering university is to be better equipped for society", has been, since its founding, actively serving the needs of social and economic as well as environmental development in the region, contributing in particular to the green development of the Hainan free trade zone. Its strong ESD orientation has earned increasingly high social awareness and a strong reputation through its internationalized educational ideal, its educational and research practices integrated with regional economic and social development, and its application-orientated talent cultivation (Tang, 2014). USY ranks in the top 3 of China's Private University List and was cited by the Chinese Ministry of Education (MoE) as one of the top 50 universities nationwide for graduate employment rate as well as China's top 50 universities for entrepreneurship and innovation in 2016.

4 Integrated Educational Approach

USY differentiates itself, from the start, from HEIs which focus on what Geoff Scott (2014) calls "the traditional 19th-century fixed-timetable, content-focused, institutionally delivered and single-discipline-based model of higher education" (p. 231). With an awareness of the key role of education for sustainable development, it has developed an educational system that includes *seven* platforms for talent cultivation, namely, (a) Humanistic general education platform; (b) Theory teaching platform; (c) Practice teaching platform; (d) Multi-level and multi-form talent training and teaching platform; (e) Healthy personality education platform; (f) Curriculum reform and innovation platform; (g) Quality monitoring and assurance platform. Such a comprehensive educational system aims at cultivating a capacity system which includes "five qualities" (tool, specialty, humanism, personality, action power) and "five career development abilities" (learning ability, practical ability, adaptability, innovation ability, and sustainable development ability).

With the *7-platform* educational system and the *double-5* capacity system, USY prioritizes a humanistic horizon, multi-disciplinary knowledge, values and competencies required for the change-makers of sustainable development. In terms of the *double-5* capacity system, values rank higher than other crucial competences including thinking mode, professional method, technical ability and professional ability. Indeed, as is particularly emphasized in the UNESCO education agenda for sustainable development, a holistic and humanistic view of education should be upheld, which considers education as "a global common good", mobilized by "principles of respect for life and human dignity, equal rights and social justice, respect for cultural diversity, and international solidarity and shared responsibility" (UNESCO, 2015, p. 14). It is precisely with such a holistic view of education that humanistic values and the vision of sustainable development are integrated into the curriculum design and actual teaching in- and outside the classroom at USY, i.e. in the "five-module curriculum design" of the theory teaching platform, covering general basic courses, discipline specialized basic courses, specialized courses, specialized elective courses, and general elective courses.

Besides, to achieve the goal of empowering students with integrated knowledge, skills, values and attitudes required for sustainable social-economic-environmental development, USY ensures its motto to "better equip students for society" by adopting a student-centered approach. By student-centeredness, three basic requirements are involved, namely, "student-centered development, student-centered learning, and student-centered learning outcome" (Hong, 2017, p. 88). The first among the three (the latter two are reserved for later discussion) views the development of students as central. According to Hong (2017), the former vice-president of USY,

> The essence of education is to promote human development, and education promotes human development with the guidance of human growth. In order to realize the development of students as the center, the first step is to understand the development status, development demand and growth pattern of students, and implement education and teaching according to the development status, development needs and growth pattern of the students, so as to facilitate their growth. (p. 89, author's translation)

Here ethical and psychological qualities in student development are clearly emphasized in the student-centered approach, which is essential for cultivating well-rounded talents for society.

5   Innovative Educational and Research Approach

Apart from its adoption of an integrated approach and student-centered approach, as one of China's top 50 universities for innovation and entrepreneurship, USY has established a close connection with the world surrounding the university. Tackling the increasing problem of a "disconnection between formal education and training and the world of work" (UNESCO, 2015, p. 59), USY keeps strengthening university-enterprise cooperation in order to equip students with entrepreneurial capacity through application-oriented education. Over the past decade, USY has developed cooperation projects on regional, national and international levels, promoting deep industry-university-research integration, with local and national government agencies and institutes, domestic and international universities, local scientific research institutions, various industry associations and well-known enterprises. Cooperation project types cover student internship training, social services, and collaborations on talent development, scientific research, resource sharing, and university development strategy design, etc.

Sponsored by the Geely Holding Group, one of the world's top 500 enterprises, the Automobile Engineering Department of the School of Science and Technology at USY best exemplifies the close industry-university-research integration promoted by the institution. Working together with engineers from the top car-making enterprise Geely Auto Group, faculty members and students strive for innovative car designs that prioritize environmental friendliness and green development, guided by China's carbon-neutrality pledge. Also, the Vehicle Engineering Experimental Center at USY combines the actual automobile world with campus teaching and learning, best illustrating the "whole-institution approach" (see Figure 4.1, UNESCO, 2017, p. 53) as suggested in the UNESCO Education 2030 agenda, where students live with what they learn.

Located on China's tropical island Hainan, an international tourism destination, the International Hospitality Management School of USY closely works with municipalities of Hainan province, public organizations, hotels, resorts, tourist attractions and travel agencies to ensure USY's active role in contributing to the construction of "Hainan Free Trade Island" and regional socio-economic and environmental development. "The Academy of Hainan Tourism Consumption" set up through a joint effort between USY and the National Development and Reform Commission, "Hainan Cultural Industry Development Research Center" co-founded with the Hainan Provincial Department of Culture and Sports, "Hainan Tourism New Business Research Center" with the Provincial Tourism Commission, and "Hainan Provincial Ecological Civilization Research Base" with the Ecological Civilization Center of National Forestry Bureau, etc., all demonstrate the industry-university-research integration which stipulates research on the development policy and strategies of the regional tourism industry, tourism investment resources, internationalization of service management, and talent cultivation of the tourism industry. It is by means of such a strong partnership with industry that a student-centered

THOUGHTS ON HESD AMID THE PANDEMIC

double-5 capacity system mentioned above is realized, which in turn also creates career opportunities for students.

6   Student-Centered Quality Development

Such a transformative holistic approach involving all sectors of the institution, from the governance body to educators and learners and to the support environment, has over the years been adopted in the running of all 21 schools of USY, where social-economic-environmental concerns are incorporated into every fabric of the educational mechanism. However, innovation for sustainable development cannot be ensured without including the important aspect of quality development in HESD.

Picking up the other two basic requirements of the student-centered approach mentioned above, namely, student-centered learning and student-centered learning outcomes, USY set up its new quality management system focusing on both student learning and learning outcomes, rather than merely on teaching. With the focus on student learning, special attention is paid to the student learning process, as Hong (2017) writes,

> Students grow in their studies. Institutions of higher learning should focus on student learning, first of all, by meeting students' learning needs and providing a supportive environment and conditions, second, by following students' learning patterns. The learning process is the process of students' active building of knowledge. It is a process in which students actively generate meaningful information through interaction with the outside world by virtue of their acquired knowledge and experience. In teaching, teachers should take students' existing knowledge and experience as the growth point of new knowledge and guide students to continuously develop new knowledge and information from existing knowledge and experience. (pp. 89–90, author's translation)

Likewise, student learning outcomes, which matter more than teaching itself and constitute the crucial aspect in the evaluation of teaching quality, are predominantly evaluated from the perspective of student learning. Hong (2017) suggests three aspects: student self-evaluation, supportive environment of student learning, and student development (p. 90). Student self-evaluation refers to students' evaluation of their own learning status, including students' evaluation of their own learning participation and academic achievement (Hong, 2017, p. 90). The former includes course learning, extracurricular learning, teacher-student and student-student interaction, whereas the latter refers to the results obtained by students through learning activities based on the course objectives and course standards. Student learning outcomes include both the outcomes for in- and outside classroom course learning and extracurricular learning which encompasses participation in research projects, subject competition, publication of papers and patent application etc. (Hong, 2017, p. 90). The evaluation of the supportive environment of student learning refers to the evaluation of students' satisfaction with the learning support and service provided by the university, including students' evaluation of the learning influence exerted by teachers and learning services and resources of the university (Hong, 2017, p. 90). Student development evaluation refers to the evaluation of students' improvement of their competences after participating in the educational activities, which can be conducted with regard to their knowledge acquired and their ethical and psychological qualities (Hong, 2017, p. 90).

Such a student-centered and learning outcomes-based approach as practiced at USY enables the development of a quality standard system that focuses on the development of students' individuality, respects students' unique personality and individual experiences, and takes students' needs into specific account. By keeping a balance between tailoring teaching to the individual needs of student learning and maintaining the general requirements of the institution, a fundamental change in quality development and management is realized, which in turn ensures, together with other measures discussed above, the cultivation of all-rounded talents with individuality and creativity needed for sustainable development.

7   Challenges and Countermeasures amid the COVID-19 Pandemic

Like all other universities in China and around the world, USY was affected by the pandemic by closing down its campuses and starting online teaching during the early months of the spring semester in March, April and early May, 2020. It was an abrupt and difficult start for almost everyone, both faculty and students, some of whom felt lost due to inadequate technical skills, whereas others were psychologically burdened due to the sudden change and isolation. In general, despite efforts and supports on all fronts, internally and externally, particularly the open access to top-quality online courses offered by HEIs throughout China via network, the initial stage of online teaching was a bumpy ride. Fortunately, owing to the effective control of the pandemic in China, USY and most of the Chinese universities, except the hardest-hit epicenter of Wuhan and Hubei Province, reverted to classroom teaching in mid-May and the autumn semester in the year of 2020. However, due to the uneven situation across the country and, particularly, sporadic rebounds of Coronavirus cases in some regions, USY has been, up till the spring semester of 2021, resorting to the blended teaching model which combines classroom teaching with live video streaming to cater to the needs of students back in the classroom and dozens of students involuntarily or voluntarily staying at home.

Over time, such a blended teaching method has become a routinized way of teaching and learning for USY faculty and students, with each classroom equipped with the necessary network facilities. At the same time, more alternative educational activities, such as short winter and summer programs with guest lectures, training workshops, even onsite and virtual internship practices with business sectors or cross-border HEIs, are integrated into the regular curriculum to enrich the blended on- and offline teaching and learning, as well as to maintain the set objectives of the university. For instance, whereas the tourism sector was heavily hit by the pandemic where student internship had to be temporarily halted, internship with some other sectors through university-enterprise collaboration continued through the pandemic, such as the talent training business, the Geely car industry, and some government-funded organizations, albeit by observing strict protective regulations against COVID-19. Over forty students from the School of Foreign Languages at USY were even able to carry on online translation training with Lipetsk State Pedagogical University (LSPU) in the autumn semester of 2020, as part of the trans-border HEI cooperation.

In spite of the gradual normalization of applicable educational practices under the current situation in China, as the fight against the pandemic continues around the world, the still indeterminate prospect of having to live with the Coronavirus poses huge challenges for both the sustainable development of HE and HE for sustainable development. The experiences of USY, along with many other Chinese HEIs, in handling teaching and learning amid the pandemic, call for long-term measures to be taken to tackle two pressing issues raised in the context of this chapter, first, how online teaching under lockdown can keep up with quality expectations of HE if not the issue of survival considering the huge loss of revenue with many HEIs mentioned earlier; second, how the transformative shift in HESD as discussed above in the case study of USY can be sustained, at present and in the foreseeable future.

It is true that online teaching in HE had become a common practice even before the pandemic in the technology-driven digital age, when multimedia facilities are widely used in classrooms and MOOCs (Massive Open Online Courses) circulated around the world. However, online teaching in the context of the COVID-19 pandemic is a completely different scenario, as it took all staff and faculty as well as students by surprise, giving them no choice and, for many, no necessary training and even no means. So, in this respect, the COVID-19 pandemic triggered an urgent need not only for long-term training and integration of online teaching and learning into HESD, but also for multiple and mobile forms of teaching and learning. Good and consistent training in mastering technology devices, learner-responsive online course design and learning outcome assessment, among others, are important factors for quality guarantee and can also be done with affordable budgets.

At the same time, as the UNESCO (2015) publication on education points out, "The world is changing – education must also change. Societies everywhere are undergoing deep transformation, and this calls for new forms of education to foster the competencies that societies and economies need, today and tomorrow" (p. 3). One of the biggest changes is human mobility, both internally and internationally, which has "important consequences for education and for employment" (UNESCO, 2015, p. 62). Thus, apart from focusing on important aspects of recognition, assessment and validation of the learner's knowledge in cross-region and cross-border education (UNESCO, 2015, p. 63), alternative educational means have to be considered and promoted, such as correspondent data-based mobile learning programs designed for mobile gadgets so as to be easily accessed anywhere away from traditional classroom teaching. This helps to tackle issues associated with a huge number of mobile learners around the world in the midst of the pandemic, as well as realizing the long-term humanist vision of flexible, affordable, life-long education for "a global common good" (UNESCO, 2015, p. 64).

On the other hand, the COVID-19 pandemic, while posing huge challenges for education around the globe, also highlights the importance of HESD. Precisely because of the natural disaster and possible future pandemics yet to come, changes have to be even more urgently implemented in HESD. The USY case study above, which exemplifies the transformative shift from mainly three aspects, i.e. integrated educational approach, innovative educational and research approach, and student-centered quality system, hopes to generate more ideas and share good practices for promoting HESD. Meanwhile, to reinforce the innovative motion for HESD as well as sustainable development of HE quality, USY issued in recent years and amid the pandemic what is called the "three criteria for curriculum development" (三度) namely, "effectiveness, depth, intensity" (饱和度、深度和紧张度), in order to substantiate its student-centered quality development in teaching and learning (Tang, 2019). Over more than 1,000 courses have adopted the "three criteria" to enable long-term curriculum construction and build systematic knowledge and quality management. Together with the other innovative practices, the "three criteria" measure works to provide students with a solid foundation in knowledge and aims at achieving the learning outcome compatible with the competences required for future change-makers of sustainable development.

References

Burns, J. (2020, July 6). *Coronavirus: 13 UK universities 'could go bust without bailout'.* BBC News. https://www.google.com/amp/s/www.bbc.com/news/amp/uk-53280965

Education and Training Update. (2020, May 4). *The Government has announced £2.6bn support to protect students and the higher education sector from the impact of coronavirus.* FENews.co.uk. https://www.fenews.co.uk/fevoices/46729-the-government-has-announced-a-range-of-measures-to-protect-students-and-the-higher-education-sector-from-the-impact-of-coronavirus

Hong, Y. (2017). Constructing quality standards for 'student-centered' undergraduate teaching [构建"以学生为中心"的本科教学质量标准]. *University Teaching in China* [中国大学教学], *10*, 88–91.

Schermele, Z. (2020, June 3). *Some colleges are closing permanently because of the coronavirus pandemic.* teenVOGUE.com. https://www.teenvogue.com/story/colleges-closing-permanently-coronavirus-pandemic

Scott, G. (2014). Quality management of education for sustainability in higher education. In Z. Fadeeva, L. Galkute, C. Mader, & G. Scott (Eds.), *Sustainable development and quality assurance in higher education* (pp. 230–254). Palgrave Macmillan. https://doi.org/10.1057/9781137459145

SDG – Quality in higher education: Developing a platform for sharing of ideas and practices within the universities. (2020, January). Report from working group. Retrieved September 18, 2020, from https://www.uib.no/sites/w3.uib.no/files/attachments/sdg_-_quality_in_higher_education_-_report_feb_2020.pdf

Tang, W. (2014). Internationalization in HE: Procedures of internal and external cultivation [大学国际化是内外兼修的过程]. In S. Chen & Y. Chen (Eds.), *Academics' view of higher education* [大学人的大学畅想—我心中的理想大] (pp. 205–209). Fudan University Press.

Tang, W. (2019). Thoughts on the three criteria for curriculum development in the new era [新时代教学管理者关于"三度"建设的思考]. In S. Shanshan (Ed.), *Curriculum quality and construction of the three criteria* [(课程质量与"三度"建] (pp. 25–30). Shanghai Jiao Tong University Press.

UNESCO. (2015). *Rethinking education. Towards a global common good?* http://unesdoc.unesco.org/images/0023/002325/232555e.pdf

UNESCO. (2017). *Education 2030: Education for sustainable development goals: Learning objectives.* https://unesdoc.unesco.org/ark:/48223/pf0000247444

UNESCO. (n.d.). *COVID-19 impact on education: Global monitoring of school closures caused by COVID-19.* https://en.unesco.org/covid19/educationresponse

United Nations. (2005, September 20). *2005 World summit outcome.* https://digitallibrary.un.org/record/556532

CHAPTER 5

Digitalization of Higher Education in Turkey and COVID-19

Nilüfer Pembecioğlu

Abstract

The trust in education perhaps was higher in earlier times when people had lower literacy rates. Whereas the increased capacity, systems, methodology, techniques of the modern world help education in various ways to be valuable, there seems to be some loss regarding motivation and participation. Thus, education needs to be restructured, functionalized, and repositioned into the digital world specifically due to the COVID-19 pandemic.

This research looks at how Turkey's transition to digital higher education has been reported in newspapers during the COVID-19 pandemic. It also raises concerns about the value of education in the twenty-first century, as well as values re-positioned in a digital world with modern supply and demand relationships in the context of the learning vs. knowledge dilemma. To collect data for this study, qualitative and quantitative methods were used to focus on the cause and effect relationships of educational improvements, as well as negotiation and persuasion mechanisms involving policy decisions and public reactions. The news coverage highlights how educational ideals are changing right before the entire population, and how more participatory education, digital education, and inclusive education permeate all levels.

1   Introduction

For centuries people have devoted themselves to learning and teaching. It is interesting to see how different people and different societies in different cultures attributed different meanings to learning. For many years, schools were assumed to be the place where learning took place, according to Nabavi (2012), who describes learning as "the relatively permanent shift in a person's knowledge or actions due to experience" (Mayer, 1988, p. 1040). Shuell, looked at learning as "an enduring change in behavior, or in the capacity to behave in a given fashion, which results from practice or other forms of experience" (Shuell, 1986, p. 412). Driscoll calls it "a persisting change in human performance

© KONINKLIJKE BRILL NV, LEIDEN, 2022 | DOI:10.1163/9789004512672_005

or performance potential ... (brought) about as a result of the learner's interaction with the (social) environment" (Driscoll, 1994, pp. 8–9).

People have been seeking knowledge since the dawn of time. Different cultures put different standards on specific forms of expertise and skills. People were looking to improve living conditions by realizing the self in different ways and creating products for consumption, taking into account the geography, climate, and habitat of the given society. There seems to be a tendency to assume that earlier periods had better standards, traditions, and educational quality. Elders in almost all communities assume that they received the best education available at the time, and that education is now becoming sloppy and unimportant. Some people link educational quality to job opportunities, or the amount of money new graduates get. Some people also claim that private education has the same meaning as clickbait news. You can get a certificate anywhere in the world as long as you pay. People, on the other hand, need more jobs and better skills in a digital environment. Several different methodologies and textbook designs have been attempted in the last few decades to raise consciousness, with the belief that it could only be accomplished through education. As a result of the COVID-19 pandemic, the definition of schooling has been restructured, functionalized, and repositioned.

Universities in the modern era, according to Gümüşoğlu (2017), should continue to use emerging information technologies that will maintain the transfer of knowledge from space and time constraints while also adding new ones. Via digitalization, new information technologies have a significant impact on education. Education is now possible thanks to synchronous and asynchronous teaching resources and interfaces. It can now be done "anywhere", "at any time", and by "all". The university tuition fee is another thing to remember. Higher education institutions must also offer high-quality education at affordable prices. Technical advancements in the digital era have made this possible. Educational institutions are also going through a period of transformation and restructuring.

2   Learning during COVID-19

This transition is not referred to in all countries as a "change from conventional to digital education". During the COVID-19 outbreak, for example, the Chinese Ministry of Education introduced the "Disrupted Classes, Undisrupted Learning" program, offering flexible online learning to over 270 million students from the comfort of their own homes, emphasizing "flexible learning" with vivid examples and touching tales. These strategies are presented based on six dimensions, namely (a) infrastructure, (b) learning tools, (c) learning resources, (d) teaching and learning methods, (e) services for teachers and students, and (f) cooperation between government, enterprises, and schools (Huang et al., 2020).

According to Shaw et al. (2020), this was a period when different cultures and communities took similar steps in different ways. Although various countries have different governance structures, it was discovered that a few governance decisions made in each country, as well as strong community solidarity and behavior, made a difference. Emerging innovations are used extensively in conjunction with medical and health-care treatment. Despite the fact that the pandemic was global, the responses were local, based on local government, socioeconomic, and cultural factors. People understood the value of awareness and information in the face of fear and anxiety. Missing information, as well as accepting disinformation, misinformation, or false news can result in death. Consequently, education is now viewed as a top priority.

Lee and McLoughlin (2010) defined flexible learning as a "set of educational approaches and systems concerned with providing learners with increased choice, convenience, and personalization to suit their needs. In particular, flexible learning provides learners with choices about where, when, and how learning occurs, by using a range of technologies to support the teaching and learning process". Therefore, providing the possibility of making learning choices is crucial to learners. These learning choices can cover class times, course content, instructional approach, learning resources and location, technology use, the requirements for entry/completion dates, and communication medium (Collis, Moonen, & Vingerhoets, 1997; Goode, Willis, Wolf, & Harris, 2007). And when added to the further development of technologies, flexible delivery is considered as a critical component (Lundin, 1999).

Later, the scope of flexible learning has been further extended beyond the dimension of delivery to cover flexible pedagogy (Gordon, 2014; Ryan & Tilbury, 2013). Flexibility is not only an attribute of students but also a feature of educational strategies at the institutional level.

Characteristics of flexible learning have several steps, as follows: First, it offers learners rich learning choices through multiple dimensions of study (Goode et al., 2007). Second, it applies a learner-centered constructivism approach which is indicated by a shift, taking learning responsibilities from the teacher to the learner (Lewis & Spencer, 1986; Goode et al., 2007). Lastly, learners are granted a variety of choices and take more responsibility for their own learning. Therefore, flexible learning requires learners to be more skilled at self-regulation in terms of goal-setting, self-monitoring, and making necessary adjustments, and instructors to promote active learning so that learning in such situations can be engaging and effective (Collis et al., 1997).

When and where the learning occurs depends upon the learner's choice. What and how students learn is more characterized through the institutes and people. Binbei School (Shandong, China), for example, opened up a "Course Supermarket" that offers courses with a broad range of topics (Binbei School, 2020). When examined closely, their content reflects information function and usage rather than conventional theoretical understanding. Similarly, several schools in Denmark and Norway offer open-air courses that teach a variety of skills to students (Noack, 2020).

There are lots of platforms that can reach the students and get their immediate and delayed feedback. The use of technologies to enhance teaching and learning, (Gordon, 2014) and helping instructors and departments to process administrative work within institutions (Casey & Wilson, 2005) can be flexible.

There is also the possibility of versatility in the evaluation of education. All of these things contribute to a more supported, regulated, and quality-based educational system. This also allows teachers and learners to be evaluated on a competitive and performance-based basis. The problem of personal privacy is also critical. It's not just about the students' and instructors' privacy, but also concerns the students' and instructors' safety. In Turkey, for example, everything is under control; the learning consoles allow for special correspondence between the instructor and the student, ensuring familiarity as well as timely and effective feedback. These online environments were intended to foster the creation of social and collaboration skills, as well as personal relationships among participants.

On a voluntary basis, the participants may take charge of their system and give lectures, presentations, or even role-playing sessions. The change in value from conventional, teacher-centered, lecture-based classes to more student-centered class events, such as group activities, pair discussions, and hands-on learning activities, is reflected in the online learning opportunities.

There are times when there are lectures, pre-planned by the teacher. Even if the notes and slides were already uploaded into the system, these are meant to be the crucial and introductory part of the course to be followed by case studies, discussions, or debates. Having instant feedback becomes important for the participants and they are motivated to perform even better the next time. Contrary to belief, online classes are not dull as they were expected to be.

This kind of open structure could even help better socialization of the classes, through "virtual networks". In their daily life, they suddenly come across something and they find it useful for their classmates as well and share it. Thus, on one hand, we may talk about a very independent study but on the other hand a kind of cooperative and collaborative learning. They feel more responsible and prepared for the courses. The ECTS (European Credit Transfer System) provides courses involving not only class time but also extracurricular

DIGITALIZATION OF HIGHER EDUCATION IN TURKEY AND COVID-19

TABLE 5.1   Distance education agenda in the COVID-19 period

Resources – objects	Basic education	Higher education	Public education
National Public platform for educational resources EBA archives were opened to all.	National Public Service Platform for Educational Resources: A specific teacher, one excellent course or anonymous writers, one regular book.	Support system from leading universities to the others (some universities provided help to the other universities, open access materials and courses provided).	Free electronic books, magazines, academic journals, films, games, etc. open access material for public use.
Establishing public platforms for educational resources. Local, regional and national access to learning platforms.	The educational cloud platforms of provinces and regions.	Open University. Online courses. Digitalization.	Courses for in-service teachers, parents, youth. Courses for public training.
School based courses at all levels (radio, TV channels and internet platforms).	K12 courses, pre-school courses, University courses via EBA, TRT. National curriculum, national general exams and grading.	The school-based learning resources. Open classes, online materials and online exams. Project type assessment models. Zoom classes and exams. Second university chance, providing education without exams.	Campaigns for needy participants (tablet, PC). Government providing 500 thousand PCs and free internet. Parents' Academy.
All types of resources by online educational schools and other collaborators (museums, libraries, tours, etc.).	All kinds of online conferences, seminars, skills and certificate courses.	International education courses (for those Erasmus incoming and outgoing students), tailored courses, online internships etc.	Hobby/skill courses for youngsters and adults: Repairing furniture, free online tourism-travel seminars and digitalization courses offered by agencies and institutions.

activities such as reading, exploring, applications, and even internships related to the course. These might refer back to the different types of motivation that Hayamizu (1997) defines. Each member is actively involved in learning and aims to help the whole community. So, no one is redundant or extracted from the group. In a way, they assume control of their own learning management system and have a say in the system design, content and context. They may also implement their own understanding and experience.

This resulted in sensitivity towards those seeking education in disadvantaged conditions. People got together to provide second-hand computers or TV sets for those lacking them. It provided an online collaboration and network atmosphere. This also emphasized how important education is.

In Turkey, everyone has the chance of enrolling in two departments once they secure a seat at the university. The second one is optional and run by both the traditional universities and open universities providing distance education. It might be a minor or major degree depending upon the choice of the students. Usually, the students could have a seat depending upon their marks in the exams and might not be able to get into the departments they loved most. Yet, this "Second Chance" is provided to them to improve themselves in another discipline as well, if they are willing to take the burden of following both departments' courses. It is all free. Sometimes the students and their parents are enrolled in the same department through this second chance provided for the parents on the online education format.

In Turkey, online education is used not only in universities but also in primary and secondary schools. As a result, digital learning has largely replaced the conventional educational system. As Zhou et al. (2020) state, the school was out but the courses were on! Education measures from previous years, as well as government-based interventions, were extremely useful in this regard. To improve the standard of education, millions of PCs and tablets were given away for free to students. More technical personnel were brought into the system to provide immediate assistance to those who were struggling. In addition to providing a collection of usable books and theses for online courses as reliable content, YOK also provided a collection of usable books and theses for newly formed universities missing any of the substructure.

Disaster encounters (see Sadeka et al., 2020), are critical in promoting early preparedness and rapid response, as well as raising public awareness. In almost all cultures, COVID-19 brought education problems to a head. There was a thirst and a deep hunger for information everywhere. Everyone wanted to know more and learn more, whether formal or informal, structural, linear, or cyclical, in certificate courses or modules, in educational institutions or in social circles! Perhaps this century has never seen such a voracious appetite for information.

Not only technology, but also attitudes and values, as Casey and Wilson (2005) pointed out, play a role in learning and learning materials. They define open learning, distance learning, student-centered learning, self-directed learning, resource-based learning, flexible learning, and e-learning as distinct learning genres. It is necessary to use a form of blended or hybrid teaching that requires various types of contributions from both the learner and the instructor. However, learner attitudes are often more critical than anything else. Regarding the input-output relation, education is perhaps one of the unique disciplines in which input cannot guarantee output and *autonomous learning* refers to a situation in which learners are responsible for their own learning (Pinto-Llorente, 2020).

3 Aims and Methodology

The purpose of this chapter is to evaluate the fluctuation of higher education in Turkey, as well as the shift in the values attributed to education as a result of media coverage. The aim of this study is to reflect the media's coverage of higher education in Turkey during the COVID-19 pandemic transition period. The evolving structure of education is reflected in the news coverage, which focuses more on the ties between tradition and modernity, social media and conventional media. The importance of curriculum changes, as well as negotiation and persuasion mechanisms in relation to government decisions and public reactions, should be highlighted here.

Since some news broadcasters tend to incorporate citizen or parent comments in order to make it more interesting, the news does not represent what happens but how it is viewed by a particular group of people. However, in this chapter, all of these opinions were omitted, leaving only the focus on education as the distinct point.

4 Findings

When I searched the word 'education' the number of items surpassed 241,000 and refining the search to 'higher education' there were still 65,000 items even in a single newspaper during COVID-19. This might provide an idea regarding the importance attributed to education in Turkey. The 'education' labeled news either reported on government restrictions during the pandemic or the parents' perspective who found it too difficult to cope with their children at home and sincerely wished to return to the days of face-to-face education immediately. The parents heavily felt their responsibilities during the lockdown and coping with the little ones as well, as Arnett (2000) emphasized, proved to be very challenging.

Those starting their university education, on the other hand, were taken aback because they thought they would have to pay rent or stay in a university dormitory but instead, they ended up staying at home and enrolling online. When a family member enrolls in a university in Turkey, the whole family usually visits the school. They are particularly proud of their freshman if it is the first one to leave home (Whiteman et al., 2010). In Turkey, only one out of every hundred students is accepted to a university. As a result, the family participates in the admission process as a kind of ritual. To inspire their children, some of them even attend the opening ceremonies and first day classes. Leaving home for the first time, university students assume the burden of living in a big city, which for the majority of them means more friends, more books, and new experiences. The freshmen hoped to move on their own for the first time in their lives to see a different city and a new world filled with new friends (Işık et al., 2020). All of the dreams, though, were in vain. Due to COVID-19 limitations, this was never possible.

The media, on the other hand, do not cover missed dreams or opportunities. They are more concerned with other issues, such as digitalization of courses. Several articles were published in newspapers or shown through other media formats presenting the digitalization of higher education. Most of the elements included brief video clips or photos to draw the audience's attention to the story's visual aspects. However, due to this study's limitations, these visuals were often not included for the purposes of this research. In the following section I provide selected reports from various media over the past year related to the developments in program delivery for HE. I consulted various news and media sources drawing especially from Hürriyet [Daily News], one of the most reliable sources of news, and present the most salient reports regarding digitalization of education and the effects on students and parents below.

1. The news was full of stories about the benefits of online education. Khan Academy, which has been owned by a group of young entrepreneurs since 2008 and offers global education all over the world, offered 200 million lessons in Turkish online school courses during the pandemic (Hürriyet, October 27, 2020). According to estimates, this online education program benefited 18 million people in our country.

2. Due to its non-profit digital platform structure, more than 200 million lessons were accessed by students and teachers. STFA, a well-known foundation supported the Turkish infrastructure and produced 10 thousand video lectures and 100 thousand interactive exercises to reach the Turkish people. This news also shows that education is a competitive field; if you are not prepared, others will step in and fill in the gaps. It also demonstrates that knowledge is becoming increasingly global, and

information is available everywhere. Borders, languages, and roots are no longer relevant considerations; instead, quality and accessibility have become more critical.

3. During the pandemic, regular meetings and social events were usually held on social media pages or popular sites such as Instagram or YouTube, in order to respect social distancing laws. Zoom has been widely employed due to its ease of use, and it has made its way through almost all university infrastructures (Hürriyet, November 17, 2020). Some of the universities are expected to develop their own Distance Education Platforms to be used in the same way as the distance education platforms like Zoom, Microsoft Teams, or Google Meet. This action underlines the importance of improving the infrastructure of universities, given that there are at least 200 separate courses in universities in relation to the number of faculties and students, and that at least 200 concurrent courses are held at the same time. It seems that creating a new infrastructure in a short period of time for at least 7000 students to compete in a slot would be exceedingly difficult. However, for example, Sakarya University did its best and managed to perform as one of the leading universities in the short period of two months (Şanlı, September 28, 2020). Called Perculus, today this platform is used in most of the prominent universities of Turkey.

4. Individual institutions, as well as national and international organizations, have worked hard to promote distance learning. For example, the World Bank-funded Safe Schooling and Distance Education project implemented an initiative that prioritized the education of children aged 4 to 8 (Hürriyet, November 11, 2020). At the meetings, the past, present and future education system and other topics were discussed.

5. Critiques were made of intensive lessons, continuous computer work, and non-ergonomic working conditions. Experts emphasized that eye problems will be one of the downsides of excessive screen use (Hürriyet, November 25, 2020). Newspapers and magazines provided insights on practical home placement solutions for parents (Hürriyet, November 27, 2020) to turn homes into healthy and comfortable learning spaces to maintain distance education. Little practical information was provided for multi-child families. Experts recommended general ergonomic rules that the distance from the screen should be 35–40 cm and young people should wear glasses with blue light protection for long-term screen use (Hürriyet, December 9, 2020). It was recommended that children and teenagers should have their eyes examined on a regular basis.

6. Computer sales also increased by 40% (Öztürk, November 18, 2020) even if it had declined just last year in comparison to mobile phone sales due

to high social media usage. While the frequency of phone renewals took 2–3 years, the computer renewal rate was expected to be in the range of 9–10 years. However, much like bicycles and used vehicles, demand for computers increased dramatically this year.

7. Municipalities were expected to support their infrastructure for those regions, which are still connected to television broadcasts via land networks or where the internet is not accessible at all. They provided quick support to ensure attendance in distance education. Public spaces were opened where distance education could be carried out in the outskirts of the city (Hürriyet, November 21, 2020).

8. Outgoing Erasmus students who had wanted to spend a semester studying in a different country were shocked during the pandemic. COVID-19 restrictions banning mobility, delayed or canceled flights, and closed borders really scared them. After all, according to some, studying abroad is now becoming only a dream since coronavirus is everywhere. Few students seem to opt for an overseas experience where the program is conducted through distance education with various restrictions (Şenkoyuncu, November 21, 2020).

9. TÜSİAD (Turkish Industry and Business Association) addressed the COVID-19 epidemic and discussed how they could contribute to distance education, especially those who are trained in vocational education and children-oriented branches took immediate action (Hürriyet, November 24, 2020a). For higher education, they have already started to create future projects with stakeholder institutions.

10. All evidence indicates that no other aspect has as much of an effect on a student's performance as a teacher. Garanti BBVA, one of Turkey's private and foreign banks, founded the Teachers Academy Foundation several years before the outbreak. It was a project that aimed to improve teachers' skills through in-service training. This initiative, which took place during the pandemic crisis and was inspired by the 'Doctors without Borders' Organization, reflected a similar point of view. With the "Teachers Without Boundaries" initiative, they were in charge of training 13 thousand teachers in instructional methods and media use during the pandemic (Ergu, 2020). Founded in 2008 by the Garanti Bank, ÖRAV (Teachers' Academy Foundation), is the first non-governmental and non-profit organization in Turkey, whose main and only focus is the personal and professional development of K-12 teachers in Turkey. During the pandemic, they also promoted teachers' personal and professional growth by offering an efficient distance education structure and activities through webinar under 17 different titles. All of the seminars were held in Turkey's

81 provinces, with topics tailored to the needs of local teachers. Since the pandemic began, online assistance has been provided in a number of fields, in addition to the seminars.

11. As the pandemic progressed, it impacted not only the health, transportation, food, and tourism industries, but also education. State institutions had an easier time developing their infrastructures, while private universities and modern, small systems had more difficulty. Due to this problem, which occurred during the placement part of the program for university students, families and young people favored institutions that could provide digital education. Hence, many institutions have lost or gained credibility as a result of digitalization (Hürriyet, November 24, 2020b).

12. The controversy about subjects that should be digitalized has arisen as a result of digitalized education. In the field of medicine, for example, distance education decisions were also made for courses requiring practical training, laboratories, and personal attendance. All were shocked and surprised by these distance education courses (Hürriyet, December 1, 2020). They claimed that by shortening the learning process, minimizing risk, and being cost-effective, digital programs improve education quality, giving it more impact. Virtual reality glasses (VR) can be used with the system, or it can be used in 2D from any device or tablet.

13. Students with chronic illnesses or disabilities faced a variety of challenges when continuing their education at a distance, in a digital world during the global epidemic, and progress on these issues was accelerated. The Higher Education Council – Disabled Student Commission Working Group, according to information collected from YK officials, facilitated disabled university students' access to educational activities. Such applications already existed. In this sense, since 2018, higher education institutions that have been carrying out programs and initiatives to solve the problems of disabled people have been given 'Barrier Free University Flags' in three separate categories: 'accessibility in location', 'accessibility in education', and 'accessibility in socio-cultural activities' (Hürriyet, December 3, 2020). According to YÖKSİS data, there are 51,647 disabled students in higher education institutions. 27,782 of these students are at the associate degree, 23,581 are undergraduate, 236 are graduate, and 48 are at the doctoral level. 89% of students are in open education programs. As a result, 115 universities (58.98%) indicated that their demands for disabled students' educational and psychosocial needs related to distance education had been determined, while 80 universities (41.02%) had not. The number of universities providing individual education services

for disabled students by distance education remained unchanged at 39 (20%). In Turkey, 150 universities (76.92%) planned to educate students by foundations, clubs, or units for disabled students. Email or text messages are used to deliver the information. Applicants with disabilities applied to universities using social media tools or other online channels.

14. Generally, during their first registration cycle, some universities provide free computers to all enrolled students. Others are offering free computer use in dorms, campuses, and libraries to allow all to use a computer and reduce risk. The Ministry of Education has agreed to offer 200,000 computers to underprivileged children (Hürriyet, December 14, 2020a). Due to the overwhelming number of applications, an additional 500,000 tablets were given away for free (Hürriyet, December 13, 2020b). Many NGOS worked on this issue as well.

15. YÖK (Council of Higher Education) and MEB (Turkish Republic Ministry of Education) have become two magic words during the pandemic, and their every decision has been turned into a piece of news that the world pays close attention to. With the opening of the EBA education system to distance education students, millions of families began to enroll their children in classes, becoming so active that institutions developed parent-specific services. According to MEB info, EBA became the world's most visited education site with 10.3 billion clicks between March 23 and November 27. Besides, digital question packages prepared for students who will take the exam were viewed 38,578,273 times. In total, the EBA's mobile application has been downloaded 26.3 million times. Mobile devices were used by 65% of visitors to EBA, 27% by PCs, and 8% by tablet computers. The institutional bodies have advised elders to bring their cellphones to class to help with attendance (Hürriyet, November 29, 2020).

16. For distance education, many universities have built new evaluation systems. For example, Turkey's first private university, Bilkent, in Ankara, has confirmed that it does not use distance or remote examinations (Şanlı, November 30, 2020). Some colleges, on the other hand, demand that the exams be taken with the camera and microphone turned on. Others were attempting to solve the issue of digital constraints. Yıldız Technical University, for example, has introduced a system that prevents students from signing up for multiple sessions during an exam. All students would be able to take a single session. However, there is a chance that the electricity or internet might go off. Many universities believed that some courses' exams are only project-based, and presenting the semester's projects would be enough. Exams were a challenge for graduate and

doctoral students as well as undergraduate students. Written tests were photographed or scanned to make them available for different jury members. After the written exams, the candidates took oral exams in front of an online jury.

17. Meanwhile, following the decision to publicize those who attempted to cheat on digital tests, it was revealed that a student from the Akdeniz University Faculty of Medicine took the exam with four of his colleagues, and the case was reported in the press (Uzun, 2020). All seemed to be fine in the videos. When they found out that the exam was taken from four different IP addresses in four different sessions, it was discovered that the student did nothing but move his cursor in front of the camera while the other students answered the questions. With the development of various software that captures such cheating incidents, studies continue to make digital exams more accurate and stable. As universities build more sensitive software, they distribute it on open access sites and with other universities, which helps to keep education at a high level.

18. Akdeniz University developed a virtual university by integrating artificial intelligence and new types of applications for distance education systems in the most successful way possible (Hürriyet, December 14, 2020b). The virtual university is well-known for designing three simultaneous Academic Exam Automation Systems. Prof. Dr. Özkan, the Rector, promised to implement these systems in other universities for free. Experts sought to meet the need to prioritize the concepts of safety and quality, stating that their workload has risen with digital tests and that they are dealing with a density of 70,000 people at the same time.

As new flaws emerge, it will be important to find solutions to issues such as cyberbullying (Hürriyet, December 14, 2020c) and copyrights. Many university professors were responsible for both content preparation and lecture delivery. The copyrights of the course's instructor are also noted. Only registered students could participate in the sessions since each lesson was encrypted and clustered. If they skip a class for an extended period of time, they must retake the course. The course material offered by the teacher is covered by law and cannot be changed, published, or replicated, according to the intellectual and creative works act. The course material, as well as the registered course, is legally shielded from unauthorized recording and copying. Without the written consent of the rightful persons, any kind of transmitted notes to the public through sound or picture can result in 1 to 5 years in prison or a judicial fine.

19. Distance education may be viewed as a total trauma by university students. These young people are referred to as "emerging adults" by Jeffrey

Jensen Arnett. They want to be away from their families and have the opportunity to pursue their dreams and goals between the ages of 18 and 29. However, staying at home and taking online classes does not meet their needs and desires (Işık-Akın, 2020). According to studies, young people who leave home for university establish stronger relationships with their parents and daily conflicts are reduced (Whiteman, McHale, & Crouter, 2010). However, staying home can create a degrading situation and trauma enough to cause conflict within the family.

20. The topic of how resources are invested is also raised by digital transformation. Turkey's total Internet bandwidth output is about 10 terabits/sec. The Ministry of Education makes use of its 1 terabit/second bandwidth. When the present situation is taken into consideration, this might not be enough. EBA teaches approximately 3 million students every day (Hürriyet, December 13, 2020a). To better control the distance education phase, efforts are being made to increase bandwidth to 4 terabits/second. Higher education institutions tend to have similar substructure specifications.

21. Innovations and augmented reality technologies were also highlighted in distance learning (Hürriyet, December 2, 2020). High school students created a mobile application that allows students to connect in a virtual classroom. Teachers and students will meet in the same space using virtual reality glasses thanks to this application. From their homes, up to 20 students can interact and explore any environment that has been modeled and drawn for the course. It may be a laboratory, a place in the world, a space, or a museum. In a similar setting, the community will have the opportunity to communicate with their teachers. Thus, VR glasses could contribute to distance education in order to allow students to experience more colorful course contents and almost real experiences.

22. Young people gain life experience by moving to another city, spending long periods of time on public transit, and living in dormitories or in shared houses with friends. Nowadays there is no time to look outside the window because everybody is cooped up in their homes due to the epidemic. The number of people who complain about having to stare at a laptop for more than half of the day rather than sipping a cup of coffee or tea with friends is very high (Özel, 2020). Newspapers are full of stories of teachers sacrificing a lot for education (Hürriyet, December 10, 2020; Özdemir & Fidancan, 2020). All these bits and pieces are very important to see and understand the meaning and importance of these new conditions attached to education.

23. Prof. Dr. Kıvılcım Yıldız, Head of the Musicology Department at Mimar Sinan Fine Arts University, reminds people to make time for music and

art in their lives. She stresses the importance of seeking academic knowledge without neglecting the arts. She is referring to the results of the most recent poll proving that people listened to music less during the pandemic lockdown. People who usually listen to music in their spare time are not doing it as much as they used to because they are always online and in front of the screen (Yıldız, 2020).

24. In 2014–2015, the number of students per academician in state universities was 21.7, according to statistics. It is 22.4 per academic today. In foundation universities, there was one academician per 20.6 students in 2014–2015, but there are now 24 (Hürriyet, November 24, 2014).

Turkey's total population is 83,154,997, with 7,940,133 people in higher education covering 8% of the total population, according to statistics. Adding in the number of scholars, 174,494, there is a total of 10% of the population involved in higher education. As a result, the widespread coverage of educational topics in the press may be clarified in this way. Education, in general, is something most people are interested in, and it has been regarded as important for millennia, as even the holy book begins with the word "Read".

Many of these students have been accepted into either State or Private Foundation Universities. There are 129 State Universities (62%) across the country, and 78 Private Foundation Universities (38%) are spread across the country. Every year, over 2.5 million young people compete for a place at a university. According to figures, a student's chances of getting into college are about 30%. The people who scored the highest on the exam could get the best jobs, but the rest will be competing for the least desirable options. When one considers the large number of people in HE whose programs have been affected by the pandemic, one can understand the importance of providing workable alternative

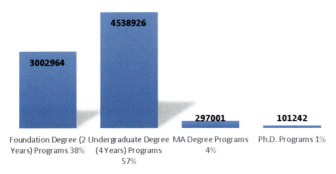

FIGURE 5.1   Distribution of the HE students in Turkey (2019–2020)

means for schooling via digitalization. Even when the pandemic is over, YÖK (Council of Higher Education) and the Ministry of Education have indicated that the distance education model will be continued, with institutions investing more in technological infrastructure as well as human capital to maintain digitalization and to increase the competitiveness at both local and global levels in the field of education.

5   Discussion: How Has Digitalization Played out in Higher Education?

The European Association of Distance Education Universities (EADTU) hosted the "Innovating Higher Education Conference" (IHE2020), and Turkey was a cofounder of the event alongside 28 other member universities. And after the pandemic crisis is over, it seems that future schooling will become a kind of integrated education for everyone. Digital education has the potential to provide more opportunities for future generations. The quotas set for physical and face-to-face education capacities should be re-evaluated, and many more students could be given the opportunity to attend university. The core ingredients of digital education, on the other hand, will remain unchanged. The candidates would be learning using a variety of resources. They should be willing to take charge of their own education and, in certain cases, select their courses accordingly. This will almost certainly lead to a type of personalized education, with a unique curriculum that takes into account each student's unique learning process and needs. The online courses would be providing the core of the information, yet, digital platforms only support learning outside of school. If the situation improves and face-to-face schooling returns, a hybrid approach to teaching can be used. Artificial intelligence can play a role in education as well. Counselors will advise participants on each phase, deciding their particular learning plan using learning analytics, and so on for potential learning. As a result, the teacher will be shaping the students' regular or weekly curriculum. There would most likely be more space for beginners if learning was independent of time and place. People would not take four years to complete their BA degrees; education could be more compact and effective. Multiple diploma courses will be in higher demand. As a result, people will be enrolled in various fields and graduate with a varied range of skills. There will most likely be more performance-based tests in the future, which will aid students in developing and gaining knowledge in the topics they select. It will be important to support student-centered instructional activities in the classroom. Future students may not have the ability to meet in person, and they may not be able to retain old friendships or share the same campus space. Communication skills must be strengthened in this situation. To provide teamwork and flexibility, critical thinking skills are needed. There is understanding of information management, ethics and accountability, and independent learning after gaining digital skills. In today's job market, more than 85% of employers are searching for workers with digital skills. While this ratio rises to 90% for intermediate members, it rises even further to 95% for senior members. Individuals must possess digital skills for both their own work and to supervise and communicate with their employees.

Blended education facilities would open up new opportunities on a global scale in the future. Perhaps education would occupy less time and people would receive an education without borders, with multilingual, multicultural young and old people participating. Multi-skilled citizens will be employed solely for pleasure for those counting on a potential "universal basic income".

Even before the pandemic, after completing the application process, research candidates with adequate academic scores were eligible to become associate professors (Hürriyet, February 16, 2015). Only scholarly papers presented online are now assessed, and the jury members make their judgments online, without seeing the other jury members. As a result of the automated platforms, more objective and straightforward assessment has occurred. Another development in the higher education system was the digitization of both MA and PhD theses during the process. Later, YÖK revealed that during the outbreak, the number of master's and doctoral theses downloaded for free increased by 110%. This was an important demand for science and research. As a result, digitalization is more scholarly, encouraging more study and open access to everyone.

In order to keep distance education as sustainable and beneficial, uninterrupted, safe, fast and high-quality internet is required more than ever (Hürriyet, August 19, 2020). Many people want to maintain the hybrid educational model long after the pandemic is over. In the field of education, this implementation will include a change, objectivity, and long-term sustainability. This demonstrates that the pandemic has resulted in a significant shift in higher education. However, higher education would need greater budgets in the future due to infrastructure and other costs. For example, in Turkey, the budget allocation for universities for 2021 was approximately 45.3 billion Turkish liras (4,759,866,200.40 Euros – March 2021).

The e-citizenship scheme, which has been on the table since before the pandemic and is increasingly evolving, produces extremely effective solutions. Many things can be accomplished with e-government applications, from scheduling a hospital appointment to requesting a diploma sample or transcript. Despite the negative feedback and concerns, there is a 93% occupancy rate, according to the university student placement survey, which was published when application and occupancy rates for this term's universities were reported. According to the YKS Placement Study, 781,165 study places were filled out of a total of 838,221 this year. According to this figure, university occupancy rates have surpassed 93% (Ülkar, 2020). However, since all accepted students do not actually enroll, only 80 out of every 100 university candidates became students this year.

The Digital Transformation Project in Higher Education created the Distance Education Platform, which was put into use at 15 universities as pilot studies (Hürriyet, August 28, 2020). Prior to the global epidemic, in 2018, a significant initiative related to future distance education, "Digital Transformation in Higher Education", began as a program to develop the digital competencies of faculty and students in 16 newly developed universities in the Eastern and Southeastern Anatolia Regions. Around 10,725 lecturers were given an online program called "Learning and Teaching in the Digital Age" in partnership with Anadolu University. For a single semester, 61,346 students were enrolled in "Digital Literacy" classes. As a result, the universities participating in the project were better prepared for the global epidemic. In partnership with YÖK, CISCO, and METU, lecturers from 5 technical universities and 3 universities in Anatolia received training in "Cyber Security and Network Management" as part of the project that began in March 2020. Under the coordination of YÖK and in collaboration with TÜBİTAK-ULAKBIM, Sakarya University's Distance Education Platform was made available to 15 universities. 15 universities in the project's reach began offering distance education courses through this local network in the fall semester of the 2020–2021 academic year.

Since the pandemic took a different route in each province, YÖK clarified that decisions including whether to remain open or closed, whether to provide face-to-face services, and whether to provide distance education during the pandemic will be made by each university. So, based on their own dynamics, academic committees will determine how to provide distance education. Nonetheless, close to the universities' opening dates (Hürriyet, September 5, 2020), the ministry of health stressed the importance of theoretical courses being as remote and digital as possible. This was merely advice; however, Istanbul University, the first name that comes to mind when universities are named, has announced that all associate and undergraduate programs will be delivered through distance education (Hürriyet, September 8, 2020). By taking the requisite health measures, certain realistic and clinical practice lessons may be done face-to-face. Following that, several other universities made the same decision and declared that they would pursue distance learning (Hürriyet,

September 9, 2020). The initial reactions piqued the interest of society, especially students. They had not anticipated so many universities offering this service. They didn't know how well-developed the workers or facilities are, and they wondered how it was possible. Almost every university announced its support for digitalization one after the other. The majority of the institutions that favored distance education did so because they had no previous experience with it. In a limited period of time, however, highly successful distance education programs were developed and began to operate. Even the newest, tiniest colleges have begun to upload their courses to virtual platforms. As a result, higher education services in Turkey were almost exclusively provided by digital learning.

Enrollment week (Hürriyet, September 10, 2020) came only a week after the declaration of this digitalization decision. 627,000 students enrolled at the university via e-registration processes in less than a week. With this first step, all of the new university students decided to adopt digitalization. As a result, there were paper, workers, time, and energy savings.

Meanwhile, the 'Distance Education Policies Committee' was created with the participation of academicians from various disciplines and universities within the body of the Higher Education Council (YÖK) (Hürriyet, September 17, 2020).

Aside from that, in the first stage of the Digital Transformation Initiative, the YÖK Virtual Laboratory technology was made available to approximately 15,000 students enrolled in different science and engineering programs at 18 universities and vocational schools participating in the project (Hürriyet, September 22, 2020). The Virtual Laboratory will allow students to conduct 14 chemistry experiments and 10 physics experiments in a virtual world.

Universities have been assessed against 32 metrics under the headings of 'Research Ability', 'Research Quality', and 'Interaction and Cooperation' since 2018, and a target performance scale has been established (Hürriyet, November 5, 2020). The following are the details of the total scores of the 'study universities' and candidate research universities in 2019 and their rankings as a result of the assessments made within the framework of the index created: Middle East Technical University, Istanbul Technical University, Bogazici University, İzmir Institute of Technology, Ankara University, Hacettepe University, Istanbul University, Yıldız Technical University, Ege University, Gebze Technical University, Bursa Uludağ University, Erciyes University, Çukurova University, Gazi University, Istanbul University-Cerrahpaşa, Selcuk University. The fact that so many universities were research universities and would be eligible to receive more financial grants was important. This would allow them to do more and higher-quality research.

In the meantime, incoming international students were a bit worried (Hürriyet, December 5, 2020). Turkey is quickly becoming a popular destination for international students pursuing higher education. In 2018, it ranked among the top ten countries in the world in terms of the number of foreign students, indicating that it is on its way to becoming a university and education hub. Turkey ranked among the top ten countries with 125,138 students in higher education, according to data released by the United Nations Educational, Scientific, and Cultural Organization (UNESCO). According to UNESCO data from 2018, the United States of America hosts 987,314 of the world's 5,571,402 foreign students (USA). In recent years, the number of international students in Turkey has risen by two and a half times.

UNESCO's data on higher education, prepared with various reports and studies, are 2–3 years behind. That is why we have the results of 2018 now in 2020. According to UNESCO's 2018 data, the top 10 countries in the world that attract the most international students are as follows: USA (987,314), England (452,079), Australia (444,514), (Germany 311,738), Russia (262,416), France (229,623), Canada (224,548), Japan (182,748), China (178,271), Turkey (125,138).

Reich et al. (2020) looked at state education department policy recommendations on remote learning that had been released by the end of March 2020 in all 50 US states. They found many points of agreement, including the cancellation of testing, suggestions to continue some sort of remote learning, consideration of digital and non-digital alternatives, and a desire to provide a fair and adequate education for students with disabilities.

They also questioned whether the primary objective of continuous learning during a pandemic should be to make forward progress in standards-aligned new content or to revisit and enrich skills. They suggest that, based on their results, they continue to emphasize equity, take into account the unique complexities of home-based learning, and create succinct communications for different target audiences.

After the initial shock, people in Turkey realized the value and role of education. For the most part, getting together and exchanging thoughts face to face was once thought to be very tedious. However, parents are now expressing their views in the media, claiming that it was the best method of teaching and learning for the children. The condition is not that different for those enrolled in higher education.

6 Conclusions

Via media attention, this chapter aimed to examine the fluctuation of higher education in Turkey and analyze the change in the principles assigned to education. Due to changes in higher education standards and realities, there were some restrictions on education in Turkey, as in any other country, even at the higher education levels. Each of the road's small hillocks were smoothly crossed. Returning to old ideals now seems to be almost impossible. As a result, most higher education experts agree that in the future, it will be a hybrid scheme since the quality maintained through the digital education could not be sacrificed for the sake of face-to-face education. However, there will be face-to-face classes as well. The means and infrastructure appear to have been meticulously designed to cover all aspects of higher education through interactive, virtual learning styles. The authorities do not want to step back to the days when tutors and participants were running from one class to another. The convenience of being able to communicate to anybody, anytime, with only one click, solve any problem with a zoom meeting, or sign electronic documents appears to be simpler and faster than spending hours upon hours in an office or school setting. This new approach, however, necessitates a high level of participation and commitment on the part of the participants, whether they be tutors, academics, students, or parents. University years spent in a big city might provide participants with a wealth of cultural, social, and economic perspectives. They can, however, benefit from staying at home with their parents and family members in their small towns while taking the theoretical part of education. In any case, a virtual environment will be possible to create and participate in from any place, at any time. Blended learning will begin in elementary school. As a result, they will graduate from high school earlier and have more time to learn about the world.

References

Arnett, J. J. (2000). Emerging adulthood: A theory of development from the teens through the twenties. *American Psychologist, 55*, 469–480.

Binbei School. (2020, February 25). SOHU. https://www.sohu.com/a/375788276_508621

Bryant, P. (2012). *The modern university in the digital age.* Greenwich Connect Key Documents. Educational Development Unit, University of Greenwich.

Casey, J., & Wilson, P. (2005). *A practical guide to providing flexible learning in further and higher education.* Quality Assurance Agency for Higher Education Scotland. http//www.enhancementthemes.ac.uk/documents/flexibleDelivery/FD_Flexible_Learning_JCaseyFINALWEB.pdf

Collis, B., Moonen, J., & Vingerhoets, J. (1997). Flexibility as a key construct in European training: Experiences from the TeleScopia project. *British Journal of Educational Technology, 28*, 199–217. doi:10.1111/1467-8535.00026

Driscoll, M. P. (1994). *Psychology of learning for instruction.* Allyn & Bacon.

Duderstadt, J. J. (1998). Transforming the University to serve the digital age. *Cause/Effect, 204,* 21–32.

Ergu. (2020, December 11). Uzaktan eğitim için öğretmen eğitimi. *Hürriyet.* https://www.hurriyet.com.tr/ekonomi/uzaktan-egitim-icin-ogretmen-egitimi-41685555

Goode, S., Willis, R., Wolf, J., & Harris, A. (2007). Enhancing IS education with flexible teaching and learning. *Journal of Information Systems Education, 183,* 297–302.

Gordon, N. A. (2014). *Flexible pedagogies: Technology-enhanced learning.* The Higher Education Academy. https://doi.org/10.13140/2.1.2052.5760

Gostin, L. O., Friedman, E. A., & Wetter, S. A. (2020). Responding to COVID-19: How to navigate a public health emergency legally and ethically. *Hastings Center Report, 502,* 8–12.

Gümüşoğlu, E. K. (2017). Yükseköğretimde dijital dönüşüm. *Açıköğretim Uygulamaları ve Araştırmaları Dergisi, 34,* 30–42.

Hayamizu, T. (1997). Between intrinsic and extrinsic motivation: Examination of reasons for academic study based on the theory of internalization. *Japanese Psychological Research, 392,* 98–108.

Huang, R. H., Liu, D. J., Tlili, A., Yang, J. F., & Wang, H. H. (2020). *Handbook on facilitating flexible learning during educational disruption: The Chinese experience in maintaining undisrupted learning in COVID-19 outbreak.* Smart Learning Institute of Beijing Normal University.

Işık-Akın, R. (2020, December 7). Evde Üniversiteli Olmak. *Hürriyet.* https://www.hurriyet.com.tr/egitim/evde-universiteli-olmak-41681359

Işık Akın, R., Breeman, L. D., & Branje, S. (2020). Motivation to leave home during the transition to emerging adulthood among Turkish adolescents. *Journal of Youth Studies,* 1–18.

Lee, M. J. W., & McLoughlin, C. (2010). Beyond distance and time constraints: Applying social networking tools and Web 2.0 approaches to distance learning. In G. Veletsianos (Ed.), *Emerging technologies in distance education* (pp. 61–87). Athabasca University Press.

Lewis, R., & Spencer, D. (1986). *What is Open Learning?* (Open Learning Guide, Vol. 4, pp. 9–10). London Council for Education Technology.

Lundin, R. (1999). *Flexible teaching and learning: Perspectives and practices* [Paper presentation]. UniServe Science Workshop. http://science_uniserve.edu.au/pubs/procs/wshop4/

Mayer, R. E. (1988). Learning strategies: An overview. In R. E. Mayer (Ed.), *Learning and study strategies* (pp. 11–22). Academic Press. doi:10.1016/B978-0-12-742460-6.50008-6

Nabavi, R. T. (2012). Bandura's social learning theory & social cognitive learning theory. *Theory of Developmental Psychology,* 1–24.

Noack, R., (2020, September 16). In Denmark, the forest is the new classroom. *Washington Post.* https://www.washingtonpost.com/world/2020/09/16/outdoor-school-coronavirus-denmark-europe-forest/

Özdemir, S., & Fidancan, N. (2020, December 14). Koronavirüs tedavisi gören babasına refakatçi öğretmen bahçede uzaktan eğitim veriyor. *Hürriyet.* https://www.hurriyet.com.tr/gundem/koronavirus-tedavisi-goren-babasina-refakatci-ogretmen-bahcede-uzaktan-egitim-veriyor-41687797

Özel, S. (2020, December 4). Uzaktan eğitim ve yaşanan sorunlar. *Hürriyet.* https://www.hurriyet.com.tr/teknoloji/yazarlar/doc-dr-serkan-ozel/uzaktan-egitim-ve-yasanan-sorunlar-41679484

Öztürk, S. (2020, November 18). Pandemi süreci bilgisayar satışlarını olumlu yönde etkiledi. *Hürriyet.* https://www.hurriyet.com.tr/teknoloji/pandemi-sureci-bilgisayar-satislarini-olumlu-yonde-etkiledi-41665585

Pinto-Llorente, A. M. (2020). A digital ecosystem for teaching-learning English in higher education: A qualitative case study. In S. Meri Yilan & K. Koruyan (Eds.), *ICT-based assessment, methods, and programs in tertiary education* (pp. 257–276). IGI Global. http://doi:10.4018/978-1-7998-3062-7.ch013

Reich, J., Buttimer, C. J., Fang, A., Hillaire, G., Hirsch, K., Larke, L. R., & Slama, R. (2020). *Remote learning guidance from state education agencies during the COVID-19 pandemic: A first look.* https://doi.org/10.35542/9sf.io/437e2.

Ryan, A., & Tilbury, D. (2013). *Flexible pedagogies: New pedagogical ideas.* Higher Education Academy.

Sadeka, S., Mohamad, M. S., & Sarkar, M. S. K. (2020). Disaster experiences and preparedness of the Orang Asli families in Tasik Chini of Malaysia: A conceptual framework towards building disaster resilient community. *Progress in Disaster Science, 6,* 100070.

Şanlı. (2020, November 30). Üniversitelilere online Sınav Nasıl Olacak? *Hürriyet.* https://www.hurriyet.com.tr/egitim/universitelilere-online-sinav-nasil-olacak-41675370

Şanlı. (2020, September 28). 'Zoom'a yerli rakip. *Hürriyet.* https://www.hurriyet.com.tr/ekonomi/zooma-yerli-rakip-41647618

Şenkoyuncu. (2020, November 21). Pandemide yurt dışında eğitim görmek hayal mi? *Hürriyet.* https://www.hurriyet.com.tr/yerel-haberler/bursa/pandemide-yurt-disinda-egitim-gormek-hayal-mi-41668055

Shaw, R., Kim, Y. K., & Hua, J. (2020). Governance, technology and citizen behavior in pandemic: Lessons from COVID-19 in East Asia. *Progress in Disaster Science, 6,* 100090.

Shuell, T. J. (1986). Cognitive conceptions of learning. *Review of Educational Research, 564,* 411–436.

Ülkar. (2020, August, 26). Üniversitelerde doluluk yüzde 93'ü aştı. *Hürriyet.* https://www.hurriyet.com.tr/egitim/yok-yks-2020-raporunu-acikladi-41596090

Uzun. (2020, December 14). Fakülte bu olayı konuşuyor ... Profesörü bile şaşırtan kopya: 'James Bond filmi gibi çekti'. *Hürriyet.* https://www.hurriyet.com.tr/gundem/fakulte-bu-olayi-konusuyor-profesoru-bile-sasirtan-kopya-james-bond-filmi-gibi-cekti-41687723

Whiteman, S. D., McHale, S. M., & Crouter, A. C. (2010). Family relationships from adolescence to early adulthood: Changes in the family system following firstborns' leaving home. *Journal of Research on Adolescence, 21*(2), 461–474.

Yıldız. (2020, December 10). Uzaktan eğitimde müzikten uzak kalmayalım. *Hürriyet.* https://www.hurriyet.com.tr/egitim/uzaktan-egitimde-muzikten-uzak-kalmayalim-41681366

Zhou, L., Li, F., Wu, S., & Zhou, M. (2020). "School's out, but class's on", the largest online education in the world today: Taking China's practical exploration during the COVID-19 epidemic prevention and control as an example. *Best Evidence in Chinese Education, 4*(2), 501–519. https://doi.org/10.15354/bece.20.ar023

Media Articles Consulted

Hürriyet. (2014, November 24). Türkiye'de 20 üniversiteliye bir akademisyen düşüyor. https://www.hurriyet.com.tr/egitim/turkiyede-20-universiteliye-bir-akademisyen-dusuyor-27640493

Hürriyet. (2015, February 16). Doçent adaylarına 'elektronik jüri'. https://www.hurriyet.com.tr/gundem/docent-adaylarina-elektronik-juri-28188509

Hürriyet. (2020, August 19). Uzaktan eğitim için güvenli kablosuz ağ şart. https://www.hurriyet.com.tr/teknoloji/uzaktan-egitim-icin-guvenli-kablosuz-ag-sart-41590822

Hürriyet. (2020, August, 28). Üniversitelerde dijital dönüşüm https://www.hurriyet.com.tr/egitim/universitelerde-dijital-donusum-41597695

Hürriyet. (2020, September 5). Sağlık Bakanlığı'ndan üniversitelere uzaktan eğitim tavsiyesi. https://www.hurriyet.com.tr/egitim/saglik-bakanligindan-universitelere-uzaktan-egitim-tavsiyesi-41603786

Hürriyet. (2020, September 8). İstanbul Üniversitesi'nden uzaktan eğitim açıklaması. https://www.hurriyet.com.tr/egitim/istanbul-universitesinden-uzaktan-egitim-aciklamasi-41606318

Hürriyet. (2020, September 9). Üniversitelerden 'uzaktan eğitim' kararı. https://www.hurriyet.com.tr/egitim/universitelerden-uzaktan-egitim-karari-41606732

Hürriyet. (2020, September 10). https://www.hurriyet.com.tr/egitim/627-bin-ogrenci-e-kayit-ile-universiteli-oldu-41607746

DIGITALIZATION OF HIGHER EDUCATION IN TURKEY AND COVID-19   83

Hürriyet. (2020, September 17). YÖK'te 'Uzaktan Öğretim Politikaları Komisyonu' oluşturuldu. https://www.hurriyet.com.tr/egitim/yokte-uzaktan-ogretim-politikalari-komisyonu-olusturuldu-41614296

Hürriyet. (2020, September 22). Üniversitelilere 'YÖK Sanal Laboratuvarı'nda deney imkânı. https://www.hurriyet.com.tr/egitim/universitetilere-yok-sanal-laboratuvarinda-deney-imkani-41642742

Hürriyet. (2020, October 27). Online okulda 200 milyon ders verildi. https://www.hurriyet.com.tr/egitim/online-okulda-200-milyon-ders-verildi-41647082

Hürriyet. (2020, November 5). https://www.hurriyet.com.tr/egitim/arastirma-performansinda-ilk-16-universite-41654921

Hürriyet. (2020, November 11). Güvenli okul ve uzaktan eğitim çalıştayı. https://www.hurriyet.com.tr/egitim/guvenli-okul-ve-uzaktan-egitim-calistayi-41659772

Hürriyet. (2020, November 17). Zoom uygulamasından eğitimle ilgili önemli iş birliği. https://www.hurriyet.com.tr/teknoloji/zoom-uygulamasindan-egitimle-ilgili-onemli-is-birligi-41664308

Hürriyet. (2020, November 21). 928 Mahalleye internet sözü. https://www.hurriyet.com.tr/yerel-haberler/ankara/928-mahalleye-internet-sozu-41668706

Hürriyet. (2020a, November 24). https://www.hurriyet.com.tr/egitim/egitimde-donusum-icin-zorluklar-ve-firsatlar-41670981

Hürriyet. (2020b, November 24). Salgınla birlikte dijital eğitim veren kurumlar değer kazandı. https://www.hurriyet.com.tr/teknoloji/salginla-birlikte-dijital-egitim-veren-kurumlar-deger-kazandi-41670243

Hürriyet. (2020, November 25). Aşırı ekran kullanımı kuru göz sendromunu tetikleye-bilir. https://www.hurriyet.com.tr/sosyal/cocuk-aile/asiri-ekran-kullanimi-kuru-goz-sendromunu-tetikleyebilir-41671647

Hürriyet. (2020, November 27). https://www.hurriyet.com.tr/aile/galeri-uzaktan-egitimde-calisma-odasi-icin-dekorasyon-onerileri-41673990

Hürriyet. (2020, November 29). https://www.hurriyet.com.tr/egitim/10-milyar-bu-rakam-ebayi-dunyanin-zirvesine-tasidi-41675115

Hürriyet. (2020, December 1). Tıp alanında sanal gerçeklik eğitimi başlıyor. https://www.hurriyet.com.tr/teknoloji/tip-alaninda-sanal-gerceklik-egitimi-basliyor-41676415

Hürriyet. (2020, December 2). Uzaktan eğitim 'sanal gerçeklik' boyutuna taşındı. https://www.hurriyet.com.tr/sosyal/tekno/uzaktan-egitim-sanal-gerceklik-boyutuna-tasindi-41677731

Hürriyet. (2020, December 3). YÖK, engelli öğrencileri mercek altına aldı. https://www.hurriyet.com.tr/egitim/yok-engelli-ogrencileri-mercek-altina-aldi-41678677

Hürriyet. (2020, December 5). Türkiye yabancı öğrenci sayısında ilk 10 ülke arasında. https://www.hurriyet.com.tr/egitim/turkiye-yabanci-ogrenci-sayisinda-ilk-10-ulke-arasinda-41680731

Hürriyet. (2020, December 9). Uzaktan eğitim gören çocuklar rutin göz muayenesinden geçirilmeli. https://www.hurriyet.com.tr/aile/uzaktan-egitim-goren-cocuklar-rutin-goz-muayenesinden-gecirilmeli-41683972

Hürriyet. (2020, December 10). Öğretmenden kahreden haber! Öğrencileri 112'yi aradı. https://www.hurriyet.com.tr/gundem/ogretmenden-kahreden-haber-ogrencileri-112yi-aradi-41685508.

Hürriyet. (2020a, December 13). Milli Eğitim Bakanı Ziya Selçuk:"EBA TV 3 bin 2 saat yayın yaptı". https://www.hurriyet.com.tr/gundem/milli-egitim-bakani-ziya-selcuk-eba-tv-3-bin-2-saat-yayin-yapti-41687613

Hürriyet. (2020b, December 13). Son dakika haberi: Bakan Selçuk'tan yüz yüze eğitim ve tablet açıklaması! 200 bin tablet dağıtılacak. https://www.hurriyet.com.tr/gundem/son-dakika-haberi-bakan-selcuktan-yuz-yuze-egitim-aciklamasi-41687528

Hürriyet. (2020a, December 14). MEB 500 bin tablet başvurusu nasıl ve nereden yapılır? Bakan Selçuk tarih verdi! İşte Ücretsiz tablet başvuru yapma ekranı ve formu. https://www.hurriyet.com.tr/galeri-meb-500-bin-tablet-basvurusu-nasil-yapilir-ucretsiz-tablet-basvuru-yapma-ekrani-ve-formu-41687541

Hürriyet. (2020b, December 14). 'Yapay Zekâyla' Sanal Üniversite. https://www.hurriyet.com.tr/yerel-haberler/antalya/yapay-zekayla-sanal-universite-41687807

Hürriyet. (2020c, December 14). Uzaktan eğitimde izinsiz kayıt yapıp bunu yayanlar hakkında işlem yapılabilir. https://www.hurriyet.com.tr/sosyal/cocuk-aile/uzaktan-egitimde-izinsiz-kayit-yapip-bunu-yayanlar-hakkinda-islem-yapilabilir-41688113

CHAPTER 6

Switching to Online Teaching within a Teacher Training Programme during the COVID-19 Pandemic

Dana Crăciun and Monica Oprescu

Abstract

During the education crisis generated by the COVID-19 pandemic universities and schools were forced to adapt and resort consistently to online technologies for continuing the teaching and learning process. The UNESCO report published June 2020 stressed the importance of free and open source technologies available to teachers and students, alongside access to public education and equal opportunities.

This chapter provides an overview of the emergency remote teaching strategy adopted by the West University of Timișoara, Romania during the pandemic crisis, which opted for digital courses and online learning and the manner in which the Department of Teacher Training met the challenge of preparing future teachers for the integration of digital resources and online activities in their teaching activity. Approaches previously used before, such as the BYOD approach in education (Bring Your Own Device), the need for learning in a hybrid/mixed environment, the integration of Open Educational Resources (OER) and Practices (OEP) and the importance of pedagogical models in integrating ICT in classes, have been readapted in this new context. Flexible learning, a student-centred approach, choosing free digital resources and appropriate delivery methods were a priority both in the strategy of the university and that of the department.

1 Introduction

1.1 *West University of Timișoara: Technology Adaptation and General Strategy*

In Romania, the COVID-19 pandemic crisis resulted in the closure of face-to-face courses in all higher learning institutions, including the West University of Timișoara.[1] From this starting point, the focus at the university level has been on continuing a qualitative educational process which has moved completely online. The change has been sustained by the fact that our university has benefitted from an intensive digitalisation programme in the past years,

© KONINKLIJKE BRILL NV, LEIDEN, 2022 | DOI:10.1163/9789004512672_006

all teaching personnel receiving technology and access to online e-learning (Google, Microsoft, Moodle)[2] and the network EduRoam[3] which is available in all teaching spaces, all these aspects facilitating the online didactical process from a technical perspective.

To ensure the continuity of the teaching and learning process, a crisis committee was constituted in the university, which was meant to manage the didactic and administrative situations and to establish general measures for remote teaching. As the material basis was there, the focus was on training in order to identify the online teaching strategy which allowed access for all students of the university and the continuation of the teaching and learning process. The following steps were taken:

1. Webinars on technical possibilities were offered by university specialists, tutorials and information posted online.[4] Also, a series of webinars "Împreună online" in partnership with the Polytechnic University of Timișoara was organised.[5]
2. The face-to-face timetable was kept, considering the complex situation of courses, of transversal disciplines and the teacher training programme, with the possibility to readapt the teaching and learning process for each faculty according to its specificity.
3. Open educational resources (OER) and training courses were offered, and both teachers and students were offered the possibility to freely participate in online courses on Coursera.[6]

The preoccupation in the West University of Timișoara for using OER (Open Educational Resources) and knowing OEP (Open Educational practices) was also shown through the participation of our colleague G. Grosseck from the Faculty of Sociology and Psychology in the adaptation and translation of the UNESCO guide for the use of Open Educational Practices during the coronavirus pandemic (Huang et al., 2020). At the same time, students received support for switching to remote learning through the Centre for Counselling and Career Orientation (CCCO), the Facebook, Instagram pages of the university and also with the help of student organisations, in order to become accustomed to online learning, a description of all these beginning measures being presented in Bran and Grosseck (2020). In addition, the focus was on correct information, as the phenomenon of fake news was rampant during the pandemic, especially as concerns COVID-19 (Grosseck & Malita, 2020).

1.2 Teaching and Learning at the Teacher Training Department, West University of Timișoara

Although the training programme of future teachers in Romania has a unique structure at the national level (O.M.E.N. no. 3850/2.05.2017), important steps were taken in the past years for adapting the training of future teachers to the process of digitalisation at the pre-university level, by reconsidering the methods of teaching and learning and of the didactic resources of most subjects in the teacher education programme. The changes derived from two premises:

1. The reality that future teachers will face includes digital native students who were educated during the digital age and shaped by the exposure and use of technology, (Dingli & Seychell, 2015) with a growing need for flexibility and diversity in learning (both in school and throughout their lives), ICT in the classroom and the ubiquity of mobile devices, which implies a rising necessity of technology-assisted teaching to meet the training requirements in this context.

2. The infusion of technology in education has generated new pedagogical models, such as SAMR (Substitution – Augmentation – Modification – Redefinition) (Puentedura, 2009), TPACK (Technological Pedagogical Content Knowledge) (De Rossi & Trevisan, 2018; Mishra & Koehler, 2006) or BYOD (Bring Your Own Device), the appearance of new concepts in education, such as mixed or hybrid learning, and Open Educational Resources (OER), which reflect a change in approaching teaching and learning in traditional classes (NMC Horizon Reports, 2014–2020).

1.3 Measures Taken in the Teacher Training Department before the Pandemic Crisis

Technological practices in education in the digital age, which have been presented before, formed the basis of the digital transformation of the teacher training programme in the past years. The teaching staff of the department was interested in the manner students are capable of integrating a variety of digital resources and applications, which would increase the value of the programme and offer an active teaching learner-centred approach. Thus, first we adopted a BYOD approach for the entire training programme, familiarising the pre-service teachers with this strategy and at the same time facilitating its integration in their future didactical practices. Hence, they had the opportunity to experiment with hands-on activities with the BYOD strategy, recognising its impact on teaching, becoming flexible and modern in learning. Another step was the technology integration model, which was done within the Computer Assisted Instruction/CAI discipline, all students analysing the use of the SAMR (Puentedura, 2009) and TPACK (Mishra & Koehler, 2006) models, highlighting the need for an efficient integration of resources and tools or various digital applications useful for the specialisation area of future teachers.

The results of a study published in 2019 (Crăciun, 2019) showed significant increases in all areas of TPACK skills, proving that future teachers understood the need to develop digital skills, integrate technology into specific teaching and transform learning tasks designed for students raised in the digital age. Therefore, pre-service teachers were offered the opportunity to adapt to distance learning and teaching during the crisis situation, understanding the pedagogical implications of the online didactic process.

A third direction follows the creation of educational resources in a digital format. Within the pre-service teacher training programme, enrolled students created various educational resources in digital format, including applications of augmented reality (Crăciun, 2018), starting from existing textbooks and/or resources used by teachers at the pre-university level. The resources were created both for face-to-face, online and blended activities, students being prepared for teaching in both physical and virtual environments.

A fourth direction represents the integration of OER (Open Educational Resources) and OEP (Open Educational Practices) within the curriculum of the teacher training programme. This referred to both teachers but also pre-service teachers in order to identify, use correctly and create OER. Although the level of licencing Creative Commons (CC) of the educational resources created is still low in our university, every generation of future teachers participates in instruction sessions on this topic within the CAI course.

Regarding the adoption of OERs, a study conducted in our university during 2017–2018, which involved future teachers in the Mathematics and Natural Sciences specialisations in the curriculum showed that by using OERs teachers can compare their own resources with those made by other teachers in the country or abroad, improving the quality of their teaching, encouraging pedagogical innovation and reducing the costs of accessing educational resources (Crăciun & Bunoiu, 2018). The study also revealed that the use and/or creation of OERs should be promoted throughout the initial psycho-pedagogical training programme in order to increase the probability that future teachers would use such resources in their own pedagogical practice.

These actions carried out over the past year contributed to optimal development of the didactic process in the period of crisis generated by COVID-19, the department already having integrated and adopted technology strategies, aimed at preparing future teachers to use technology in teaching, which formed the basis of distance teaching and learning activities for the past university year.

1.4 The Strategy of the Teacher Training Department in the Times of Crisis

To make the transition to remote teaching, due to the crisis situation, the council of the department established a strategy based on the university recommendations and on the experience of the universities that have already been confronted with this challenge (Bao, 2020) and the recommendations of international organisms: UNESCO (2021a, 2021b) in two materials, *Education: From disruption to recovery* and *Education in a post-Covid world: Nine ideas for public action* and the European University Association (2020) in *Resources for digital learning and teaching during the coronavirus pandemic*. The members of the department identified the most appropriate didactic strategy for the period of remote teaching, focusing on the following:

1. Communicating online with students both on the university platform, through institutional e-mail and also through social media, WhatsApp or Skype.
2. Choosing a single platform, Google classroom and the application Google Meet for synchronous and asynchronous communication with students, an exception being CAI, for which communication was done on the platform Edmodo.
3. Reorganising teaching and learning activities (both as methods and digital resources) to make accessible and facilitate online student engagement (Huang et al., 2020; McAleavy & Gorgen, 2020).
4. Rethinking the evaluation manner, with the accent on diverse formative and summative assessment (portfolio, multimedia projects, open-book or oral exam) in accord with the principles of Universal Design for Learning (UDL) at the university level (La, Dyjur & Bair, 2018).
5. The reinforcement of the online presence of teachers, by posting short pieces of information, introductory videos and prompt feedback for assignments.
6. Short preparation sessions in group or individual format of the teaching staff in the department by the colleagues who teach CAI and the Didactics of Informatics.

The measures were put into application so that by the end of April all courses took place online, 87% of teachers using Google Classroom and 100% Google Meet (Bunoiu et al., 2020). Students were proposed digital instruments for communication, interaction and learning which are frequently used at the pre-university level, as well, trying to value the period as one of experiential learning (especially in teaching practice which was also done online). Students were instructed synchronously, for those topics difficult for individual learning, but also asynchronously, for specific topics/themes, leading to complex learning activities (presentation of the subject – exercise – evaluation – self-evaluation), without making substantial curriculum changes for this period of emergency remote teaching (Hodges et al., 2020). Parallel with asynchronous learning, students benefitted from collaborative sessions, both synchronous and asynchronous, guided by the teacher. Therefore, communication competences, the improvement of self-regulated learning and the development of students' abilities to work collaboratively were improved (McAleavy & Gorgen, 2020). All measures taken aimed at completing the pre-service teachers' programme during the university year and the training programme. For the exam sessions and final exams, the decision was made at the university level for students to take all exams online; in the department all exams took place synchronously through the application Google Meet.

1.5 Experiences in the Teacher Training Department: The Strategy Adopted for Teaching Practice

As Teaching Practice was coordinated at the level of the department, it was decided to have distinct classes on Google classroom for each specialisation and level, co-teachers being the tutors from the application schools. The activity was modified minimally, keeping all didactic activities and the same manner of evaluation (portfolio) as before. The organisation was done by the teaching staff in the department, considering each specialisation and its particularities. Therefore, students had different experiences, the instruments that facilitated the learning process being diverse: WhatsApp, e-mail, Google Classroom, Moodle or the school platform.

In order to replace the effective teaching, which in some schools could not be done synchronously online, the traditional activities for Teaching Practice were replaced with activities that aimed at creating didactic resources for teaching. These included Science online (presentations, interactive videos, activity sheets, online tests), also the collaborative analysis of assistance forms and of the created didactic materials by pre-service teachers with the help of different applications (Wordwall,[7] Kahoot,[8] Quizlet,[9] Quizizz,[10] Google Forms etc.), besides the analysis and evaluation of filmed lesson sequences realised by students. The videos, having as topic the teaching of lesson sequences, were posted asynchronously on Flipgrid.[11] Afterwards they were discussed in synchronous sessions together with group colleagues, coordinators and tutors, in accordance with the principles of flexible learning (Huang et al., 2020). In order to create resources pre-service teachers accessed autochthonous OER,[12] CRED,[13] and digital textbooks.

1.6 Computer Assisted Instruction

During the Computer Assisted instruction/CAI course, the online activities designed entirely for the new situation were lectures which were moved online, and in order to value the synchronous interaction with students, a

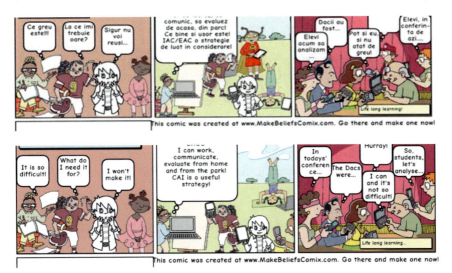

FIGURE 6.1   Comic created by students during the CAI course

flipped-classroom strategy was adopted, the course resources being posted in advance. During the activities electronic presentations were used as a basis for discussions, alongside quizzes Mentimeter,[14] Quizzes,[15] for motivating students and collaborative activities such as Padlet,[16] collaborative maps Coggle[17] or done with the Google suite. Also, to keep students motivated, they were asked to create resources (comics, animations) and the whole course was gamified, cumulative badges being given.

2 Perceptions of Teachers and Future Teachers on the Didactic Process in the Second Semester of the Academic Year 2019–2020

Another aspect of interest at the university level and also in our department was the identification of the degree of accessibility to online education, technical problems and learning issues of students, the manner in which this situation affects their academic situation and not least the manner in which they perceive this difficult period in rapport to their future teaching career.

1. The study realised in our university showed that some of the teaching staff in the department considered that the first two great difficulties were: efficient communication with students and the lack of instruments to manage groups of students in order to evaluate and give feedback. (Bunoiu et al., 2020). Also, teachers considered that online teaching requires much more preparation and the use of professional development with the help of colleagues, specialised articles and webinars. The

greatest difficulty in learning was considered to be the lack of practice in using new technologies, but they also believed that students could work autonomously, most of them succeeding in finishing online courses (Bunoiu et al., 2020).

Regarding the transferability of skills in this period, teachers considered that distance learning was easy to switch to, useful for the facilitation of students' learning and the manner in which it is structured was considered to be clear and easily understood by the students. The great majority of respondents affirmed they would also use the online instruments in face-to-face teaching, the digital competences acquired being useful for their future didactic activity (Bunoiu et al., 2020).

2. In order to identify the perspectives of the students on the didactic process in the Teacher Training Department, we used an online questionnaire for the students completing the first level of the programme, post-university level, which highlighted the technology used, accessibility to education, technical/learning problems and the opportunities/concerns generated by remote learning. 59% of the 102 students enrolled in

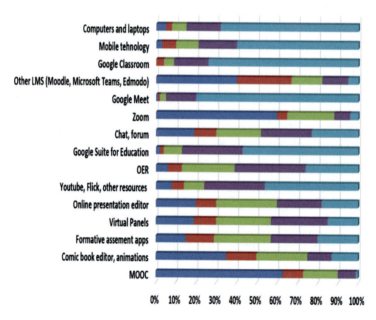

FIGURE 6.2   Pre-service teachers' responses regarding the use of technology

the CAI course answered the questionnaire 30% male and 70% female, 21% also working as substitute teachers at the pre-university level.

Here are the answers of the respondents regarding the dispositive and the digital resources used in didactic activities, both in the training programme and in the schools where they were teaching.

Regarding applications, 87% of respondents declared they often used Google suite for education, followed by resources deposits – YouTube, Flickr, presentation editors, collaborative panels, applications for tests and online questionnaires, open educational resources and also diverse applications for formative assessment. Applications for simulations, animations or MOOCS were less utilised.

The biggest problems concerning technology were the lack of familiarity, the access to resources and the unclear expectations regarding the use of technology for didactic activities. Comparing the answers of the respondents we notice different opinions regarding the manner in which teachers perceive the use of technology in teaching and the manner this is perceived by the participants in the courses. Since this was a new situation, we consider that we must follow some steps to form digital competences for the effective integration of adequate technology during remote teaching. Participants in the course identified parallel courses and activities as the greatest difficulty, as many of them worked and this affected their learning time. Personal learning obstacles proved to be the difficulty to concentrate and the allocation of time for these activities. The greatest concerns of respondents were connected to the possibility of fulfilling all course requirements and also possible delays in graduating from the programme due to the pandemic crisis.

We were also interested in the opinion of future teachers on the teaching competencies acquired within the Teacher Training Department, particularly after completing their online learning period (Table 6.1).

All answers received to this question, as a percentage, are presented in Figure 6.3.

It can be observed that pre-service teachers are confident that they can create adequate educational resources, they have formed digital competences, they can apply diverse applications to teach content and to motivate students inclusively in online teaching activities and they became conscious of the necessity of adequate class management or the necessity of pedagogic fundamentals for useful ICT in the classroom. All these are the premises of future didactical activity adapted to online or mixed teaching in the pandemic crisis where children have little access to school.

94 CRĂCIUN AND OPRESCU

TABLE 6.1   Competences formed after the teacher training programme (1 totally disagree – 5 totally agree)

	Preservice teacher competence	Score	Stand. dev.
1.	I can create educational resources useful in my own teaching activity	4.689	0.696
2.	I have become aware of the necessity of appropriate class management (including online activities)	4.607	0.665
3.	I know how to use online applications to facilitate the teaching of the content of my discipline	4.590	0.616
4.	I have become aware of the necessity of forming a network of learning to improve my teaching skills and to manage a crisis situation	4.541	0.647
5.	I have improved my digital and media skills	4.475	0.808
6.	I know useful applications for motivating students for online learning	4.475	0.887
7.	I have become aware of the necessity of pedagogical background for the efficient use of ICT in teaching and learning activities	4.459	0.886
8.	I can plan learning sequences using ICT for online teaching	4.410	0.783
9.	I can integrate useful applications to motivate my students for online learning in their specialisation	4.377	0.799
10.	I can apply and assess viable strategies for using computers /mobile devices in online didactic activities	4.361	0.731
11.	I know how to search, select and integrate open educational resources accessible online	4.344	0.854
12.	I know various e-learning strategies (synchronous/ asynchronous, individual/collaborative etc.) and can apply them selectively according to the advantages of each of them	4.197	0.872
13.	I have developed effective communication skills (verbal, written, and multimedia in a variety of styles and contexts)	4.082	1.005
14.	I can integrate a diversified palette of collaborative web 2.0 applications in the teaching process	3.820	1.057

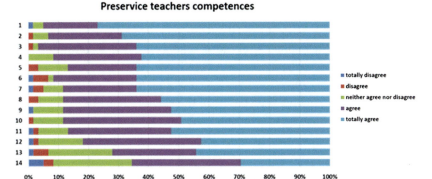

FIGURE 6.3   Preservice teachers' competences formed during completing the initial teacher training programme

Other points of interest were the problems and also the opportunities created in education by the pandemic crisis. The lack of technology in school or the support in using it was the biggest issue, pre-service teachers being confident in the capacity to select adequate technology and to offer students learning resources and varied communication channels, also diverse possibilities to express what they have learnt.

Major opportunities identified by pre-service teachers as a follow up of the online Teaching Practice activities (with reference to their future didactic activity), aim at accelerating the integration of technology in classes, the development of student autonomy and the creation of an environment that offers teachers the opportunity to be creative and to plan motivating activities for their students. The first two opportunities identified were also in accord with international opinions (United Nations Report, 2020).

Nevertheless, future teachers consider that this period did not lead to the formation of a stronger relationship with their students. This could reflect the experience during Teaching Practice when the activity was most of the times centred on sending didactic materials and evaluation, tutor teachers having minimum contact with students.

3   The Changes in the New Academic Year for the Teacher Training Department

For the new academic year, the faculties of the West University of Timișoara, taking into account the national situation, have decided to remain online for the first semester of the academic year 2020–2021. Also, the Teacher

Training Department decided to continue activities online (the department's programme is offered to students of all faculties) except for Teaching Practice which depended on the manner application schools decided to continue their activity.

In order to improve online teaching and learning, the department offered five webinars for the teaching staff, based on the EU requirements for blended learning activities and the UNESCO recommendations for flexible learning and Open Educational Resources. The documents were discussed and a unitary strategy for teaching – evaluation was set, useful applications were analysed both for synchronous and asynchronous activities and OER were identified. This step was a necessary one as the strategy for emergency remote teaching from the first semester had to be reconsidered and established on the principles of classical online learning in conformity to the recommendations of international organisations, but also adapted to the particular situation in the university and within the department.

4 Conclusions

This study provides a sketch of the activity of the Teacher Training Department at the West University of Timișoara in the second semester of the academic year 2019–2020, during the period of remote emergency teaching, following the technology and strategy adopted for teaching and learning and the opinions of teaching staff and students on the problems and opportunities identified for that period and for the future, as well. Out of all the questionnaire data we identified different opinions about online learning of both teaching staff and students, whose analysis could lead to an improvement of the teaching activity and a growth in the satisfaction of students with the programmes offered by the department. Still it is satisfying that although half of the teacher education programme took place online, pre-service teachers still considered they got the necessary competences to teach, considering they are well prepared for online education.

Still, some aspects need to be reconsidered: rethinking resources also for mobile learning, considering that some students use mobile devices; continuous training of the departments' staff to lead interactive synchronous activities online; rethinking teaching activities and formative evaluation in order to achieve better communication with students and offering prompt feedback in the online environment.

Notes

1 For details see the decision nb. 7/11.03.2020 of Comitetul Național pentru Situații Speciale de Urgență/National Committee for Special Emergency Situations, https://gov.ro/ro/masuri
2 https://elearning.e-uvt.ro/
3 https://www.eduroam.org/
4 https://resurse.e-uvt.ro/
5 https://elearning.upt.ro/en/impreuna-online/
6 https://www.coursera.org/
7 https://wordwall.net/ro
8 https://kahoot.com/
9 https://quizlet.com/
10 https://quizizz.com/
11 flipgrid.com
12 https://www.digitaliada.ro/, https://digitaledu.ro/
13 https://digital.educred.ro/
14 https://www.manuale.edu.ro/, https://www.mentimeter.com/
15 https://quizizz.com/
16 https://padlet.com/
17 https://coggle.it/

References

Bao, W. (2020). COVID-19 and online teaching in higher education: A case study of Peking University. *Human Behavior and Emerging Technologies, 2*(2), 113–115. https://doi.org/10.1002/hbe2.191

Bran, R., & Grosseck, G. (2020). Press RESET: Digitalising education in disruptive times. *Revista Românească Pentru Educație Multidimensională, 12*(1 Supp 2), 39–48. https://doi.org/10.18662/rrem/12.1sup2/245

Bunoiu, M., Ilie, M., Cimpoca, B., Smarandache, I., & Chereches, V. (2020). *Carrying out the teaching process in online regime at Western University from Timișoara – The perspective of the staff teaching.* https://cda.uvt.ro/wp-content/uploads/2020/05/UVT-proces-didactic-online-Raport-mai-2020

Crăciun, D. (2018). Class orchestration in an augmented reality based environment. In M. M. Crișan & R. A. Toma (Eds.), *Beliefs and behaviours in education and culture.* Pro-Universitaria.

Crăciun, D. (2019). Training future language teachers to educate the digital generation, *Journal of Educational Sciences, 20*(1), 90–107.

Crăciun, D., & Bunoiu, M. (2018). Teacher training in the context of open science and science education, In I. Roceanu (Ed.), *The 14th international eLSE conference proceedings* (Vol. 4, pp. 319–326). Carol I NDU Publishing House.

Decision nb. 7/11.03.2020 of Comitetul Național pentru Situații Speciale de Urgență [National Committee for Special Emergency Situations]. https://gov.ro/ro/masuri

De Rossi, M., & Trevisan, O. (2018). Technological pedagogical content knowledge in the literature: how TPCK is defined and implemented in initial teacher education, *Italian Journal of Educational Technology, 26*(1), 7–22.

Dingli, A., & Seychell, D. (2015). *The new digital natives*. Springer Verlag.

European University Association. (2020, April 23). *Resources for digital learning and teaching during the coronavirus pandemic*. Retrieved March 9, 2021, from https://eua.eu/resources/news/494-resources-for-digital-learning-and-teaching-during-the-coronavirus-pandemic.html

Grosseck, G., & Malita, L. (2020). Insights from Romania's reaction to coronavirus info-demic. Towards an educational approach. *Logos Universality Mentality Education Novelty: Social Sciences, 9*(1), 119–138. https://doi.org/10.18662/lumenss/9.1/38

Hodges, Ch., Moore, S., Locke, B., Bond, A., & Aaron, M. (2020). *The Difference between emergency remote teaching and online learning*. Retrieved March 16, 2021, from https://er.educause.edu/articles/2020/3/the-difference-between-emergency-remote-teaching-and-online-learning

Huang, R. H., Liu, D. J., Guo, J., Yang, J. F., Zhao, J. H., Wei, X. F., Knyazeva, S., Li, M., Zhuang, R. X., Looi, C. K., & Chang, T. W. (2020). *Guidance on flexible learning during campus closures: ensuring course quality of higher education in COVID-19 outbreak*. Smart Learning Institute of Beijing Normal University.

Huang, R., Liu, D., Tlili, A., Knyazeva, S., Chang, T. W., Zhang, X., Burgos, D., Jemni, M., Zhang, M., Zhuang, R., & Holotescu, C. (2020). *Ghid pentru aplicarea Practicilor Educaționale Deschise în timpul pandemiei de coronavirus. Utilizarea Resurselor Educaționale Deschise în conformitate cu recomandările UNESCO* (G. Grosseck, D. Andone, & C. Holotescu, Trans.). Smart Learning Institute of Beijing Normal University.

La, H., Dyjur, P., & Bair, H. (2018). *Universal design for learning in higher education*. Taylor Institute for Teaching and Learning, University of Calgary.

McAleavy, T., & Gorgen, K. (2020). *Report overview of emerging country level response to providing educational continuity under COVID-19*. Best practice in pedagogy for remote teaching, EdTech and coronavirus (COVID-19) series. Retrieved March 9, 2021, from https://edtechhub.org/coronavirus/resources-and-tools/

Mishra, P., & Koehler, M. (2006). Technological pedagogical content knowledge: A framework for teacher knowledge. *Teachers College Record, 108*(6), 1017–1054. https://doi.org/10.1111/j.1467-9620.2006.00684.x

NMC Horizon Reports, 2014–2017. Retrieved March 9, 2021, from https://www.nmc.org/nmc-horizon/

O.M.E.N. No. 3850/2.05.2017. Retrieved March 16, 2021, from https://www.edu.ro/sites/default/files/fisiere%20articole/ORDIN%203850-2017_0.pdf

Puentedura, R. (2009). *As we may teach: Educational technology, from theory into practice*. Retrieved March 9, 2021, from http://www.hippasus.com/rrpweblog/archives/000025.html

UNESCO. (2021a). *Education: From disruption to recovery*. Retrieved March 9, 2021, from https://en.unesco.org/covid19/educationresponse

UNESCO. (2021b). *Education in a post-COVID world: Nine ideas for public action*. Retrieved March 9, 2021, from https://en.unesco.org/sites/default/files/education_in_a_post-covid_world-nine_ideas_for_public_action.pdf

United Nations. (2020, August 4) *Policy Brief: Education during COVID 19 and beyond*. Retrieved March 9, 2021, from https://www.un.org/development/desa/dspd/wp-content/uploads/sites/22/2020/08/sg_policy_brief_covid-19_and_education_august_2020.pdf

CHAPTER 7

The Pandemic and the End of the Lecture

Pete Woodcock

Abstract

The COVID-19 pandemic has forced higher education institutions to rethink and adjust the ways in which their regular activities are carried out. This chapter addresses the issue of the lecture, a quintessential element of traditional university life, and speculates on the format of the lecture in universities post-pandemic or whether the university lecture as we knew it will cease to exist altogether. An online survey was distributed to university educators which invited them to share experiences of teaching since the start of the pandemic, and to reflect on changes in their practices once and if university life returned to normal. Most predicted a return to normal albeit in a blended model of learning. Although COVID-19 has contributed to certain transformations in the delivery of academic content, many questions remain to be addressed regarding the future of academic activities in Higher Education Institutions.

∙ ∙ ∙

Some people talk in their sleep. Lecturers talk while other people sleep.

ALBERT CAMUS

∙ ∙
∙

1 Introduction

The COVID-19 pandemic has had a significant impact on the university sector, and the way it conducts its teaching and learning activities in particular. This chapter focuses its attention on just one of these teaching and learning activities, namely the lecture. With campuses initially closed for face-to-face teaching from late spring until autumn 2020, and then perhaps operating on a much lower capacity when they reopened, traditional lectures delivered face to face have largely vanished. They have been replaced with online lectures,

THE PANDEMIC AND THE END OF THE LECTURE   101

some delivered in a synchronous manner, others in an asynchronous manner –
it is perhaps not too large a hyperbole to say that the COVID-19 pandemic has
been single handedly responsible for the biggest shake up to the university
lecture in half a millennium.

The traditional university lecture had already been under attack from two
directions in the years before the pandemic. One critique is that technology
renders it obsolete, and the other suggests that its didactic nature renders it
an unhelpful educational tool. Indeed, some academics have promoted the
'flipped classroom' as an alternative to the traditional lecture. These critiques,
coupled with the enhanced training and experience colleagues have received
in online learning since the commencement of the pandemic, have led many
colleagues to question whether we will ever return to the lecture in the post
pandemic world. Is the lecture as we have understood it dead?

This chapter will argue that the death of the lecture is greatly exaggerated.
It will outline the main critiques of the lecture, then provide a pen picture of
how the sector coped with teaching and learning in the pandemic. It will then
suggest that the lecture is likely to return for a variety of reasons. It will be
suggested that the lecture as an institution will return as academic staff think
that this is what their universities will want, and because one can foster more
interaction on campus than online. Sure enough in a post pandemic world academics are likely to augment their teaching with more online materials, and
are mindful of the need for interactivity; however, there will be a place for the
lecture in the post pandemic teaching and learning world.

2   **The Lecture and Its Critics**

The traditional university lecture has come under a pincer attack in the last
two decades, with some critics attacking its anachronistic on campus presence,
and others focusing on its didactic focus and its lack of interactivity that makes
it a less than useful educational tool. So, one criticism focuses on the ability of
technology to free us from the campus for lectures, the other focuses on the
didactic nature of the traditional lecture, suggesting that this is a poor form
of education. One thing is certain is that critics of the lecture have an uphill
battle to fight to persuade academics and students of the need for change in
the chief method of teaching that has dominated education in universities in
the twentieth and twenty-first century.

The lecture and a university education are perhaps indivisibly linked in
the popular imagination. From Jasper's advice to Charles Ryder in *Brideshead
Revisited* 'to go to the best lectures ... irrespective of whether they are ... [on

your course] or not' (Waugh, 2000, p. 21), to Mark Zuckerberg leaving a lecture whilst solving an equation in *The Social Network*, the notion that going to lectures is what undergraduate students do seems inescapable. Indeed, in UK universities, most academic staff are called either Lecturers, Senior Lecturers, or sometimes Principal Lecturers, and even the title 'Reader' holds an historic link with the lecture.[1] That conducting lectures is a central element of what academics are supposed to do seems bound up in their job identity. Thus, when we think of a university education, the image persists of a tiered theatre on a campus, with a lecturer at the front speaking didactically to a group of students whose job it is to listen and take notes. Certainly, the equipment available to the lecturer to aid their presentation and students to take notes changes with time, as do the fashions sported by everyone in the room. The chalkboard gave way to the overhead projector, which in turn was rendered obsolete by PowerPoint, just as the notebook and pen gave way to the laptop, but the image of the lecture persists.

Many have predicted that we have been on the cusp of a radical overhaul of the way in which universities conduct their teaching for some time. As far back as 2001 Duderstadt, for example, noted the potential for technology to 'have a profound impact on teaching, freeing the classroom from the constraints of space and time' (Duderstadt, 2001, p. 55). The lecture need not take place in a tiered lecture theatre, with students being able to access lectures online. Indeed, in the same year, when outlining his famous dichotomy of digital natives and digital immigrants, Prensky noted that today's 'students are no longer the people our education system was designed to teach' (Prensky, 2001, p. 1). Therefore, for some time there have been those that imagined that technology and connectivity could free us from the physical presence of much of our current HE practice, and that our students were more in tune to this technology than educators or administrators in higher education were.

The other chief criticism of the lecture focuses less on them as being events in space and time, but rather in their form and style; that is to say, the type of teaching that often goes on within them. It argues that lectures, when they are didactic in nature (that is, that the lecturer presents information and the students simply receive this information rather than engage in any manner of active learning) is a poor teaching and learning technique. As such one could argue that this criticism is not of lectures *per se*, but rather a critique of a manner of carrying out lectures (admittedly one that is perhaps dominant in the sector).

Freeman et al.'s influential and startling study of 2014 compared STEM courses that had traditional lecturing with those that had some element of active learning. Its results were stark, and heavily support the notion that

THE PANDEMIC AND THE END OF THE LECTURE 103

lectures with an element of active learning are superior to those perhaps more traditional didactic lectures:

> These results indicate that average examination scores improved by about 6% in active learning sections, and that students in classes with traditional lecturing were 1.5 times more likely to fail than were students in classes with active learning. (Freeman et al., 2014, p. 8410, emphasis added)

Unsurprisingly, they concluded that:

> The results raise questions about the continued use of traditional lecturing as a control in research studies, and support active learning as the preferred, empirically validated teaching practice in regular classrooms. (Freeman et al., 2014, p. 8410)

This discovery and those like it led Eric Mazur to declare that 'it's almost unethical to be lecturing' (Mazur, cited in Worthen, 2015). Not only does lecturing in a traditional format lead to worse marks and more failures, it also hits certain students harder than others. In traditional didactic learning courses, there is a gap between male and female students, in courses with active learning both genders do better, but female students gain disproportionately and close the gap (Lambert, 2012).

So, this critique of the lecture looks at the type of learning that goes on within it and shows that traditional didactic lectures perform much worse than those with elements of active learning within. It is a call therefore to reexamine how to conduct a lecture rather than an attack on the lecture itself. It is a critique though that has radical implications for what will go on at the university, however. Firstly, staff training and discussion of pedagogical elements is a necessity but in many ways this is the easy part, the second and harder part would involve universities to reexamine their estates and room booking procedures. 'Most classrooms' on university campuses, Mazur points out 'are built with just one purpose: focusing the attention of many on the professor' (Mazur, cited in Lambert, 2012). And this is clearly true – even if most rooms are not auditoriums in the traditional tiered form, often the furniture is laid out as if it were one. Oftentimes the complicated timetabling systems that exist in all universities struggle to allocate the room which makes student discussion possible to the academic who wishes to conduct their session in that manner.

Whereas I have presented in this chapter hitherto the 'time and space' and the 'content' critiques as being discrete and separate arguments, this is not necessarily the case, and perhaps crucially the solutions to these critiques heavily overlap. They are both present in the notion of the 'Flipped Classroom' (also sometimes referred to as the 'Inverted Classroom') approach to Higher Education that has gained many adherents in recent times and has perhaps provided the main model of academic delivery to challenge the standard lecture. In this, the explanation of concepts (the didactic information giving element of any module course) is taken out of the classroom and put perhaps online by way of video, narrated PowerPoint, audio file and the like. Students then access this in their own time, and as time is then freed up on courses by not having lectures, more seminar/workshop time is created.

Here lectures are no longer events in the sense that students and academics need to travel onto campus and occupy the same time and space as one another – they are accessible online – and as such satisfy the criticisms of those who see the lack of technology used as being a chief problem with the lecture. Additional time is then made for seminars and workshops, on campus, to promote active learning. So, this model would go some way to addressing the critiques of the lecture as a didactic method. The lecture in this model is seen as being primarily about inputting information – which is perhaps problematic; one does not need to be a wholehearted supporter of the traditional didactic lecture to see that building arguments, connecting ideas, and carrying out certain forms of analysis are at least an equal part to a lecture as giving information; especially in the humanities and social sciences. The Flipped Classroom, however, illustrates that the lecture is in the process of being modified in higher education at the moment and has not remained static, although the change has been led by a small but committed group of colleagues.

3 The Lecture and the Pandemic

The COVID-19 pandemic, and the lockdowns that followed, forced the Higher Education sector's hand to address issues around the physical location of lectures, as it was no longer permissible to hold them on campus. As campuses were closed, lectures and seminars were speedily switched online, with educators rapidly having to learn new technological skills and pedagogical methods. It dragged universities and academics, technology enthusiasts might argue, kicking and screaming into the 21st century. Institutionally universities rapidly needed to take inventory of the online learning platforms and subscriptions that they possessed. Academics, whether technologically savvy or not, had to ensure that they had the necessary skills to teach at distance. Training courses were hastily arranged, hardware tested, broadband connections checked; in

THE PANDEMIC AND THE END OF THE LECTURE   105

terms of infrastructure and skills, the pandemic forced a rapid reevaluation of universities' teaching offer that was unprecedented in modern times.

However, there was variation amongst academics and institutions in how online lectures would be delivered; online delivery is not, in and of itself, a pedagogical formula and different practices emerged around the sector, each with its own advantages and disadvantages. Perhaps one of the key dilemmas faced by academics is that of the two chief approaches to delivering online lectures (online synchronous and online asynchronous), the former allows for the interactivity that pedagogical critics of the lecture would like, whilst remaining online, the latter loses that interactivity, but frees the lecture not only from space but also from time. Online delivery provides no magic bullet from the perspective of overhauling the lecture.[2]

Some lecturers made their lectures available online asynchronously, recording their lectures and distributing them to students via a Virtual Learning Environment.[3] This form of lecture meant that students could view them at a time that was convenient to them, no longer having to timetable their day around lectures; it freed the lecture from time and space, but the cost was the lack of interactivity. Sure, enough interactivity might be built onto other areas of modules or courses, but the lecture remained didactic; perhaps even more so than in person. Students could not ask questions, could not discuss concepts with fellow learners live, and lecturers were consigned to speaking into a camera with no immediate feedback on their lecture. The portability of education has its costs, and it changed for many what it meant to be a lecturer. Often the lecturer leading an asynchronous course might find themselves more of a recorder and curator of learning resources than a lecturer. This should not surprise us as research on this model of education often found that lecturers spent 'a great deal of time gathering and organizing materials and getting them into digital or other media formats' (Coppola et al., 2002, p. 180).

Other educators choose to hold their lectures online synchronously on platforms such as Zoom, Microsoft Teams, or Google Hangouts. Perhaps the availability of platforms allowing multiple users to log into a video event is the most significant recent advance in computing technology educationally speaking. These allowed the possibility of interaction to remain between lecturer and student (even when the latter were unwilling or unable to switch on their cameras, the chat function remained a popular vehicle for discussion), but lectures were not freed from time. Students and lecturers had to log on at the same time and were dependent on their broadband connections and technological skill to participate in the sessions. But this method of lecture kept the notion of it being an event. Students and lecturers were participating in something together at the same time. Lecturers battled on as best they could, experimenting with breakout room discussion where the technology and know-how allowed. An often-reported challenge to the interactiveness made possible with online synchronous activities was that students were often nervous to participate, and would switch their cameras and microphones off, so the process of giving a lecture was not too dissimilar to an asynchronous one. Lecturers often felt, to stretch Sherry Turkle's phrase, alone together (Turkle, 2012). They were online together with students, but they felt alone delivering the lecture.

Of course, synchronous activities could also be recorded and made available online asynchronous for students unable to make the specific time slot (or indeed those who wanted to watch an element of the lecture again). However, it is not only the lecturer who is recorded, it is also the student contributions, and recording these raises interesting discussions around privacy and barriers to participation in lectures.

So the pandemic has forced us as professionals to examine ways to deliver our material that does not involve us being all in the same (physical) room at the same time. But does this mean necessarily that post the pandemic, when delivery could return to how it had been prior to lockdown, that the lecture will be altered or remain the same? The purpose of the remainder of this chapter is to discuss this.

4 Business as Usual? The Lecture after the Pandemic

In November/December of 2020 I created and distributed an online survey aimed at university educators to share their experiences of teaching since the start of the pandemic, and to outline their reflections as to how their practice might change when university education could, theoretically return to normal. Thirty-nine colleagues completed this questionnaire. I asked the respondents out of online synchronous, online asynchronous and on campus face-to-face which had been the most effective teaching they had conducted during the pandemic. 44.12% responded online synchronous, 14.71% online asynchronous, 26.47% responded on campus face-to-face, and 14.71% said they were all the same. There is a clear bias here towards methods of education in which the possibility of interaction between lecturers and students exists with online synchronous and on campus face-to-face combined receiving 70.59%. The notion of freeing the lecture from both time *and* space via asynchronous online lectures seems to have little support from the respondents to my survey.

When asked if they intend to return to deliver their lectures on campus face-to-face when things return to normal after the pandemic the respondents to my survey are unequivocal with 64.10% saying yes, and 15.38% saying no (with the rest responding that either they do not have lectures, or that it is too early to say). However, whereas they intend to return to delivering their lectures face-to-face on campus, this does not mean to say that there is a desire for things to return to exactly the same way as prior to the pandemic. It appears that their exposure to online learning tools has whetted their appetite as when asked if they anticipate continuing to use some of the learning methods they have employed in the pandemic 84.21% responded that they would, and only 2.63% saying they wouldn't (with 13.16% saying it was too early to tell). So whereas it appears that the experience of the pandemic has not led (yet) to the respondents of my survey to conclude that lectures on campus should be abolished, it has led them to conclude that there are interesting and useful distance learning tools available for them to employ in their courses.

When asked why they had responded the way they had to the question asking if they intended to return their lectures to campus after the end of the pandemic, some interesting themes emerged. The first one was that they did not imagine that they would have all that much choice in the matter, and as one respondent suggested 'there will be an expectation that face-to-face lectures recommence'. So, universities would be keen for them to return onto campus regardless of how individual lecturers thought about it, indeed, another responded that their 'university is keen to return to face-to-face as soon as possible'. Another said that lectures would return to campus as 'politically and economically the pull of the lecture is too strong regardless of the evidence against it', another that 'I think my institution will make colleagues do so', another that 'I will likely use some asynchronous lectures post-COVID, but suspect the wider institutional timetable will dictate a return to mostly traditional lectures'. So these are not pedagogical points, but rather an acceptance that academics do not have full agency on this issue, and that universities are likely to want a return to campus to create as one respondent sums it up that management will want to see a return to 'the university experience, which happens in expensive buildings'.

Despite this skepticism, academics are very keen to return to a blended model of learning. This might include on campus face to face lectures, but that might be only a part of the educational experience as opposed to the crucial element of it. As one respondent sums it up:

> Blended and modular education for skill and knowledge enhancement is the need of the hour. A good mix live (face-to-face/synchronous) as well as asynchronous delivery is critical in a fast paced world filled with the need of continuous educational enhancement. It helps in providing

value-based learning cutting across the constraints of time and geographies (time zones).

This notion that we are at a point in time when we should not turn back to the methods of education we employed prior to the pandemic is echoed by another respondent who suggests that we 'shouldn't be considering going back to how things were. We need a hybrid. Let's pick the best bits of both'. Another simply suggests that 'I think the combination of pre-recorded content followed by in-person taught sessions will work well'.

Even those academics who wished to return to on campus face-to-face lectures saw the benefits of incorporating more technology into the business of the university. For example, this respondent who suggested:

> The good thing about face-to-face lectures is that you get a sense of how well people are following your lesson. You can pick up signals from the audience that can't be gathered in an online session. That said, I will definitely continue to do one-to-one meetings by Teams. This is because students find it more convenient and are more likely to accept study support meetings if they can be done virtually.

So, whereas this respondent gives their endorsement to the on campus face-to-face lecture due to their ability to better 'read' the students whilst in the room with them, they also suggest that there is a place for more technology in education even if that isn't replacing the lecture itself.

I asked the respondents if they felt that they had received sufficient training on online teaching and learning methods, and here the results were mixed with 52.78% saying yes, and 47.22% saying no. So, whereas the majority say yes, it is hardly a ringing endorsement of the training made available to them. A slight nervousness about using the technology can be detected from the responses. One respondent noted that they were 'still adapting to online delivery. *I would like to think it's something I will get better at going forward*' (emphasis added). Another noted that lecturing 'online is ok but has its limitations – I just can't do everything I would like to do or have the resources available that I would like'. Another pointed to the time commitment needed to record asynchronous learning resources and noted that doing lectures in this manner took 'almost five times as long to prepare' and that consequently next year, 'I may instead simply record my live lectures [instead]'. So, there is a sense of unease at the moment about the role of the technology, if they have had sufficient training, if they had the time to do things perfectly, and perhaps that sometimes a reasonable effort is more likely than striving at perfection. Of course, this nervousness

THE PANDEMIC AND THE END OF THE LECTURE   109

is entirely understandable. The respondents to this survey had had less than a calendar year since lockdowns and reduced capacities at university had made online learning necessary. Likewise, institutions had had limited time to get the appropriate equipment, software licenses and the like up and running, still fewer developed appropriate training and support for staff. If we returned with a similar set of questions to our respondents in a year or two's time, we may get a different set of responses.

So, what the respondents to my survey seem to be telling us is mixed. There is an expectation that lectures will return to campus post pandemic. For some this is something to be welcomed, for some it is something to be accepted. Some respondents think that having on campus face-to-face adds something to the educational experience, others think that it will be a *fait accompli* imposed by the organisation of their university. But there is an expectation that the lecture will endure and return to campus when the pandemic is over. This does not mean to say that academics expect things to return the same way as before the pandemic as nearly all of my respondents saw some role for online learning when the ability to meet face-to-face resumes. This might mean recording some lectures or adding additional resources, or it might mean making office hours or student one to one support meetings online using Microsoft Teams, Zoom, and/or Google Hangouts. This is combined with a slight nervousness, a sense that they are feeling their way through something new and they are not entirely convinced they know what will be the end result. Not only do they have this sense, but a significant minority feel that they have received insufficient training from their institution. There were also respondents that are clear supporters of the blended learning method; but even if one is not (or did not pre-Pandemic regard themself as a supporter of the blended learning method) there is a sense that using these tools has created blended learning adherents of us all.

5   Conclusion

This chapter has suggested that despite the criticisms levelled at the lecture as an institution, and the experiences of online learning that professionals at universities have been forced into, the feeling amongst academics is that after the pandemic is over, on campus face-to-face lectures will resume. So, the potential death of the lecture has been greatly exaggerated. That does not mean to say, however, that education as a whole will return to normal post pandemic. The feeling is amongst colleagues that on campus lectures will be supported with a variety of other online methods, so a more blended approach be taken, and perhaps interactivity being built into courses in ways other than the lecture.

This chapter is only intended as a brief 'think piece' on what might happen to the lecture, and numerous questions still remain that would form the basis of some interesting further research. Firstly, bearing in mind that one of the key criticisms of the lecture as an educational tool is its lack of interactivity, it would be interesting to see precisely what academics are doing in lectures. The notion of the lecturer speaking and everyone else listening seems a touch like a straw person to me; are there colleagues who teach in this manner, or is interactivity standard and if so, what activities are colleagues doing with students? Secondly the voice of students has been noticeably absent in this piece. What are their reflections on the role of the lecture in their studies? Which form of online lecture did they prefer in the COVID-19 lockdown? Do they want to spend their studies using online learning more or would they like to be on campus? Thirdly and finally, what should the institutional response to these issues be? We have seen discussions that academics feel that on campus face-to-face lectures will return post pandemic as it is what university management will want. Also, that the layout of the majority of rooms on campus is not conducive to the interaction that some pedagogical theory demands. Is this true? And if so, what should we as academics do about it?

Notes

1   The more American nomenclature of Assistant Professor, Associate Professor, and Professor is used in some UK Universities, but not in most.
2   Of course, whereas asynchronous lectures do not contain much by the way of interactivity with the lecture itself, this does not mean to say that interactive elements cannot be introduced within a diet of education in some manner (with other activities, an online seminar at another time, for example, addressing the same topic as the lecture). This essay is, however, focused on the lecture as an object of study rather than a schedule of teaching as a whole.
3   Asynchronous learning is not, of course, synonymous with the internet. Lectures in the past have been delivered via video cassettes, and in the case of the British Open University, via late night television. What recent developments in Internet and Computing technology has done, however, is make the recording, distribution, and viewing of asynchronous materials easier.

References

Coppola, N. W., Hiltz, S. R., & Rotter, N. G. (2002). Becoming a virtual professor: Pedagogical roles and asynchronous learning networks. *Journal of Management Information Systems, 18*(4), 169–189. https://doi.org/10.1080/07421222.2002.11045703

Duderstadt, J. J. (2001, March). The future of the university in the digital age. *Proceedings of the American Philosophical Society, 145*(1), 54–72. https://www.jstor.org/stable/1558325

Freeman, S., Eddy, S. L., McDonough, M., Smith, M. K., Okoroafor, N., Jordt, H., & Wenderoth, M. P. (2014). Active learning increases student performance in science, engineering, and mathematics. *Proceedings of the National Academy of Sciences of the United States of America, 111*(23), 8410–8415. https://doi.org/10.1073/pnas.1319030111

Lambert, C. (2012, March/April). Twilight of the lecture. *Harvard Magazine*. Retrieved November 19, 2020, from https://harvardmagazine.com/2012/03/twilight-of-the-lecture

Prensky, M. (2001, September/October). Digital natives, digital immigrants. *On the Horizon, 9*(5), 1–6. https://www.emerald.com/insight/content/doi/10.1108/10748120110424816/full/pdf?title=digital-natives-digital-immigrants-part-1

Turkle, S. (2012). *Alone together: Why we expect more from technology and less from each other*. Basic Books.

Waugh, E. (2000). *Brideshead revisited*. Penguin Modern Classics.

Worthen, M. (2015, October 17). Lecture me. Really. *The New York Times*. https://www.nytimes.com/2015/10/18/opinion/sunday/lecture-me-really.html

CHAPTER 8

Facing Adversity at the University

A Case Study to Reflect on Pedagogical Challenges in Times of Pandemic Risk

Aurora Ricci and Elena Luppi

Abstract

In a few months, the coronavirus (COVID-19) affected a large part of the world, forcing a huge number of extremely different countries to face common challenges. One of the most interesting and crucial challenges is being played out in the educational field. This chapter focuses on describing how the University of Bologna (UNIBO) is facing the pandemic emergency by presenting, in particular, empirical research on a study program. By exploring the first results of a survey (pre- and post-emergency distance learning) addressed to a target group of Veterinary Medicine students, we are going to highlight some emerging trends and to reflect on the impact of this emergency on teaching and learning practices.

1 Introduction

At the end of December 2019, the World Health Organization (WHO) received the first official bulletin related to the presence of a pneumonia case with unknown etiology in Wuhan city (China) (WHO, 2020a; Zhu et al., 2020). Three weeks later the Chinese government implemented in Wuhan and then in twelve other cities in Hubei province (Rubin & Wessely, 2020) the strictest form of quarantine ever seen in the world since the "Spanish flu" one hundred years earlier. The presence of the first pneumonia cases of COVID-19 in Italy were detected at the end of January and the first consistent cluster of Italian cases was identified during the first half of February, in the north of Italy. Despite the fact that the outbreak of the pandemic was officially declared by WHO on March 11, 2020 (WHO, 2020b), the Italian government already started to impose severe restrictions as of March 9 (Loli Piccolomini & Zama, 2020). Strict risk reduction and prevention measures such as national lockdowns, quarantine, physical distancing, and travel restrictions were extensively implemented (Yanes-Lane et al., 2020) particularly for Italy, the first country in Europe to be affected by the spread of COVID-19, and which suffered the greatest losses during the first wave of the pandemic.

© KONINKLIJKE BRILL NV, LEIDEN, 2022 | DOI:10.1163/9789004512672_008

Starting from the 24th of February 2020, all Italian Universities were forced to suspend any teaching activity in order to reduce the danger of contagion. One week later the University of Bologna transferred online 70% of the lectures and then after two weeks 100%, in synchronous mode, using the Microsoft Teams platform. More in detail, 3,667 lectures, 215,880 examinations and 10,069 graduations have been provided online from early March to the end of the semester in July 2020. Despite both the unprecedented demand linked to workforce efforts in public health services and economic contraction which affected companies, internships have not been interrupted. Indeed, agreements with the hosting organizations and the provision of alternative activities monitored by academic supervisors, allowed the internships to be carried out remotely.

An intense program of events and activities for communication, cultural entertainment, sport, and community networking was launched during the lockdown, but the greatest efforts of the UNIBO involved innovation in teaching and learning. In particular, the emergency outlined the need to face several new educational and pedagogical challenges. The lockdown period and the subsequent social distancing restrictions forced universities to transfer their teaching activities to virtual environments, without any trial or piloting time.

This contribution is part of a wider project on the innovation of teaching and learning practices conducted in the UNIBO. The aim of this work was to explore the first results of a survey (pre- and post-emergency distance learning) addressed to a target group of Veterinary Medicine students, in order to highlight some emerging trends and to reflect on the impact of the emergency on teaching and learning practices.

2 The University of Bologna's Innovation in Learning and Teaching

During the last few months, the University of Bologna implemented a plan for monitoring, research, and training, with the aim of promoting and increasing the quality and innovation of teaching and learning practices during the emergency. The activities related to Innovation in Teaching and Learning at the University of Bologna have been designed and implemented in the last few years by drawing inspiration from the theoretical-methodological framework of Formative Educational Evaluation (House & Howe, 2003; Lincoln, 2003; Scriven, 2003; Stake, 2003; Stufflebeam, 2003), in particular, from Training Research (Betti & Vannini, 2013; Betti et al., 2015). These processes are characterized by the involvement of stakeholders (students, teachers, and administrative staff) in data analysis and project redesign, with a particular focus on improvement

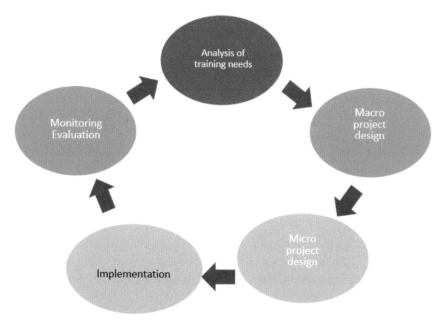

FIGURE 8.1   Phases of the learning and teaching innovation process (from Luppi et al., 2021)

(Vertecchi, 1976), in order to promote diagnostic, decision-making, and project design skills (House & Howe, 2003). In other words, students and professors have been involved, as active participants, in a process of analysis and reflection on their transversal competencies, roles, and teaching beliefs.

The process can be condensed in the following phases: needs analysis, macro and micro-project design, planning, and implementation of the training activities, mid-term, and final evaluation (e.g. Figure 8.1).

According to this method, specific monitoring and training activities have been introduced in order to support professors and lecturers in teaching and learning innovation. From February to June 2020 the University of Bologna promoted some specific research and evaluations on innovation in learning and teaching and 21 training initiatives were provided, with 81 hours of training, for a total of 590 teachers involved. Finally, based on the results of the analysis of online teaching experiences, additional training is under design.

With the spread of the pandemic and the consequent lockdown phase, a monitoring process was activated both through surveys addressed to students (technical and learning aspects) and to teachers (online teaching practices). In particular:

– Almost 10,000 students arising from all study programs answered a short online survey launched two weeks after the beginning of online teaching. Preliminary results have shown a relatively low incidence of technical

FACING ADVERSITY AT THE UNIVERSITY

difficulties (internet access quality and the use of online learning platform) and medium-high satisfaction levels concerning learning aspects as interaction with teachers, attention during teaching activities (the average score, in this case, is lower) and the overall experience in online lessons (Luppi et al., 2020). These early results motivated reflection on the opportunity to innovate online teaching practices, thus a formative video with the main results summarized has been distributed to the entire UNIBO Community. The same survey was proposed again at the end of the semester and at the beginning of the following academic year.

- A survey of teaching practices was sent out to explore the learning and teaching practices and to encourage collegial debate on them. Data obtained from 600 respondents have been analysed and the teaching practices described have been clustered by scientific and thematic areas. Using insight gained from this study, in May and June 2020 experts in disciplinary didactics conducted five virtual training workshops, in order to prepare the teaching staff for the blended synchronous phase starting from September 2020.
- Almost 400 teaching staff answered an online questionnaire launched between July and November 2020 concerning beliefs, attitudes, and practices during the pandemic emergency. Data analysis is ongoing.

3   Case Study on a University Program during the Pandemic

The current case study is part of a wider project on the innovation of teaching and learning practices conducted in the School of Veterinary Medicine of UNIBO. Within this Research Training's longitudinal study design, several observations of the same learning variables were repeated. In particular, the first quantitative measurement was planned for January 2020 during the first assessment period[1] and the second quantitative measurement was planned for the end of June 2020 (and lasted one month) during the second assessment period.

The spread of the pandemic emergency affected the research design and the research focus shifted to monitoring emergency distance learning. This chapter seeks to address the following research questions: (1) how did the academic study programs face emergency online learning? and (2) what are the next challenges after the pandemic?

The new objective of the investigation was to explore the impact of the pandemic emergency on teaching and learning dimensions through a short term longitudinal research design following the pre-test/post-test logic (Janson, 1981; Jöreskon, 1981; Fraccaroli, 1998); indeed, comparing results of the *face to face learning* phase (T1) to the results of *emergency distance learning*[2] phase (T2), a reflection based on students' beliefs, motivations, skills and opinions can be started, and generalizations with the other study programs can be done.

In order to answer the research questions, procedural choices and methods were shared with lecturers from Veterinary Medicine and with lecturers who are members of the Quality Assurance Committee of the study program. In fact, according to the initial research design, each data collection was embedded in a Formative Educational Evaluation framework, and ensured that:

- the objectives and tools of the survey are designed and chosen in collaboration with the study program's coordination group;
- data collection procedures, data analysis, and reporting activity are carried out by the research group;
- results interpretation, in the different research phases, is carried out in collaboration with the study program board.

Thus, according to the theoretical-methodological framework of Formative Educational Evaluation, in order to identify lecturers' teaching methods and to support at the same time their reflection on the importance of alignment between teaching objectives, lesson management methods, and evaluation functions (Brinko, 1993), tools and procedures consistent with the profile of the course of study itself have been created. Therefore, the current study tried to explore the effect of the pandemic on a University Program with a view on motivations, beliefs, transversal skills, opinions, and satisfaction of students with learning. Innovation in learning and teaching is, in fact, very much focused on the previous mentioned dimensions; indeed, coherently with the skills-based teaching approaches, universities nowadays promote the development of a combination of both disciplinary skills and transversal competences as a synergy of cognitive and metacognitive components, interpersonal and intellectual attitudes and ethical values characterizing professional profiles. In order to investigate teaching and learning dimensions, this study used the CIPP Evaluation Model (Stuffelbeam, 1983, 2003) taking into account:

- input evaluation, focused on motivation, metacognitive strategies, attributional styles, self-efficacy, students' attitudes as key criteria for assessing needs, problems, area assets, and opportunities,
- context evaluation, focused on needs assessment, problems, assets, and opportunities within a defined environment
- process evaluation, control over the implementation of a plan and process reporting (e.g. students' opinion on teaching), and
- product evaluation, a measurement, interpretation, and judgement about a study program's achievements (e.g. students' satisfaction) (e.g. Figure 8.2).

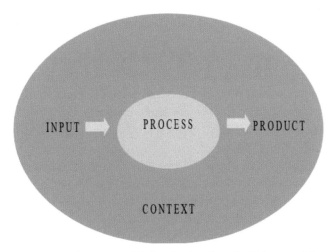

FIGURE 8.2 The CIPP model of evaluation (from Stufflebeam, 1983)

Getting inspiration from the above mentioned CIPP model (Stufflebeam, 1983) the following variables have been selected for monitoring the emergency situation:

– Input: learning self-efficacy, academic motivation, and two transversal skills useful to cope with an emergency like independence and flexibility. The reason for such choices is that several studies have determined the effects of motivation (Mayer, 2014), metacognition (Moreno & Mayer, 2007), and students' attitudes (Scheiter & Gerjets, 2007) towards learning effectiveness; furthermore, of concern to the online learning condition, a number of studies revealed that in online learning, motivation plays an important role with regard to both students' attitudes and learning behaviors (Fairchild et al., 2005; Ryan & Deci, 2000). In parallel, transversal skills play an important role in facing adversity; on the one hand, flexibility defined by the ability to plan ahead involves workable and realistic planning of learning goals and involves also the ability to adapt plans to sudden changes (Kyndt & Baert, 2015); on the other hand, independence defined by the ability to choose and determine for oneself what to do as well as taking responsibility for one's actions (Rauch & Frese, 2007; Wagener et al., 2010; Kyndt & Baert, 2015). Finally, according to Panigrahi and colleagues (2018), online education requires more self-discipline of students than classroom education.

– Process: students' *opinions on teaching*. Indeed, even though teaching evaluation activities by students have been implemented by many universities, beyond formative educational evaluation studies, only a small amount of evidence shows that teaching evaluation activities are systematically used by staff to develop and improve teaching (Smith, 2008).

- Product: students' *satisfaction*. Concerning this, Eom and colleagues (2006) found that motivation in an online environment affects satisfaction, even though a direct connection with perceived learning was not noticed. Furthermore, the literature showed that the ability of learners to interact, collaborate, and build relationships with peers was a source of student satisfaction (Biasuttie, 2011). Finally, the present study embraces the growing body of research showing that engagement in learning communities significantly affects student learning (Tinto, 2000).

Data have been collected using a self-administered questionnaire rolled out online via Qualtrics' online surveys software. The questionnaire was sent via e-mail by the study program coordinator to all students of the study program. Only those who gave full informed consent were included in the study.

The following scales are used in order to assess the learning dimensions:

Intrinsic motivation: the Academic Motivation Scale (Vallerand et al., 1992) with 8 items in a Likert scale 1-7 (1 = does not correspond at all, and 7 = corresponds totally) has been used to measure the tendency to carry out an activity for themselves and the pleasure and satisfaction derived. Examples of the item are "Because I feel pleasure and satisfaction learning new things" and "For the pleasure, I feel when I surpass myself in one of my personal goals".

The scale scored the following Cronbach Alpha T_1 = .92; T_2 = .89.

Extrinsic motivation: the Academic Motivation Scale (Vallerand et al., 1992) with 8 items on a Likert scale 1-7 (1 = does not correspond at all, and 7 = corresponds totally) has been used to measure the tendency to carry out an activity for the satisfaction derived from the rewards perceived. Examples of the item are "Because it allows me to make a better choice about my career orientation" and " Because even with graduation, I will not find a well-paid job".

The scale scored the following Cronbach Alpha T_1 = .73; T_2 = .81.

Self-efficacy: was measured through College Student Self-Efficacy Scale – CSSES (Couvillion, 2003), in particular with 10-items of self-efficacy for self-regulated learning (SESRL) (Zimmerman et al., 1992) and 2-items of self-efficacy for academic achievement (SEAA) (Roeser et al., 1996). Likert scale 1–5 (1 = very weak, and 5 = very strong).

The scale scored the following Cronbach Alpha for SESRL: T_1 = .75; T_2 = .77; and for SEAA: T_1 = .72; T_2 = .70.

Independence: was measured through the Kyndt and Baert (2015) scale with 5 items on a Likert scale 1-6 (1 = never, and 6 = always). Examples of items are "I prefer to determine what I do and don't do myself" and "I take responsibility for my actions".

The scale scored the following Cronbach Alpha: T_1 = .80; T_2 = .78.

FACING ADVERSITY AT THE UNIVERSITY

Flexibility: was measured through the "planning for the future" scale (Kyndt & Baert, 2015) with 5 items on a Likert scale 1-6 (1 = never, and 6 = always). Examples of items are "If a situation changes, I adjust my plans" and "I adjust my planned approach when new opportunities arise".

The scale scored the following Cronbach Alpha: T1 = .84; T2 = .85.

Teaching evaluation: was measured through a scale on student evaluation of teaching methods already applied by UNIBO Quality Assurance Sector for the Evaluation of Study Programs. This is a 7 items Likert scale 1–4 (1 = no, almost none, and 4 = yes, almost all). Examples of items are "They can explain clearly and understandably" and "They are capable of stimulating the students' interests".

The scale scored the following Cronbach Alpha: T1 = .88; T2 = .87.

Students' satisfaction: was measured through a scale on satisfaction for the study program (Lodini et al., 2004). Examples of items are "Are you satisfied with the relationships you have established with your teachers?" and "Are you satisfied with the relationships you have established with your fellow students?".

The scale scored the following Cronbach Alpha: T1 = .78; T2 = .73.

375 questionnaires were collected. Participants provided an anonymous identification code to allow their acknowledgment between T1 and T2. We decided to consider valid only questionnaires that could be paired up, excluding those that did not fill in one of the two observations (T1 or T2). Thus, our research consists of 173 observations, 49.1% on T1 and 50.9 on T2. The vast majority of participants were female (80.7%) with an average age of 23.1 (19–45 years old) and with a class enrolment as described in Table 8.1. SPSS software (21.0) was used for data analysis.

TABLE 8.1   Distribution of participants by class enrolment

Class	%
1°	20.7
2°	17.2
3°	11.5
4°	17.5
5°	19.5
1° opt	6.9
2° opt	6.9
Total	100

Note: opt = outside prescribed time

A paired sample t-test has been run to analyse the pre-post emergency distance learning differences.

4 Main Results Comparing the Face to Face and Emergency Distance Learning

This is a summary of the first main results on input variables.

The descriptive statistics (mean and standard deviation) showed medium-high levels for each variable in both face-to-face learning as well as emergency distance learning. The results of the t-test for paired samples used to detect differences between input variables in face-to-face learning (T1) and distance learning (T2), showed that significant differences are not appreciable (see Table 8.2). Indeed, although the levels of motivation (intrinsic and extrinsic), learning self-efficacy, independence, and flexibility increased during emergency distance learning, the difference between T1 and T2 was not statistically significant. We can observe that data analyses showed a general pattern of stability in all input variables; indeed, it appears that the unexpected change in learning environment had no influence on students' motivations or beliefs concerning their competence to reach learning goals or their awareness about competences related with coping.

This is a summary of the first main results obtained about *the process variable*.

TABLE 8.2 Input variables: Paired t-test comparing the face to face and emergency distance learning

	FL (T1) M (SD)	EDL (T2) M (SD)	t
IM (1–7)	5.27 (1.23)	5.30 (1.09)	.18 (ns)
EM (1–7)	5.48 (.80)	5.48 (.93)	–.06 (ns)
SESRL (1–5)	3.62 (.62)	3.68 (.59)	–.66 (ns)
SEAA (1–5)	3.77 (.83)	3.82 (.72)	–.41 (ns)
IND (1–6)	4.93 (.79)	4.98 (.75)	–.39 (ns)
FLEX (1–6)	4.71 (.85)	4.82 (.79)	–.84 (ns)

Note: FL = Face-to-face Learning; EDL = Emergency Distance Learning;
IM = Intrinsic Motivation; EM = Extrinsic Motivation; SESRL = Self-Efficacy
for Self-Regulated Learning; SEAA = Self-Efficacy for Academic Achievement;
IND = Independence; FLEX = Flexibility; TEACHEV = Teaching Evaluation;
ns = no significance

FACING ADVERSITY AT THE UNIVERSITY   121

The descriptive statistics (mean and standard deviation) showed medium-low levels for each teaching evaluation's item in both face-to-face learning as well as emergency distance learning. The results of the t-test for paired samples used to detect differences between *process variable* in face-to-face learning (T1) and distance learning (T2), showed that significant differences are not appreciable for the majority of items except for one (see Table 8.3). Indeed, although the levels of teaching evaluation during emergency distance learning increased, the difference between T1 and T2 was statistically significant only for the item concerning "the evaluation of clearness about how they are assessed". This result could suggest that the shift to online teaching requires adaption in teaching practices and in the way in which professors and lectures explain learning goals and examination modalities.

This is a summary of the first main results obtained about *product variable*.

TABLE 8.3   Process variables: Paired t-test comparing the face to face and emergency distance learning

	Item	FL (T1) M (SD)	EDL (T2) M (SD)	t
TEVA_1 (1–4)	Teachers are able to explain clearly and understandably	1.95 (.65)	2.17 (.75)	–1.82 (ns)
TEVA_2 (1–4)	T. know their subject well	1.56 (.56)	1.70 (.77)	–1.14 (ns)
TEVA_3 (1–4)	T. listen to and understand students' difficulties in studying	2.34 (.78)	2.52 (.76)	–1.33 (ns)
TEVA_4 (1–4)	T. are capable of stimulating the interests of the students	2.36 (.78)	2.38 (.79)	–.13 (ns)
TEVA_5 (1–4)	T. stimulate collaboration and discussion between students	2.44 (.89)	2.54 (.76)	–.69 (ns)
TEVA_6 (1–4)	T. are interested in making everyone understand the arguments	2.19 (.75)	2.23 (.75)	–.34 (ns)
TEVA_7 (1–4)	T. are clear about how students are assessed	1.88 (.75)	2.26 (.78)	–2.92*
TEVA_mean (1–4)		2.10 (.57)	2.26 (.57)	–1.56 (ns)

*$p < .01$

Note: FL = Face-to-face Learning; EDL = Emergency Distance Learning; TEVA = Teaching Evaluation; ns = no significance

TABLE 8.4   Product variables: Paired t-test comparing the face to face and emergency distance learning

Item		FL (T1) M (SD)	EDL (T2) M (SD)	t
SAT_1 (1–5)	... with the academic timetable	2.88 (1.12)	2.81 (1.06)	.34 (ns)
SAT_2 (1–5)	... with the spaces and equipment	3.49 (1.15)	3.54 (1.04)	−.23 (ns)
SAT_3 (1–5)	... with the presence of teachers	4.29 (.92)	4.20 (.96)	.50 (ns)
SAT_4 (1–5)	... with the relationship established with fellow students	3.89 (1.16)	3.72 (1.21)	.81 (ns)
SAT_5 (1–5)	... with the relationship established with teachers	3.61 (1.11)	3.33 (1.15)	1.41 (ns)
SAT_mean (1–5)		3.62 (.79)	3.52 (.75)	.72 (ns)

Note: FL = Face-to-face Learning; EDL = Emergency Distance Learning; SAT = Satisfaction; ns = no significance

The descriptive statistics (mean and standard deviation) showed medium-high levels for each item during both the learning conditions, except for the satisfaction with the academic timetable (in FL and EDL) and with spaces and equipment (in FL) that was medium level. The results of the t-test for paired samples used to detect differences between *product variable* in face-to-face learning (T1) and distance learning (T2), showed that significant differences are not appreciable for any items (see Table 8.4). Indeed, although all levels of satisfaction except one (satisfaction with spaces and equipment) showed a slight decrease during emergency distance learning, the difference between T1 and T2 was not statistically significant. Thus, the satisfaction for teaching and learning remained high even after the unexpected change in learning experience.

5   A Resilient Community with Many Future Challenges

The COVID-19 pandemic forced universities to suddenly change their learning and teaching practices. The University of Bologna promptly responded to the emergency implementing several activities in terms of new teaching and learning environments/platforms, processes' monitoring and evaluation, and tutoring and training addressed to professors. The results of the case study presented above showed a good stability in students' motivations, self-efficacy and coping skills, from the face-to-face learning experience to the emergency distance learning. Furthermore, even the medium-low satisfaction on teaching practices did not have an impact on students' learning satisfaction. With a wide interpretation of the data, it appears that forced imposition of online learning was understood by students as a necessary response to pandemic and social distancing. For these reasons, it appears that UNIBO Veterinary Medicine's teaching and learning community reacted resiliently.

Results showed that, during the emergency distance learning experience (T2), the levels of learning variables on input, process, and product variables of CIPP Evaluation Model remained stable. The only exception has been detected on one process variable's item; indeed, student's assessment on lecturers' clarity on assessment methods increased significantly. Participants showed a good level of academic motivation and self-efficacy in both learning conditions; furthermore, learning satisfaction, and coping skills (flexibility and independence) demonstrated good scores, but the same is not detectable for the evaluation of teaching. This outcome also finds support in the open-ended questions of the survey conducted with the 10,000 students of UNIBO. In particular, the students' critical feedback on "a good number of students lament the tendency of teachers to explain too quickly without gradually checking whether the classroom can follow" stood out (Luppi et al., 2020, p. 52). It is reasonable to remember that online teaching classes have been a new experience for both professors and students. According to the literature (Desai et al., 2008), in an online classroom it is more difficult to "read" facial expressions, tone and pitch of the voice. Thus, as opposed to classroom with face-to-face learning, students' body language and non-verbal signals were not available in order to support effective teaching. Finally, satisfaction outcomes of the present study confirm those of the overall survey collected from 10,000 students of UNIBO. Indeed, satisfaction for interaction with teachers, on the one hand, and learning satisfaction, on the other hand, showed medium-high levels even in this research (Luppi et al., 2020).

The pandemic spread put universities into a new uncertain situation. Since the feeling of uncertainty is indispensable to experimentation and, according to Dewey (1933), such conditions represent the starting point for reflective thinking, the current situation could be seen as an opportunity for "learning through and from experience towards gaining new insights of self and practice" (Finlay, 2008). With regard to this, reflective learning practices (face-to-face, distance, and blended) will need to be increasingly encouraged and monitored in order to identify strengths weaknesses of the different types, also in relation to teaching and learning strategies. In addition, the need to react to and face new unpredictable challenges, confirms the need for long term planning in the academic institution. These new challenges could "reshape the higher education sector globally including a shift towards more intensive and diversified forms of online delivery" (Bryson & Andres, 2020, p. 611). Future challenges can be represented by blended or dual learning during transitional phases between distance and face-to-face learning. Furthermore, Universities could use a virtual environment for other learning purposes in the direction of teaching and learning innovation.

Authors' Note

Although the manuscript is a result of a collaboration among the two authors, the contribution of each author can be qualified as follows: A.R. wrote Sections 3 and 4; E.L. wrote Sections 1 and 2. Section 5 is a joint effort of the two authors. Both authors have read and agreed to the published version of the manuscript.

Notes

1 At the University of Bologna for each course unit, there are at least 6 exam dates a year, two for each assessment period. Based on the academic calendar and the periods in which the courses are held, students can take the exams as soon as all the lessons of the period are finished.
2 The term "emergency" underlines the circumstance that distance learning has been carried out without the necessary project design and during a lockdown condition, a state of isolation that is completely new for both teachers and students.

References

Betti, M., Davila, D., Martínez, A., & Vannini, I. (2015). Una ruta hacia un sistema de aseguramiento de la calidad en Educación Superior: la experiencia del proyecto TRALL (Un percorso verso un sistema di assicurazione della qualita per L'istruzione Superiore: L'esperienza del progetto TRALL). *Journal of Educational, Cultural and Psychological Studies, 12*, 77–115. http://doi:10.7358/ecps2015-012-bett
Betti, M., & Vannini, I. (2013). Valutare la qualità dei corsi di lifelong learning in America Latina. Alcune riflessioni teoriche e metodologiche sul disegno valutativo utilizzato nel progetto AlfaIII Trall. *Ricerche di Pedagogia e Didattica, 8*(2), 45–61.

Biasuttie, M. (2011). The student experience of a collaborative e-learning university module. *Computers & Education, 57*(3), 1865–1875. http://doi:10.1016/j.compedu.2011.04.006

Brinko, K. T. (1993). The practice of giving feedback to improve teaching: What is effective? *The Journal of Higher Education, 64*(5), 574–593. http://dx.doi.org/10.2307/2959994

Bryson, J. R., & Andres, L. (2020). Covid-19 and rapid adoption and improvisation of online teaching: Curating resources for extensive versus intensive online learning experiences. *Journal of Geography in Higher Education, 44*(4), 608–623. https://doi.org/10.1080/03098265.2020.1807478

Couvillion, L. C. (2003). *Self-efficacy, motivation, and outcome expectation correlates of college students' intention certainty.* LSU Doctoral Dissertations, 1254. https://digitalcommons.lsu.edu/gradschool_dissertations/1254

Desai, M., Hart, J., & Richards, T. (2008). E-learning: Paradigm shift in education. *Education, 129*(2), 327–334.

Dewey, J. (1933). *How we think: A restatement of the relation of reflective thinking to the educative process* (Vol. 8). Heath & Col Publishers.

Eom, S. B., Wen, H. J., & Ashill, N. (2006). The determinants of students' perceived learning outcomes and satisfaction in university online education: An empirical investigation. *Decision Sciences Journal of Innovative Education, 4*, 215–235. https://doi.org/10.1111/j.1540-4609.2006.00114.x

Fairchild, A. J., Horst, S. J., Finney, S. J., & Barron, K. E. (2005). Evaluating existing and new validity evidence for the academic motivation scale. *Contemporary Educational Psychology, 30*(3), 331–358. https://doi.org/10.1016/j.cedpsych.2004.11.001

Finlay, L. (2008, January). *Reflecting on "reflective practice".* PBPL paper 52, 1–27. www.open.ac.uk/pbpl

Fraccaroli, F. (1998). *Il cambiamento nelle organizzazioni.* Cortina Editore.

House, E. R., & Howe, K. R. (2003). Deliberative democratic evaluation. In T. Kellaghan & D. L. Stufflebeam (Eds.), *International handbook of educational evaluation.* Kluwer. https://doi.org/10.1002/ev.1157

Janson, C. G. (1981). Some problems of longitudinal research in the social sciences. In F. Schulsinger, S. A. Mednick, & J. Knop (Eds.), *Longitudinal research* (pp. 19–55). Martinus Nijhoff. https://doi.org/10.1037/h0099078

Jörekson, K. G. (1981). Statistical model for longitudinal studies. In F. Schulsinger, S. A. Mednick, & J. Knop (Eds.), *Longitudinal research* (pp. 118–124). Martinus Nijhoff. https://doi.org/10.1037/h0099078

Kyndt, E., & Baert, H. (2015). Entrepreneurial competencies: Assessment and predictive value for entrepreneurship. *Journal of Vocational Behavior, 90*, 13–25. https://doi.org/10.1016/j.jvb.2015.07.002

Lincoln, Y. S. (2003). Constructivist knowing, participatory ethics and responsive evaluation: A model for the 21st century. In T. Kellahan & D. L. Stufflebeam (Eds.), *International handbook of educational evaluation* (Vol. 9, pp. 69–78). Springer. https://doi.org/10.1007/978-94-010-0309-4_6

Lodini, E., Luppi, E., & Vannini, I. (2004). *La valutazione della qualità nell'obbligo formativo: un'indagine esplorativa con allievi e formatori dei Centri di Formazione Professionale della Provincia di Bologna.* Provincia di Bologna.

Loli Piccolomini, E., & Zama, F. (2020). Monitoring Italian COVID-19 spread by a forced SEIRD model. *PLoS ONE, 15*(8), e0237417. https://doi.org/10.1371/journal.pone.0237417

Luppi, E., Consolini, E., Scagliarini, A., Degli Esposti, M., & Ubertini, F. (2021). The University of Bologna during the Covid-19 pandemic: Protect, provide and innovate – Responses from a resilient community. In S. Bergen, T. Gallagher, I. Harkavy, R. Munck, & H. van't Land (Eds.), *Higher education's response to the Covid-19 pandemic: Building a more sustainable and democratic future* (pp. 155–164). Council of Europe Higher Education.

Luppi, E., Freo, M., Ricci, A., & Gueglio, N. (2020). L'innovazione della didattica all'Università di Bologna durante la pandemia: un percorso basato sulla ricerca valutativa. *Lifelong Lifewide Learning, 16*(36), 44–57. https://doi.org/10.19241/lll.v16i36.557

Mayer, R. E. (2014). Incorporating motivation into multimedia learning. *Learning and Instruction, 29*, 171–173. https://doi.org/10.1016/j.learninstruc.2013.04.003

Moreno, R., & Mayer, R. E. (2007). Interactive multimodal learning environments. *Educational Psychology Review, 19*, 309–326. https://doi.org/10.1007/s10648-007-9047-2

Panigrahi, R., Srivastava, P. R., & Sharma, D. (2018). Online learning: Adoption, continuance, and learning outcome – A review of literature. *International Journal of Information Management, 43*, 1–14. https://doi.org/10.1016/j.ijinfomgt.2018.05.005

Rauch, A., & Frese, M. (2007). Let's put the person back into entrepreneurship research: A meta-analysis on the relationship between business owners' personality traits, business creation, and success. *European Journal of Work and Organizational Psychology, 16*(4), 353–385. https://doi.org/10.1080/13594320701595438

Roeser, R. W., Midgley, C., & Urdan, T. C. (1996). Perceptions of the school psychological environment and early adolescents' psychological and behavioral functioning in school: The mediating role of goals and belonging. *Journal of Educational Psychology, 88*(3), 408. https://doi.org/10.1037/0022-0663.88.3.408

Rubin, G. J., & Wessely, S. (2020). The psychological effects of quarantining a city. *BMJ, 368*. https://doi.org/10.1136/bmj.m313

Ryan, R. M., & Deci, E. L. (2000). Intrinsic and extrinsic motivations: Classic definitions and new directions. *Contemporary Educational Psychology, 25*(1), 54–67. https://doi.org/10.1006/ceps.1999.1020

Scheiter, K., & Gerjets, P. (2007). Learner control in hypermedia environments. *Educational Psychology Review, 19*, 285–307. https://doi.org/10.1007/s10648-007-9046-3

Scriven, M. (2003). Evaluation theory and metatheory. In T. Kellaghan & D. L. Stufflebeam (Eds.), *International handbook of educational evaluation* (pp. 15–30). Kluwer.

Smith, C. (2008). Building effectiveness in teaching through targeted evaluation and response: Connecting evaluation to teaching improvement in higher education. *Assessment & Evaluation in Higher Education, 33*(5), 517–533. https://doi.org/10.1080/02602930701698942

Stake, R. (2003). Responsive evaluation. In T. Kellaghan & D. L. Stufflebeam (Eds.), *International handbook of educational evaluation* (pp. 63–68). Kluwer.

Stufflebeam, D. L. (1983). The CIPP model for program evaluation. In F. F. Madaus, M. Scriven, & D. L. Stufflebeam (Eds.), *Evaluation models: Viewpoints on educational and human services evaluation* (pp. 117–141). Kluwer. http://dx.doi.org/10.1007/978-94-009-6669-7_1

Stufflebeam, D. (2003). The CIPP model for evaluation. In T. Kellaghan & D. L. Stufflebeam (Eds.), *International handbook of educational evaluation* (pp. 31–62). Kluwer.

Tinto, V. (2000). Learning better together: The impact of learning communities on student success in higher education. *Journal of Institutional Research, 9*(1), 48–53.

Vallerand, R., Pelletier, L., Blais, M. R., Brière, N., Senécal, C., & Vallieres, E. (1992). The academic motivation scale: A measure of intrinsic, extrinsic, and amotivation in education. *Educational and Psychological Measurement, 52*, 1003. https://doi.org/10.1177/0013164492052004025

Vertecchi, B. (1976). *Valutazione formativa*. Loescher.

Wagener, S., Gorgievski, M., & Rijsdijk, S. (2010). Businessman or host? Individual differences between entrepreneurs and small business owners in the hospitality industry. *The Service Industries Journal, 30*, 1513–1527. http://dx.doi.org/10.1080/02642060802624324

WHO. (2020a, January 21). *Novel Coronavirus (2019-nCoV): Situation report* (1st ed.). World Health Organization. https://www.who.int/docs/default-source/coronaviruse/situation-reports/20200121-sitrep-1-2019-ncov.pdf?sfvrsn=20a99c10_4

WHO. (2020b, March 11). *WHO director-general's opening remarks at the media briefing on COVID-19*. World Health Organization. https://www.who.int/dg/speeches/detail/who-director-general-s-opening-remarks-at-the-media-briefing-on-covid-19---11-march-2020

Yanes-Lane, M., Winters, N., Fregonese, F., Bastos, M., Perlman-Arrow, S., Campbell, J. R., & Menzies, D. (2020). Proportion of asymptomatic infection among COVID-19 positive persons and their transmission potential: A systematic review and meta-analysis. *PLoS ONE, 15*(11), e0241536. https://doi.org/10.1371/journal.pone.0241536

Zhu, N., Zhang, D., Wang, W., Li, X., Yang, B., Song, J., Zhao, X., Hyang, B., Shi, W., Lu, R., Niu, P., Zhan, F., Ma, X., Wang, D., Xu, W., Wu, G., Gao, G. F., & Tan, W. (2020). A novel coronavirus from patients with pneumonia in China, 2019. *New England Journal of Medicine, 382*(8). https://doi.org/727-733. 10.1056/NEJMoa2001017

Zimmerman, B. J., Bandura, A., & Martinez-Pons, M. (1992). Self-motivation for academic attainment: The role of self-efficacy beliefs and personal goal setting. *American Educational Research Journal, 29*(3), 663–676. https://doi.org/10.3102/00028312029003663

PART 2

Teaching from Home: Teachers' Wellbeing

∴

CHAPTER 9

'Overall It Was OK'

COVID-19 and the Wellbeing of University Teachers

Susan Beltman, Rachel Sheffield and Tina Hascher

Abstract

The complex profession of a university academic includes a wide array of tasks and expectations in research, administration and teaching (Gillespie et al., 2001). The teaching component involves further complexity as teaching requires educating students of differing backgrounds and levels of academic and social-emotional skills (Hagenauer & Volet, 2014). Although conditions vary across nations and systems, a common concern is increased demands associated with the likelihood of burnout in university teachers, less job satisfaction and a threat to wellbeing (Han et al., 2020). The COVID-19 pandemic presented an additional layer of challenge throughout the world that might impede university teacher wellbeing. Wellbeing, however, can be supported through social and organisational as well as individual strategies (Mudrak et al., 2018). This chapter examines how the COVID-19 pandemic impacted the wellbeing of university teachers in one Australian university over the course of a semester.

1 Introduction

1.1 *The Current Context of Work in Higher Education*

The 'Fourth Industrial Revolution' features change, uncertainty and 'digital workspaces' that are likely to influence employees' mental health (Van der Walt & Lezar, 2019). Universities have experienced similar changes to other organisations with increased workloads and scrutiny, for example, leading to poorer job satisfaction, productivity, and health, as well as concerns with work-life balance (Melin et al., 2014). With increasing digital technologies, boundaries between home and work have blurred as academics have greater flexibility to work from home. A study of 918 academics in the UK and Australia revealed that they spent about one third of their day involved in various communication technologies (Fetherston et al., 2020). Although university teachers appreciated flexibility in their place of work when not conducting

© KONINKLIJKE BRILL NV, LEIDEN, 2022 | DOI:10.1163/9789004512672_009

face-to-face teaching, more than 75% reported that the work-life merge had negatively affected their psychological health.

1.2 *Wellbeing*

The World Health Organization (1948) introduced the concept of wellbeing into public awareness, defining health as a state of complete physical, mental, and social wellbeing – instead of the mere absence of disease or infirmity. In empirical psychological research, Diener (1984) defined wellbeing as a combination of subjective life satisfaction with positive and negative affect. Despite a subsequent vast array of definitions, there is agreement that wellbeing is a multidimensional construct that includes positive emotions and satisfaction as well as negative emotions and complaints. Wellbeing in this chapter is regarded as a positive imbalance in university teachers' evaluation of their professional life, where positive components are more pronounced than negative components (Deci & Ryan, 2001).

Wellbeing is a precondition, as well as an indicator, of successful fulfilment of a professional role and the meaningfulness of professional work (Deci & Ryan, 2008; Dolan & Metcalfe, 2012). Researchers have frequently investigated stress or burnout of university staff (Johnson et al., 2019; Shin & Jung, 2014; Watts & Robertson, 2011). Studies consistently report high workloads, work-life-imbalance (Catano et al., 2010) and research-teaching tension (Han et al., 2020) impacting wellbeing. Other workplace conditions such as quantitative demands, job insecurity and work-family conflicts similarly negatively influence university teacher wellbeing (Mudrak et al., 2018).

Despite high stress and burden, research generally indicates high levels of job satisfaction (Shin & Jung, 2014) and wellbeing (Mudrak et al., 2018) of university teachers. Social supports such as collaboration with colleagues and supportive leadership can foster aspects of university teacher wellbeing (Barkhuizen et al., 2014; Franco-Santos & Doherty, 2017). Individual coping strategies, such as capitalizing on personal resources, or teaching efficacy can mediate a possible negative impact of job burdens on aspects of university teacher wellbeing (Abouserie, 1996; Han et al., 2020) which is supported by having influence on one's work and autonomy (Mudrak et al., 2018). Interaction with students, the relevance of the profession to society, and feeling fortunate due to, for example, good working conditions, positively contribute to emotional wellbeing (Talbot & Mercer, 2018).

2 Context and Aim of the Present Study

Although the presence of resources supports educator wellbeing, critical situations can threaten it (Parker et al., 2012). One such situation is the COVID-19 pandemic, comprising the 'triple crisis of a global pandemic, a brutal economic downturn, and a profound social and cultural dislocation', but also featuring positive individual and collective actions protecting mental health (Evans & Evans, 2020, p. 3). In the first 16 weeks of the pandemic a UK survey of adults showed that initially anxiety and depression were higher than usual, but as restrictions eased these decreased and loneliness scores and happiness improved (Fancourt et al., 2020). In Australia, although not affected as severely as many countries, restrictions in March led to closure of schools and many businesses, with employees working at home (Australian Bureau of Statistics, 2020a). By June as cases fell, students began returning to schools, universities reopened, and in Western Australia, the location of the present study, workplaces gradually reopened (Australian Bureau of Statistics, 2020b).

In the university of the present study, large lectures were cancelled first, then all students and staff were sent home. An additional week was added before the scheduled one-week tuition-free break, for staff to prepare to deliver all courses fully online (see Table 9.1). An extra week extension on assessments was given and late penalties reduced. The university provided additional support for staff and student mental health and offered students financial support. Some courses were already regularly delivered online but

TABLE 9.1   Timeline for university and research activities

	University activity	Research activity
February	Feb 24 Semester 1 commences	
March	Mar 23 on campus classes stop	
April	Extra non-teaching week	Ethics approved
	April 6: Fully online classes begin	
May	Semester 1 continues fully online	Pulse checks
		1: May 25
		2: May 29
June	Online classes continue	Pulse checks
	June 5 last week of teaching	3–11
	June 15–26: exams (all online)	
July	Semester break but some online study	Pulse check
	periods continue	12: July 3
August	August 3: Semester 2 commences	Interview 1, 2
		Interview 3, 4

others with laboratory classes, for example, were not. Staff who were parents had to supervise their children's learning from home. All households were affected by general community restrictions. Although staff could still access their specific building to work, staff were expected to work from home where possible and university meetings were conducted online.

The aim of the study was to examine the wellbeing of university teachers during the pandemic, and to give them a voice to report challenges and resources related to their professional situation during this time. The specific research questions were: During the COVID-19 pandemic ...

1. how do university teachers appraise their wellbeing?
2. what aspects of their working conditions do university teachers appraise as challenging?
3. what resources and strategies do university teachers draw upon to support their wellbeing?

3 Methology

3.1 Research Design and Procedure

Our research adopted a socio-ecological approach that values the role of individual-context-interaction for development (Bronfenbrenner & Morris, 2006), and used a predominantly qualitative research design providing participants with a voice to share their views (Patton, 2002). We combined a short online survey ('pulse check') with follow-up online-interviews. Ethics approval was obtained and confidentiality of individuals and departments was assured. Table 9.1 outlines the timeline of research activities and how they aligned with the university teaching activities and COVID-19 response strategies.

3.2 Participants

Purposeful sampling targeted university academics with a teaching role and connected to university groups concerned with promoting excellence in learning and teaching. Twenty-seven participants completed the first pulse check with the number decreasing at subsequent survey points. The initial group comprised 16 females and 11 males from three faculties (Health Sciences, Science and Engineering, Humanities). They had 1–35 years of experience as an academic. The number of respondents for each pulse check ranged from 11 to 27, with ten completing every pulse check. In the final pulse check, there was an invitation to take part in an interview and four participants (2 female; 2 male) from the above three faculties (two from Humanities) responded.

3.3 Data collection

3.3.1 Online Survey

Participants were emailed an online biweekly survey (pulse check) through Qualtrics for six weeks. The survey was anonymous and participants created their own ID. In each post, participants rated their wellbeing from 1–10 and explained what led them to make that judgement. Surveys included an additional question each week on topics such as demographics, challenges and successes.

3.3.2 Interviews

Interviews gain detailed perceptions and reactions (Frankael et al., 2012). Four interviews were conducted online by the same researcher, recorded and transcribed. The open-ended semi-structured design included questions such as usual teaching roles and changes during the pandemic, current wellbeing rating, reflection on high or low ratings during the pandemic, and resources or strategies used during this time.

3.4 Data Analysis

Analysis occurred across participants and coding focused on aspects of working conditions appraised as challenging, and resources and strategies drawn upon during the pandemic. A second researcher reviewed categories for continuity and consistency. Analysis also occurred within participants as individual ratings, with the associated events and perceptions examined for changes over time, and plotlines developed (Crosswell et al., 2018).

4 Results

4.1 Working during the Pandemic

4.1.1 Negative Aspects

In week two, participants were asked about the main work-place challenges they had experienced as a result of the pandemic. Twenty-one separate challenges were identified and coded. Table 9.2 indicates the most prevalent challenges and an example of a response.

4.1.2 Positive Aspects

Week three included a question about successes experienced as a result of the pandemic. Twenty-three participants responded and Table 9.3 presents the categories and an example of the 16 nominated successes.

136 BELTMAN ET AL.

TABLE 9.2 Workplace-related challenges, frequency and example

Category (number of participants)	Example of response
Workload (5)	... having all the students online has definitely increased workload with collaborates and lots of emails ....
University policy on extensions (4)	The enormous amount of extensions, then extensions on extensions has irritated me ....
Communication with colleagues (3)	I have not been able to interact with colleagues personally and have those ad-hoc chats that get things done.
Student issues (3)	An escalation of emails that have often been a lot of confirmation as students have needed a high level of reassurance. ... I have also missed f2f and the regular contact and interaction with my students.
Family responsibilities (2)	Working at home while home-schooling children! But also a lot of fun ... sometimes.

TABLE 9.3 Nominated successes, frequency and example

Category (# of participants)	Example of response
Greater productivity (6)	Flexibility of work – Could get more done!
Positive student feedback (4)	Some students have sent emails thanking me for my support and kindness.
Improved skills (3)	Moving some curriculum online and learning about a new web-app that will be useful in the future.
Feelings of belonging (3)	Our team are now meeting regularly once a week online. was not happening before – safe space (online) to venture ideas.

4.1.3 Strategies and Resources

In week four, participants were asked about *the most critical thing/s that have kept you going during this time,* aiming to reveal resources and strategies implemented by individuals, their immediate workplace or the university. Seventeen participants completed this pulse check. Table 9.4 presents the categories of the 22 coded responses, the number of participants in each category and two examples of a response.

TABLE 9.4 Strategies, resources, frequency and example

Category (# of participants)	Example of response
Personal thoughts/actions (9)	I consider myself lucky when I compare my situation with others. Exercise (walking, cycling).
Work factors (8)	Being able to focus on my research. Support of colleagues. Flexibility to work from home ....
Home/community factors (5)	Happy home life. My partner has kept me going ....

4.2 Individual Experiences

There were differences between participants in the bi-weekly wellbeing ratings. For example, for the first pulse check the 27 participants' wellbeing scores ranged from 3 to 9, with an average of 7. There were also variations within plotlines of individual participants as illustrated by the following cases.

4.2.1 Andrew

Andrew had worked in the Faculty of Health Sciences for five years after coming from overseas with his family. With 19 years' experience as an academic, his first language was not English. Figure 9.1 shows the plotline of his 12 pulse check ratings and shows high ratings with one dip.

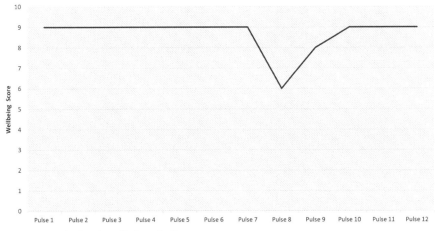

FIGURE 9.1 Andrew's wellbeing plot line

Initially Andrew rated his wellbeing as 9 due to: 'Self-esteem, uniqueness of sharing knowledge, value of what I am doing, positive feedback from students and colleagues'. In his interview, Andrew explained that he usually worked on campus because at home his wife was looking after two children, one with special needs. He said working from home would be: 'unfair for them as well as unfair for me as well as unfair for the students. It would have been a problem to deliver quality time from home. From here, it was perfect'.

Andrew did not have much experience teaching online and was part of the team that taught a very large first-year science unit. Needing to teach this online was challenging 'but we did a good job … it was a blessing in disguise because we learned to do things that we were not able to do before'. This positive attitude was reflected in the way Andrew dealt with the news that his contract would not be renewed. Although his rating dropped to 6, he immediately gave a higher rating of 8 and finally returned to 9, commenting: 'positive attitude and nice relaxing weekend just behind'. Despite needing to find a new job, Andrew reported a strong sense of wellbeing reflected in positive comments throughout his interview such as: 'Overall, it was okay, even now it's okay'.

4.2.2   Jennifer

Jennifer, experienced in teaching online, had worked as a casual teaching academic in Humanities for eight years. Figure 9.2 shows her plotline was relatively high with some decline. Comments revealed a focus on her students' wellbeing. She began with a rating of 7 and observed: 'A lot of students are overwhelmed … weary and working extra shifts. We absorb a lot of their fears

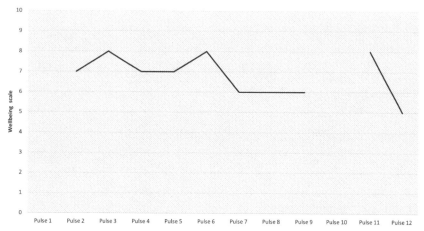

FIGURE 9.2   Jennifer's wellbeing plot line

and frustrations'. A rating of 6 was because of 'corona fatigue' and to explain her lowest rating of 5, she reported 'feeling overwhelmed'. In her interview, Jennifer explained that, as the semester progressed, she was concerned about students and their challenges revealed during online teaching sessions:

> I probably was absorbing some of what our students were going through, ... A lot had lost their jobs and so then you were sort of feeling that. A lot, or a partner had lost a job, and a lot were fleeing domestic violence.

In the interview, Jennifer rated her current wellbeing as 10: 'Because I love this job, yeah. I love this job'. When asked how she coped during the pandemic she explained that she lived alone and had no pets and this quiet time enabled her to 'refresh and rejuvenate'. Nevertheless, she was concerned about her family's situation and thought these contributed to her 'sliding scale', of decreasing ratings:

> ... so me living on my own perhaps, yeah, that contributed to my sliding scale. Somebody who was more consistent probably came home to people and could debrief or had a glass of wine or something ...

4.2.3 Peter

Peter (Faculty of Humanities) did not respond to the interview invitation, which could reflect his declining sense of wellbeing indicated in Figure 9.3. In pulse check 1 (highest rating 8) Peter explained that working at home suited him. He typically went on campus every day including most weekends. Although still working long hours he said:

> ... I am in a new house and I am enjoying the comfort of my home. I also have my own office, rather than an open plan space where I am disturbed by people having long, loud conversations, which can be stressful.

By pulse check 6 his plotline shows a steady decline and at his lowest rating of 3 he was concerned that he had spent time on his teaching and being 'absorbed' with his students instead of writing and getting published:

> I am feeling extremely tired and nauseous, at the moment, especially mid to late afternoon. I just have to stop working and cannot come back to it until the following day. I feel as though this Semester has sucked up all my energy and I have very little left.

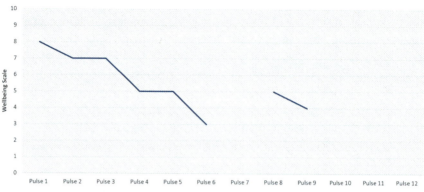

FIGURE 9.3   Peter's wellbeing plot line

Peter did not complete the final three pulse checks and his last ratings showed a decline. He had worked during most of a week's leave and stated: 'final assignments had to be marked and there is still a mountain of work to do'.

4.2.4   Sia

Unlike the other examples, Sia (Humanities) fluctuated more between pulse checks. Starting with a 3 rating, Sia wrote: 'Lack of support from the University and Faculty – School is fine, but understaffed so this creating pressure on everyone. Also mixed messages from the University leadership does not help'. By pulse check 5 her rating climbed to 6 because: 'It's Monday, a feeling we are through the worst, teaching, marking etc., nearly done and so student concerns are going down'. In pulse check 6 her wellbeing rating went down to 3 again as she commented: 'It's been a tough week with many upset students', but she returned to a final rating of 7: 'Marks are in, things have calmed down quite a bit'.

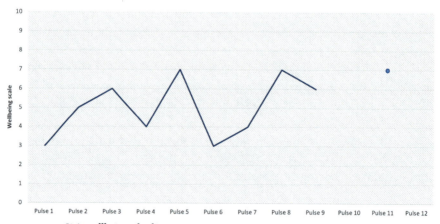

FIGURE 9.4   Sia's wellbeing plot line

5 Discussion

5.1 *Key Findings*

5.1.1 Individual Variability

A sense of wellbeing occurs when the perceived positive aspects of one's situation outweigh the negative. Participants experienced a variable sense of wellbeing, even though they were all doing similar work in the same university. The plotlines showed differences between individuals as well as within individuals over time. Large-scale data have shown, for example, increased happiness as restrictions eased, but also group differences (Fancourt et al., 2020). By gaining individual level data, our study has shown that wellbeing evaluations are nuanced and can change in complex ways depending on a mix of personal and contextual aspects. Some participants experienced potential challenges in their home and work settings (e.g. Andrew: a child with a disability and contract termination), yet still reported a positive sense of wellbeing. Even though restrictions were lifting, others felt increasingly overwhelmed by workload or concerns with students.

Participants used a variety of strategies to manage challenges. They thought positively about their situation, acknowledged and accepted support from family and colleagues, refocused on other aspects of work, and engaged in physical exercise. These align with strategies used, for example, with schoolteachers under emotional stress (Beltman & Poulton, 2019). In Van der Walt and Lezar's (2019) discussion of digital workplaces, they suggest that individuals will need to take on more responsibility for their personal and professional growth and wellbeing rather than rely on organisational structures, and the university teachers in this study were to some extent able to do this.

5.1.2 Importance of Work Situations

Extra time needed to deal with extensions and student issues, often at the expense of research, was a challenge for participants. Moving off campus meant that some missed the ongoing interaction with their colleagues. Aspects of work were also positive in relation to participants' wellbeing. They spoke of resources provided by the university to staff and students, and sometimes more effective interactions online. Others appreciated the flexibility of working from home and reported learning new skills in the online environment. The findings align with research that shows workplace conditions in universities can negatively impact staff wellbeing, while supportive leaders and colleagues, and increased autonomy support wellbeing (Mudrak et al., 2018).

5.1.3 Importance of Home Situations

Although the survey asked about workplace wellbeing, participants reported challenges and supports originating in their homes. During the pandemic this setting became even more connected to work and varied for individuals. For some, increased flexibility, a home office and few distractions at home were positive aspects. Others with young children or those living alone were challenged. This aligns with the increased blurring of boundaries of work and home (Fetherston et al., 2020) as well as a social ecological perspective that requires consideration of multiple settings (Ungar, 2012). Research on school teacher and leader resilience has extensively supported the notion that teachers' capacity to sustain their professional commitment is linked to their personal values and beliefs, to their family and social roles in their life outside school, and to the specific setting in which they work (Gu & Day, 2013). Similarly, workplace, home setting and personal characteristics of university teachers interacted in this study in complex ways.

5.1.4 Role of Students

The role of students was similarly complex. Participants reported that students had high needs and required reassurance during the semester. Escalating emails and no opportunities for face-to-face discussions created workload challenges and increasing concerns as participants empathised with students. Positive student feedback and completing marking supported wellbeing. Positive interactions with students do contribute to university teacher emotional wellbeing (Talbot & Mercer, 2018). Fetherston et al. (2020) found that about 75% of academics had a 'calling' orientation to their work which focuses on 'the enjoyment of fulfilling, socially useful work' (p. 11), positively predicting mental wellbeing in Australian academics. In the present study the wellbeing of participants such as Jennifer and Sia, was closely related to their students' wellbeing, aligning with a calling orientation.

5.2 *Implications*

Workplace flexibility supported participants managing changing conditions. For some, this meant working at home and for others, the option of continuing to be based on campus. Some appreciated not being under the watchful eye of a supervisor and others enjoyed online meetings that enabled greater individual input. In a university, such decisions are usually enacted at department level and the study highlighted the need for department heads to have the autonomy, skills and resources to create supportive work settings. Participants acknowledged additional physical and emotional resources provided during the pandemic although one commented that greater support of staff wellbeing should not require a pandemic. Such resources are essential for employees to flourish at work (Van der Walt & Lezar, 2019) but Fetherston et al. (2020) maintain it is not enough for universities to provide programs encouraging healthy lifestyle behaviours and recommend national advisory groups focused on university wellbeing. They suggest as the physical and temporal boundaries between home and work become increasingly blurred, individuals will need to take more responsibility for their wellbeing.

Some participants did appear aware of strategies to support their wellbeing. The university already offers programs for staff such as free mindfulness programs but accessing these can be difficult (Fetherston et al., 2020). Aligning with a social ecological perspective, Evans and Evans (2020) reported that positive and negative effects on wellbeing had multiple sources not just based on work-related structures, policies or colleagues. Their report showed that individuals tapped into many areas of life, such as the arts, food, homes, and green spaces to support their mental health. As communities as well as workplaces have a role in providing resources, individuals need to be aware of these and be able to access them. Given the likely increased complexity and unpredictability of future work places, 'employees should possess, apart from mental health and agility, high levels of cognitive ability, innovation and creativity' (Van der Walt & Lezar, 2019, p. 101). Individuals need to rely more on themselves to understand their sense of identity, meaning and purpose in life. How existing work structures can support or encourage this is a topic for future research and discussion. Similarly, it remains to be understood how staff wellbeing is impacted by universities' responses to the COVID-19 related issues. Staff redundancies, a freeze on new appointments and cutting of programs are being experienced across the country, with potentially negative impacts on employee wellbeing.

5.3 Limitations

The main study limitation is the small sample size sourced from one university in a specific part of Australia. Not all participants completed all research components, and their prior wellbeing is unknown. Participants were employed at the time of the study and had a high level of education, so were not necessarily typical of the general population. Nevertheless, even with this small group, interesting differences between and within individuals over time emerged, with the key role of, not only work place strategies and structures, but also participants' personal life and individual thoughts and actions.

6 Conclusion

This research examined how university teachers appraised their wellbeing, the challenges they faced and the resources and strategies that supported them during three months of the COVID-19 pandemic. Individual differences were found in the trajectories mapped through plotlines. Reasons for the differences were grounded in personal beliefs and cognitive strategies, relations with students, home and personal situations, as well as specific work settings within the university. The study adds to broader survey data to highlight that strategies to support wellbeing are not simply the responsibility of an individual or of an organisation, but both, along with the wider community have a role to play, particularly in challenging times.

References

Abouserie, R. (1996). Stress, coping strategies and job satisfaction in university academic staff. *Educational Psychology, 16*, 49–56. https://doi.org/10.1080/0144341960160104

Australian Bureau of Statistics. (2020a). *Measuring the impacts of COVID-19, Mar–May 2020.* https://www.abs.gov.au/articles/measuring-impacts-covid-19-mar-may-2020#new-high-frequency-abs-products-help-measure-the-economic-and-social-impacts-of-covid-19

Australian Bureau of Statistics. (2020b). *A series of unprecedented events – The June quarter 2020.* https://www.abs.gov.au/articles/series-unprecedented-events-june-quarter-2020

Barkhuizen, N., Rothmann, S., & van de Vijver, F. J. (2014). Burnout and work engagement of academics in higher education institutions: Effects of dispositional optimism. *Stress and Health, 30*(4), 322–332. https://doi.org/10.1002/smi.2520

Beltman, S., & Poulton, E. (2019). "Take a step back": Teacher strategies for managing heightened emotions. *The Australian Educational Researcher, 46*(4), 661–679. https://doi.org/10.1007/s13384-019-00339-x

Bronfenbrenner, U., & Morris, P. A. (2006). The bioecological model of human development. In R. M. Lerner (Ed.), *Handbook of child psychology* (6th ed., Vol. 1, pp. 793–828). John Wiley & Sons.

Catano, V., Francis, L., Haines, T., Kirpalani, H., Shannon, H., Stringer, B., & Lozanzki, L. (2010). Occupational stress in Canadian universities: A national survey. *International Journal of Stress Management, 17*(3), 232–258. https://doi.org/10.1037/a0018582

Crosswell, L., Willis, J., Morrison, C., Gibson, A., & Ryan, M. (2018). Early career teachers in rural schools: Plotlines of resilience. In M. Wosnitza, F. Piexoto, S. Beltman, & C. F. Mansfield (Eds.), *Resilience in education: Concepts, contexts and connections* (pp. 131–146). Springer. https://doi.org/10.1007/978-3-319-76690-4

Deci, E. L., & Ryan, R. M. (2001). On happiness and human potentials: A review of research on hedonic and eudaimonic well-being. *Annual Review of Psychology, 52*, 141–166. https://doi.org/10.1146/annurev.psych.52.1.141

Deci, E. L., & Ryan, R. M. (2008). Hedonia, eudaimonia, and well-being: An introduction. *Journal of Happiness Studies, 9*, 1–11. https://doi.org/10.1007/s10902-006-9018-1

Diener, E. (1984). Subjective well-being. *Psychological Bulletin, 95*(3), 542–575.

Dolan, P., & Metcalfe, R. (2012). Measuring subjective wellbeing: Recommendations on measures for use by national governments. *Journal of Social Policy, 41*(2), 409–427. https://doi.org/10.1017/S0047279411000833

Evans, A., & Evans, J. (2020). Collective resilience: How we've protected our mental health during Covid-19. *The Collective Psychology Project.* https://www.collectivepsychology.org/wp-content/uploads/2020/09/Collective-Resilience.pdf

Fancourt, D., Bu, F., WanMak, H., & Steptoe, A. (2020). *Covid-19 social study: Results release 16.* London's Global University. https://www.covidsocialstudy.org/results

Fetherston, C., Fetherston, A., Batt, S., Sully, M., & Wei, R. (2020). Wellbeing and work-life merge in Australian and UK academics. *Studies in Higher Education.* https://doi.org/10.1080/03075079.2020.1828326

Franco-Santos, M., & Doherty, N. (2017). Performance management and well-being: A close look at the changing nature of the UK higher education workplace. *International Journal of Human Resource Management, 28*(16), 2319–2350. https://doi.org/10.1080/09585192.2017.1334148

Frankael, J. R., Wallen, N. E., & Hyun, H. H. (2012). *How to design and evaluate research in education* (8th ed.). McGraw-Hill.

Gillespie, N. A., Walsh, M., Winefield, A. H., Jua, J., & Stough, C. (2001). Occupational stress in universities: Staff perceptions of the causes, consequences and moderators of stress. *Work and Stress, 15*, 53–72. https://doi.org/10.1080/02678370110062449

Gu, Q., & Day, C. (2013). Challenges to teacher resilience: Conditions count. *British Educational Research Journal, 39*(1), 22–44. https://doi.org/10.1080/01411926.2011.623152

Hagenauer, G., & Volet, S. E. (2014). "I don't hide my feelings, even though I try to": Insight into teacher educator emotion display. *The Australian Educational Researcher, 41*(3), 261–281. https://doi.org/10.1007/s13384-013-0129-5

Han, J., Yin, H., Wang, J., & Bai, Y. (2020). Challenge job demands and job resources to university teacher well-being: The mediation of teacher efficacy. *Studies in Higher Education, 45*(8), 1771–1785. https://doi.org/10.1080/03075079.2019.1594180

Johnson, S. J., Willis, S. M., & Evans, J. (2019). An examination of stressors, strain, and resilience in academic and non-academic U.K. university job roles. *International Journal of Stress Management, 26*, 162–172. https://doi.org/10.1037/str0000096

Melin, M., Astvik, W., & Bernhard-Oettel, C. (2014). New work demands in higher education. A study of the relationship between excessive workload, coping strategies and subsequent health among academic staff. *Quality in Higher Education, 20*(3), 290–308. https://doi.org/10.1080/13538322.2014.979547

Mudrak, J., Zabrodska, K., Kveton, P., Jelinek, M., Blatny, M., Solcova, I., & Machovcova, K. (2018). Occupational well-being among university faculty: A job demands-resources model. *Research in Higher Education, 59*(3), 325–348. https://doi.org/10.1007/s11162-017-9467-x

Parker, P. D., Martin, A. J., Colmar, S., & Liem, G. A. (2012). Teachers' workplace well-being: Exploring a process model of goal orientation, coping behavior, engagement, and burnout. *Teaching and Teacher Education, 28*, 503–513. https://doi-org.dbgw.lis.curtin.edu.au/10.1016/j.tate.2012.01.001

Patton, M. Q. (2002). *Qualitative research and evaluation methods* (3rd ed.). Sage Publications.

Shin, J. C., & Jung, J. (2014). Academics job satisfaction and job stress across countries in the changing academic environments. *Higher Education, 67*, 603–620. https://doi-org.dbgw.lis.curtin.edu.au/10.1007/s10734-013-9668-y

Talbot, K., & Mercer, S. (2018). Exploring university ESL/EFL teachers' emotional well-being and emotional regulation in the United States, Japan and Austria. *Chinese Journal of Applied Linguistics, 41*(4), 410–432. https://doi.org/10.1515/cjal-2018-0031

Ungar, M. (2012). Social ecologies and their contribution to resilience. In M. Ungar (Ed.), *The social ecology of resilience: A handbook of theory and practice* (pp. 13–31). Springer Science+Business Media.

Van der Walt, F., & Lezar, L. W. P. (2019). Flourishing and thriving for well-being. In M. Coetzee (Ed.), *Thriving in digital workspaces* (pp. 85–107). Springer Nature.

Watts, J., & Robertson, N. (2011). Burnout in university teaching staff: A systematic literature review. *Educational Research, 53*(1), 33–50. https://doi.org/10.1080/00131881.2011.552235

World Health Organisation. (1948). *Preamble to the Constitution of the World Health Organization as adopted by the International Health Conference*, New York, 19–22 June 1946. http://whqlibdoc.who.int/hist/official_records/constitution.pdf

CHAPTER 10

Rethinking Academic Teaching at and beyond the Pandemic

Marta Ilardo and Morena Cuconato

Abstract

In the Knowledge Societies, Higher Education (HE) has had to reconcile its educational role with the challenges of promoting employability and social cohesion. This changing mission has influenced the academic teachers who have to shift from their role of "instructor" and content-transmitter towards a student-centered teaching approach. What does this educational aim mean in the time of the pandemic? In this chapter, we discuss the set of skills and reflective practices that HE teachers need to develop in order to face the challenges that have emerged during the COVID-19 emergency.

1 Introduction

For over two decades now, the advent of the so-called Knowledge Society has put Higher Education Institutions (HEIs) under pressure to expand access to higher education as the knowledge economy needs more graduates. Furthermore, the graduates are expected to return for more studies as *lifelong learning* becomes the norm in both work and leisure time, assuming therefore also a *life-wide* dimension (Beerkens, 2008).

These are the urgent pressures that have set in motion a rethinking of the role of teaching in HE. First of all, access has been expanded and nowadays students from various backgrounds populate classrooms traditionally geared to middle-class young people. Second, a Knowledge Society implies a learning society (Beck, 2008) and a dynamic concept of knowledge is interpreted not as a fixed set of facts, but as "a constantly increasing, self-updating, interconnected whole that requires a high degree of independence, flexibility, and willingness to learn and improve well beyond one's academic degree, including the ITC skills that today are as necessary as basic literacy in order to understand the impact of digitalization on contemporary society, culture and politics" (Cuconato, 2020, p. 221). Traditionally, a degree certifies the knowledge that graduates have developed when they leave a university; however,

© KONINKLIJKE BRILL NV, LEIDEN, 2022 | DOI:10.1163/9789004512672_010

nowadays the more enduring qualities that university is expected to transmit are the skills, attitudes, and ways of thinking derived from courses. Therefore, degrees and syllabuses that are still defined in terms of subject knowledge are less adequate than the practice of high-level skills as the requirements of the Knowledge Society.

Although the paradigm change from education to lifelong learning (Crosier et al., 2012) seems to charge students with the main role in structuring a learning path, that goes beyond the requests of formal education, HEIs still play a pivotal role in the development of an individual active approach towards learning in order to enable students to achieve an independent understanding of themselves and their world including the full range of the natural, human, and social worlds as objects of understanding.

However, to maintain their core values – including research-based teaching and a curriculum that provides for the long-term cognitive needs of individuals – HEIs are required to shift radically from the standard transmission model of university teaching to adopting what Schön (1987, p. 157) defines a "reflective practicum", enabling students to be able to go beyond the rules – devising new methods of reasoning, strategies of action, and ways of framing problems (Finlay, 2008). In this way, it would be possible to equip students to do things with knowledge, using it in inventive practical ways which benefits their future careers after graduation. This was the framework that was pushing HEIs to ask academic teachers to adopt an innovative didactic, providing more suitable learning proposals, offering students learning environments based on a wide variety of educational programs, learning experiences, instructional approaches, and academic-support strategies in order to address the distinct learning needs, interests, aspirations, or cultural backgrounds of individual students and groups of students. However, have teachers really perceived the difference between a curriculum that teaches what is *known* and one that teaches *how to come to know*?

Then in 2019, the pandemic shock arrived and HEIs were compelled to "move online" fearing the consequences for their students' learning and participation activities in front of this new and unexpected imperative, and teachers were suddenly asked to reflect on how they can teach, adopting the new technology.

A year later, grounded on a literature review of European scholars' research, this chapter aims to present and analyze: (1) the challenges that European HE teacher professionalism has to face with the advent of the Knowledge Society; (2) Whether and how the COVID-19 emergency has impacted teachers with regard to the application of a more reflective teaching/learning approach, implying the possible and fruitful overcoming of the traditional transmission model. The chapter ends with some concluding remarks on the findings regarding the two above-mentioned issues.

2   Academic Teachers' Changing Role in the Knowledge Society

The advent of the Knowledge Society and the consequent need to enlarge the academic student population confronted teachers with the task of motivating a wide variety of students in order to help *all* of them to develop an autonomous approach to learning, realizing that learning, as an ability and challenge, is a lifelong process that does not end with HE and cannot be limited to the digital environments (Figel, 2006). Therefore, some scholars argue that teaching should change in order to meet the needs of increasingly diverse student cohorts. This implies reflection on the multifaceted needs of all students, discovering who these young people are, and understanding the reasons behind their actions and behaviors, which may be either cultural or economic rather than purely individual (Crul et al., 2012).

Teachers can no longer be merely considered as knowledge experts, but they are also expected to support students to develop into active members of society, promoting cooperative competencies and activities which enhance the collective intelligence of learners and collaborating with colleagues to promote their own professionalism. In this way, teachers need to be aware of what contributes to social cohesion or, on the other hand, exclusion in society, focusing on the ethical dimensions of learning and networking with other educational and societal stakeholders.

In this vein, there is a broad national and international debate on the need to improve the training offered by making it accessible, broad, diversified and student-centered (Lea et al., 2003). This implies that teachers themselves should adopt a reflexive approach in their profession in order to be aware of the implicit attitudes, beliefs, and knowledge that guide their daily activities necessitating a constant shaping and reshaping of their practices, thereby adapting it to changing students' needs. As Diamond and Mullen (1999) argue in their reflections on the professional development of post-modern educators, "Teachers can each learn to be scholars of their own consciousness and experts in the remodeling of their experiencing of the experience of teaching" (p. 123).

This approach recalls the image of "teacher-researcher" (Burns et al., 2017) and concerns the teachers' responsibility to change according to situations and needs. Doing research allows teachers to develop a new "mindset", investigating his/her own teaching/learning practice through a reflective lens in a cyclical and open process with the twin purposes of modifying his/her own practice, while contributing to the theoretical development of innovative didactics (Wang et al., 2010). Detaching themselves from their teaching practice, observing and subjecting it to criticism provides a clear framework of problems and possible solutions. The globalizing implications of the Knowledge Society invite HEIs and their teaching staff to develop sustainable networks within and outside the academic environment in order to master their tasks. The University – and HE's teachers in their classrooms– should perceive themselves no longer as a closed universe, but potentially as an open space for combining knowledge and expertise from several different sources and resources, cooperating with non-academic professionals, teacher training colleges, municipalities, and local labor markets for in-service, which helps students to prepare for their academic career as well as their future professions. This imperative recalls the focus that Wenger (1998) puts on the concept of "learning community" as space and structure for the acquisition of knowledge which – aiming at long-term students' cognitive needs and life-skills – goes beyond the well-trodden path of the traditional HE curriculum. In summary, it is not only students but also academic teachers themselves who are expected to become those "challenging, innovative and lifelong learners" (Coolahan, 2002, p. 14) who are highly needed in the contemporary Knowledge Societies.

3   Possible Side-Effects of COVID-19 on HE's Teaching

Despite the efforts of HEIs in the last twenty years, curricula and teaching methods have not developed fast enough to keep pace with what is needed by students and societies as a whole. The transmission model remains the dominant model and lectures, books and marked assignments are still the predominant learning technologies; this applies as well to digital technologies if they are used in the framework of a transmissive approach. As HEIs have not reconceptualized the meaning of "higher learning", the use of new technologies could not change what traditional learning technology has always done: transmitting the academics' knowledge to students without exploring the possibility inherent to other learning approaches such as situated learning, discovery learning, and meta-learning which are more suitable to the imperative of lifelong and life-wide learning.

Despite this, since the beginning of the pandemic crisis, implying a stop to the traditional face to face activities, there have been encouraging signs indicating that HE is more flexible than presumed, particularly when it comes to teaching and learning. The academic world has put each new – before "neglected" – technological device into the service of the transmission model of learning, coping with the many challenges due to the unexpected health crisis.

The main immediate reaction was the untested and massive shifting of teaching to the online format, the adaptation of learning content to remote learning and the consequent online assessments, often conducted on a simple trial-and-error basis. However, neither all teachers nor all students were trained to use technology and tools within an educational framework. Therefore, the transition to an "online mode" has had its share of challenges for all the actors involved in the process. These include limited access to the Internet, lack of uninterrupted connections, ill-equipped teachers, increase in screen-time and unavailability of tools to create content monitoring methods functioning from a distance, lack of confidence in creating a relationship between teachers and students, and among peers in an online experience, bridging the patchy and impersonal virtual classroom.

However, forced by the virtual experience, teachers have started step by step to wonder: "How can I teach this" and also "how can the students learn it?" as the digital distance replaces their face-to-face traditional professional praxis.

It could be due to this reflectivity that despite the initial worries about students' reaction to the forced "on-line" attendance, the digital learning techniques have not only helped students to go on learning, but they have allowed them to engage with other students, to receive immediate feedback from teachers and peers, to provide them with the opportunity to discuss and process learning materials while still in a virtual class and to increase in this way their learning motivation as they perceive themselves to be active participants in their learning process.

At this point, a question naturally arises: Could this crisis work as a sort of "bypass" button also for what concerns the application of a more reflective approach to HE? "Being ready for anything requires rethinking what HE teachers typically do in the classroom, including reframing and reconceptualizing communication, engagement, community, and more. In other words, the current crisis could create opportunities to remake institutions" (Cuconato, 2020, p. 217).

Long before the radical changes caused by the COVID-19 health crisis, scholars had suggested that educational organizations and institutions should avoid "cognitive shortcuts" (Vogus et al., 2010), that is, adopting standard solutions based on past teaching and learning experiences. In the case of universities (and schools), some of these shortcuts hold the belief that presence is better than distance; the idea that schools and universities are places where people are taught and not where they learn and the attitude that it is impossible to evaluate from a distance.

The unexpected could be governed by avoiding these shortcuts. And alternatively, it can mean, for example, to think about how to organize the digital environment; how to cope with the limits and possibilities of digital distance and how to consider classroom attendance and digital presence not as an alternative, but as coexisting dimensions.

Accordingly, teachers require constant updates of contents and need to be open to using new didactics and tools which means that "teachers must be willing to treat the process as essentially problematic, iterative, and always improvable; we must stop assuming that teaching can be theorized like a natural science, and treat it like a design science" (Laurillard, 2012, p. 82).

As argued by Rapanta et al. (2020),

> Under this teaching as 'design for learning' perspective (Dimitriadis & Goodyear, 2013), teachers act as both constructors and actors. On the one hand, they need to design the tasks, environments and resources which can help students learn. On the other hand, they must enact the designed lesson plan, shifting nimbly between roles as appropriate: e.g. as an orchestrator, a facilitator, etc. (p. 4)

From this point of view, this change also requires teachers to rethink and co-create occasions and spaces for the relationship between students and teachers.

> This involves encouraging students to engage in and create verbal, public and private chat room exchanges. This includes not only real-time student polling to guide the learning process, but also the management of students' experiences. For example, it can entail polling students on their selections of the essay questions and then discussing these questions and repolling to track alterations before, during and towards the end of an online discussion. (Bryson & Andres, 2020, p. 615)

To implement digital and pedagogical teaching skills, universities have stood out for the innovative nature of their proposals already since the "Common European Principles for Teacher Competences and Qualifications" (European Commission [EC], 2000). However, teachers still require constant updates about subject knowledge and need to redefine the key competencies they are expected to achieve in the presence of this social and educational change. From the beginning of the pandemic emergency, National and European research promoted a lot of technical and administrative training regarding teaching online targeted to teachers and students in order to open new

RETHINKING ACADEMIC TEACHING AT AND BEYOND THE PANDEMIC

debates and activate the integration of so many learning opportunities. Specific training was aimed at:

1. promoting the interactive process of knowledge construction and skill development;
2. encouraging immediate application of new knowledge;
3. maintaining and enhancing intrinsic motivation of both
4. teachers and students developed and constantly supported through emotional involvement;
5. promoting suggestive, supportive, and efficient teaching styles; immediate, objective, and stimulating feedback and continuous student support;
6. innovating the learning design (Adedoyin & Soykan, 2020).

These challenges require due consideration from program coordinators in every student-centered HEI. Teaching and learning activities could become more hybrid if the challenges experienced during this pandemic were well-explored and the opportunities provided by online learning environments maintained their capacity to be stimulating, inclusive and flexible (when designed appropriately for what regards both content and method). In order to smooth this process, one could consider the learning activity as a cycle of specific steps along which one can move forward or backward to analyze the experiences and make connections between new experiences and prior knowledge and experiences.

4   Some Concluding Remarks

The opportunity for innovative processes taking place in the EU university system, which emerged due to COVID-19, highly relates to the effective use of digital resources. Although digital technologies have been used to guarantee crucial teacher-learner interaction, today teachers' approaches should intentionally move to educational innovation in order to cope with the need of transmitting updated "higher" skills helping students to become confident in their needed "learn to learn" procedure using digital technologies as a "facilitating" tool. Under these circumstances, teachers are expected to shift from the role of "knowledge owners" and "knowledge givers", that are inherent in the transmissive model to that of "facilitators" and "researchers", achieving a totally different set of skills aimed at promoting an iterative dialogue with students. Taking first these dialogic activities as criteria for the reflective practicum, the "facilitating" teacher can then look for the most appropriate technology to be exploited to achieve this aim. Thus, it can be concluded that, the learning design derives from the learning goal and not from the capability of the technology.

However, the question is which are the main differences between the two roles (Burns et al., 2017)? First, whereas a traditional teacher mostly gives passive students a teacher-centered lesson on his/her subject matter from the front of the classroom, a facilitator activates a learning process leading the learners to get to their own understanding of the content. In this way, the focus shifts from the instructor and the content towards the learner. Second, a traditional teacher tells, a facilitator asks. While the first lectures from the front, a facilitator supports from the back. A teacher answers according to a set curriculum, a facilitator creates guidelines and designs a supportive learning environment for the learners to derive their own conclusions, challenging their critical thinking and therefore giving them the ownership of the problem and solution process.

The critical goal is to support the learner in becoming an effective thinker. However, this goal would imply that academic teachers were open to become self-reflective professionals. As suggested by Bryson and Andres (2020), in this effort "[...] the emphasis must be on formative reflection intended to inform teaching practice. Reflective practice challenges existing practices, but with a focus on enhancement" (p. 611). It is an approach that encourages proactive improvisation.

In order to support this process with regard to the online teaching experiences, Bryson and Andres (2020) argue that "faculty should consider two phases of teaching, the offline self-learning phase and the online teaching phase" (p. 611). In the first phase, due to "COVID-19, change was required as part of a reactive strategy that must be embedded within a longer-term approach to reflective practice" (Bryson & Andres, 2020, p. 611). In this sense, the first effort requires that each teacher goes beyond the concern of identifying the most appropriate technological solution, but he/she engages more critically in the module's design and in understanding the meaning of an online learning module. In the second phase, the main challenge is instead

> to ensure that an online module is designed around high levels of interactions between students and instructors. [...] This involves considering not only the importance of the voice in online teaching (Bao, 2020), but also the selection, assemblage, and packaging of resources. (Bryson & Andres, 2020, pp. 613–614)

In conclusion, the goal to find a new approach to HE teaching, making good use of what we have experimented with as a result of COVID-19, implies a gain

RETHINKING ACADEMIC TEACHING AT AND BEYOND THE PANDEMIC

in common understanding of the nature of learning at the HE level, teachers' acceptance of their role shift to "learning facilitators", the development of a reflective practicum and the commitment of the HE's governance to support and reward this innovative teaching approach. During COVID-19 teachers have learnt to use new technology, but technology without a change in the teaching approach is inadequate to cope with the educational challenges of the Knowledge Society.

References

Adedoyin, O. B., & Soykan, E. (2020). Covid-19 pandemic and online learning: The challenges and opportunities. *Interactive Learning Environments*, 1–13. https://doi.org/10.1080/10494820.2020.1813180

Bao, W. (2020). COVID-19 and online teaching in higher education: A case study of Peking University. *Human Behavior and Emerging Technologies*, 2(2), 113–115. https://doi.org/10.1002/hbe2.191

Beck, S. (2008). The teacher's role and approaches in a knowledge society. *Cambridge Journal of Education*, 38(4), 465–481. https://doi.org/10.1080/03057640802482330

Beerkens, E. (2008). University policies for the knowledge society: Global standardization, local reinvention. *Perspectives on Global Development and Technology*, 7(1), 15–36. https://doi.org/10.1163/156914907X253242

Bryson, J. R., & Andres, L. (2020). Covid-19 and rapid adoption and improvisation of online teaching: Curating resources for extensive versus intensive online learning experiences. *Journal of Geography in Higher Education*, 44(4), 608–623. https://doi.org/10.1080/03098265.2020.1807478

Burns, A. C., Dikilitaş, K., Smith, R., & Wyatt, R. (2017). Introduction. In A. C. Burns, K. Dikilitaş, R. Smith, & M. Wyatt (Eds.), *Developing insights into teacher research* (pp. 1–17). IATEFL.

Coolahan, J. (2002). *Teacher education and the teaching career in an era of lifelong learning*. OECD Education Working Papers, No. 2. OECD Publishing. http://doi.org/10.1787/226408628504

Crosier, D., Horvath, A., Kerpanova, V., Kocanova, D., Parveva, T., Dalferth, S., & Rauhvargers, A. (2012). *The European higher education area in 2012: Bologna process implementation report*. Education, Audiovisual and Culture Executive Agency, European Commission. http://doi.org/10.2797/81203

Crul, M., Schneider, J., & Lelie, F. (Eds.). (2012). *The European second generation compared: Does the integration context matter?* Amsterdam University Press. http://doi.org/10.26530/OAPEN_426534

Cuconato, M. (2020, September 24). Blended learning at Covid time and beyond. In R. K. Gil'meevoy & L. A. Shibankovoy (Eds.), *Развитие человека в эпоху цифровизации* [*Human development in the time of digitalisation*] (pp. 215–221).

Institut Pedagogiki, psikhologii i sotsial'nykh problem. https://cris.unibo.it/retrieve/handle/11585/783804/698663/ПЕДАГОГИЧЕСКИЕ%20ЧТЕНИЯ%202020%20_Cuconato.pdf

Diamond, C. T. P., & Mullen, C. A. (Eds.). (1999). *The postmodern educator: Arts-based inquiries and teacher development*. Peter Lang Publishing. https://www.peterlang.com/abstract/title/56976?rskey=bOJ4T3&result=2

Dimitriadis, Y., & Goodyear, P. (2013). Forward-oriented design for learning: Illustrating the approach. *Research in Learning Technology [RLT] Journal, 21,* 1–13. https://doi.org/10.3402/rlt.v21io.20290

EU. (2000, March 23–24). *Presidency conclusion*. Lisbon European Council. https://www.europarl.europa.eu/summits/lis1_en.htm

Figel, J. (2006). Searching for a new balance: The next frontier for higher education in Europe. *Higher Education in Europe, 31*(4), 415–420. https://doi.org/10.1080/03797720701303731

Finlay, L. (2008). Reflecting on "reflective practice". In *Practice-Based Professional Learning [PBPL] paper 52* (pp. 1–27). The Open University. Retrieved December 3, 2020, from http://www.open.ac.uk

Laurillard, D. (2012). *Teaching as a design science: Building pedagogical patterns for learning and technology*. Routledge. https://doi.org/10.4324/9780203125083

Lea, S. J., Stephenson, D., & Troy J. (2003). Higher education students' attitudes to student centred learning: Beyond 'educational bulimia'. *Studies in Higher Education, 28*(3), 321–334. https://doi.org/10.1080/03075070309293

Rapanta, C., Botturi, L., Goodyear, P., Guàrdia, L., & Koole, M. (2020). Online university teaching during and after the Covid-19 crisis: Refocusing teacher presence and learning activity. *Postdigital Science and Education, 2*(3), 923–945. Retrieved December 1, 2020, from https://link.springer.com/article/10.1007/s42438-020-00155-y

Schön, D. A. (1987). *Educating the reflective practitioner: Toward a new design for teaching and learning in the professions*. Jossey-Bass.

Vogus, T. J., Sutcliffe, K. M., & Weick, K. E. (2010). Doing no harm: Enabling, enacting, and elaborating a culture of safety in health care. *Academy of Management Perspectives, 24*(4), 60–77. https://doi.org/10.5465/amp.2010.24.4.3652485.a

Wang, Y., Kretschmer, R., & Hartman, M. (2010). Teacher-as-researcher: Theory-into-practice. *American Annals of the Deaf, 155*(2), 105–109. www.jstor.org/stable/26235034

Wenger, E. (1998). *Communities of practice: Learning, meaning, and identity*. Cambridge University Press.

CHAPTER 11

Higher Education Academics' Perspectives

Working from Home during COVID-19

Rashmi Watson, Upasana Singh and Chenicheri Sid Nair

Abstract

COVID-19 has had a disruptive effect on higher education. A number of new studies have appeared to look at the effects on student learning. In 2020, an online survey to Australian Higher Education Academics was conducted during March-May to gather information about how academics were adjusting and transforming educational practices during the Pandemic. A range of questions were asked about the use of technologies (both pre and intra COVID-19), academics' experiences with the sudden shift to working from home (WFH) arrangements and quality assurance measures for the digital technologies. This chapter focuses on the questions around WFH arrangements (sustainability, challenges and future preparedness) utilising both qualitative and quantitative data. Responses were received from 71 academics across 12 Australian universities/tertiary institutions. Academics (63%) perceived they could sustain their current WFH arrangements 'indefinitely'. A number of challenges were raised regarding WFH including: general Pandemic anxiety, communication with colleagues, internet access with students and social isolation. Academics stated they utilised many methods to support students during the Pandemic but this will require continued support from their institutions if this is to be sustained long term where most perceive their institution will adopt blended learning in the post Pandemic period.

1 Introduction

This chapter focuses on the Working from Home (WFH) component during COVID-19, in terms of: challenges, benefits, sustainability, and the impact on relationships with colleagues, and future opportunity proposals for the broader higher education academic community. With the sudden, massive global move to WFH, a focus on academics' perceptions and impact on them as they work from home is an important study for future adaptations which may be applied to the academic work and lessons. The role of digital transformation in academic work, knowledge management and higher education

© KONINKLIJKE BRILL NV, LEIDEN, 2022 | DOI:10.1163/9789004512672_011

organisational processes has been rapid and evolving in relation to the ways in which academics manage work demands.

The world is facing a new Pandemic affecting the higher education sector in multiple ways including working from home (WFH) due to COVID-19 having a disruptive and forced effect through social physical distancing in higher education requiring 'work from home' also known as 'teleworking', 'home office', 'smart working', 'agile working', 'flexible working', 'remote work' or 'virtual work'. There is no common consensus as such on the term; however, the term 'working from home' is most commonly used in Australia and will be used through this chapter. The term 'smart working' implies an emphasis on the perceived positive outcomes that the model is expected to bring about for companies and individuals (Bolisani et al., 2020). As a result of COVID-19 and the resulting imposed social distancing, most academic employees across Australia commenced working from home around March 2020 with many still working offsite and remotely as of July 2021, with many now adopting a more flexible approach to academic work. Working from home refers to an office replacement at home or offsite, away from the usual building infrastructure where higher education academics usually work and teach.

This study utilised an online survey to Australian Higher Education academics conducted during March-May to gather information about how academics were adjusting and transforming educational practices during the Pandemic. A range of questions was asked about the use of technologies (both pre and intra COVID-19), academics' experiences with the sudden shift to working from home arrangements and quality assurance measures for the digital technologies. This chapter focuses on the questions around WFH arrangements (sustainability, challenges and future preparedness) utilising both qualitative and quantitative data. Responses were received from 71 academics across 12 Australian universities/tertiary institutions. Academics (63%) perceived they could sustain their current WFH arrangements 'indefinitely'. A number of challenges were raised by academics.

2 Australian Higher Education Context

Australia, in comparison to the rest of the world, has done very well to date in managing the spread of COVID-19. Statistics from the Australian Department of Health state that there have been close to 28,000 cases with ~25,000 of these cases as recovered and approximately 900 deaths with most of these (~800) in the state of Victoria which has seen the greatest period of lock-down and work and school closures (Australian Government, 2020).

The higher education sector in Australia commenced 2020 anticipating another prosperous year (Doidge & Doyle, 2020) but instead, has been deeply affected with changes to pedagogical delivery, redesign of learning programs, assessments and how academic staff and students interact with many not being able to return to a physical campus site at some stage or throughout the year or in some cases still partially or completely working remotely. Academics stated they utilised many methods to support students during the Pandemic but that this would require continued support from their institutions if this was to be sustained long term where most perceived their institution would adopt blended learning in the post Pandemic period. The world faced a new and unknown challenge in 2020 known as the Coronavirus or better known as COVID-19 which has wreaked havoc across the globe and in November, 2020 continues to cause major disruption and changes to what was once considered normal day-to-day work arrangements. Academics' work has been impacted and current research has shown a broad range of responses from the academic community from no response, social isolation strategies on campus, rapid changes to curriculum and spike in online opportunities (Crawford et al., 2020).

Academics and students were asked to stay home as the rapid spread of COVID-19 increased across Australia and to ensure correct social and physical distancing rules were put into place by the Australian state and Federal government. Evaluating the potential and effective home based work behaviours can support future policies and formulation of reopening strategies (Bick et al., 2020).

3 Research Methodology

The current research forms part of a broader study on the impact of the COVID-19 pandemic on academics at Higher Education Institutions. Ethics approval was received from the University of KwaZulu-Natal, South Africa as per Protocol Reference Number HSSREC/00001284/2020. As per the required Ethical procedures, participants were required to provide Informed Consent before proceeding with the survey. Part of this Informed Consent highlighted that their participation in the study was voluntary, with no financial implications, and that they were free to withdraw at any stage of the study. They were also notified that data collection was anonymous, so neither their names nor the names of their Institutions would be disclosed. The focus of this study was on higher education academics in Australia. Ethics approval was received from both South Africa and Australia as part of the initial, joint collaborative research. An online survey tool through Google docs was developed to gather primary data. The survey was pilot tested with selected academics from varying countries for logic, coherence, content and understandability.

The survey was disseminated via a number of methods including: direct email invitation to academic staff from within the universities/institutions, postings on academic forums such as the Higher Educational Research Society for Australia (HERDSA) mailing list and on researchers' own LinkedIn posts. The methodology used a mixed-method approach gathering both qualitative and quantitative methods. Quantitative data were employed to analyse usage and adoption of technology for teaching, and assessment, prior to and during the pandemic; and open-ended questions to capture academics' perceptions, feedback and experiences with the transition to online teaching and assessment. In this chapter, the authors have used both qualitative and quantitative data to report on one aspect of the larger research question in the original study about the rapid transformation of Higher Education during the COVID-19 Pandemic with a focus on changes to technology use by academics which also captured data around working remotely which has been applied to this current chapter.

A total of 36 questions were asked with 11 on demographic data, 16 requiring a rating on a scale, and nine open-ended responses. Data collection was open for a period of six weeks. The online survey took approximately 15 minutes to complete and was anonymous; only demographic data was collected identifying the university, role and years of experience. The final sample was 71 academics across 12 Australian universities/tertiary institutions.

Quantitative data were analysed using statistical analysis using SPSS and the results of the full quantitative part of this study are presented in a separate paper (Singh, 2021). This chapter focuses specifically on the WFH aspects of this study, and as such includes the results of three quantitative questions from the survey and one qualitative question. Simple thematic analysis was conducted on the qualitative data and emerging themes were identified, which are summarised in word clouds and discussed with supporting respondent feedback thereafter.

4 Demographics of Respondents

A total of 71 valid responses were received in this study from both public (71.9%) and private (28.1%) institutions. The majority of the participants (59.2%) were from the ages of 41 to 60. Females (63.4%) dominated the study. Almost all respondents (97.2%) had a postgraduate degree. In terms of academic hierarchy, lecturers (40.8%) held the highest participation rate, with 43.7% of participants having experience in academia for more than 16 years. The majority (57.7%) had permanent tenure.

5 Working from Home Challenges, Benefits and Sustainability

Working from home has presented academics across the globe with many challenges including increased work hours, juggling care of young children also forced to remotely attend school from home, having to learn new technological skills rapidly or taking on new roles and responsibilities (Wells, 2020). Women in particular have been impacted by care responsibilities creating a new challenge for higher education institutions (Nash & Churchill, 2020). There has similarly been a constant clamour of forewarning of inadequate workplace policies, most notably the powerful argument for paid family leave in the United States (Connelly & Ghodsee, 2011). A lack of home office infrastructure and internet access and bandwidth to access remote content from home locations are all challenges of WFH (Crawford et al., 2020). Working from home is shown to improve or hamper organisation performance directly through efficiency, motivation, and knowledge creation of the workforce and indirectly through cost reductions that allow resources to be more readily available for productivity increasing innovation and reorganisation.

A number of challenges were raised from this study from the Australian higher education sector regarding WFH including: general Pandemic anxiety, communication with colleagues, internet access with students and social isolation.

6 Challenges Results

The effect of working at home and the impact of the lives of Australian academics was investigated in our study. The predominant challenges faced by academics in the 'forced' work-from-home arrangements during the pandemic were identified as: (i) 'General anxiety about COVID-19'; (ii) 'Communication with colleagues' equally as the highest rated challenge; (iii) 'Internet connection for students'; (iv) 'Social isolation' and (v) 'Disturbance from family members' at equal levels; (vi) access to technology; (vii) lack of knowledge and (viii) personal health issues. These are displayed in Table 11.1. None of these challenges was indicated by a significant proportion of the respondents.

TABLE 11.1   Challenges faced by academics

Challenges	Percentage
General anxiety	32
Communication	32
Internet connection	31
Social isolation	30
Disturbance (by family)	30
Access to technology	14
Lack of knowledge	14
Health issues	11

Further in qualitative data analysis, academic staff enunciated matters of concern regarding work at home. Respondent 3, stated that "handling my own kids at home is a little hard with teaching". This was further expanded upon by Respondent 48 – "... the need to set up a family friendly office space", and reiterated by Respondents 63 and 71, who state that academics are "forced to work from home" for "longer hours" now and Respondent 16 who stated "I increased my teacher presence online which was necessary through the pandemic stressors".

The provision of a supportive infrastructure, for instance childcare for working parents is critical and was addressed positively by the Australian government who provided fee-free and subsidised, income-tested child care services to families using government approved child care services from April to June 2020 to support parents during the Pandemic. The fees were means tested based on family income, hours of care used, type of care used and parents' levels of work or training which meant for many families (approximately 1 million), the service was free of charge. The cost of the subsidy for the three month period was estimated at $1.6 billion (Klapdor, 2020). Increasing WFH without complementary policies to improve supportive infrastructure could increase the burden especially on women from competing work and caretaker duties (Alon et al., 2020). The importance of offering appropriate and accessible childcare due to a higher incidence of employees working from home supports career advancement, especially for women, and supports potential improvement in equal opportunities inherent in the changing norms on caretaker duties during the crisis (Alon et al., 2020). The Pandemic has highlighted privileges of male workers in the pandemic due to the work and care

FIGURE 11.1   Themes emerging from challenges associated with the forced WFH scenario

challenges for female academics and that the Australian Higher Education sector positions this as 'private matters' for women to manage their own solutions with care challenges (Nash & Churchill, 2020).

Six themes emerged from the qualitative responses from academics in relation to the challenges they faced with WFH. These themes are presented in the word cloud depicted in Figure 11.1 showing (i) 'social isolation' as the major theme followed by (ii) 'poor communication', (iii) 'disconnected', (iv) 'decreased collegiality', '(v) stressful meetings' and (vi) 'job uncertainty'.

While a large number of academics indicated the WFH scenario did not affect their relationship with their colleagues by stating 'none' as a response, the biggest challenge outlined by others, was that of social isolation. Academics cited "no social interaction" (Respondent 2), "Easy to be left out of discussions" (Respondent 5), "limited contact" (Respondent 8), and "can't catch up face to face" (Respondent 23). While the WFH scenario has limited contact amongst academics "they are very supportive of one another" (Respondent 42). The limited contact with other colleagues can lead to "decreased visibility and poorer understanding of the workplace" (Respondent 49). While many academics were having regular Video Conferencing meetings with their colleagues, they stated they were missing the social interaction in the informal environments, "I don't see them in the tea room any more" (Respondent 50), "we don't have the casual meetings and chats in the hallways" (Respondent 70), and find the online meeting environments restrictive, "mostly we just listen and ask a few questions" (Respondent 50). There is a lack of "onsite communication and knowledge share" (Respondent 59), which can result in the "communication being degraded with colleagues" (Respondent 63). This was supported by Respondent 24 who feels that "we have lost opportunities for more regular informal discussions around T&L and assessment". Less frequent personal communication can also have negative implications for its engagements with key stakeholders such as students and peers with possible adverse effects for the overall performance of businesses (Hovhannisyan, 2019).

Being disconnected from colleagues was another emerging theme: "meant that incidental conversations tend to be shared with more people, on Teams channels, and casual chat is more likely to be written (on Teams, Twitter, etc.) than verbal, although sometimes there's casual chat after a Zoom session" (Respondent 21). However, (Respondent 21) stated that "virtual coffees don't serve the purpose of moving to another space to have a private or different kind of conversation". While the WFH has provided the basis for a "strong relationship with (my) immediate team" it is "difficult to engage in ad hoc meetings as all interactions have to be planned to some extent" (Respondent 27). Often less communication leads to "less comradery" (Respondent 55). Disruptive forms of communication may surge to compensate for the lack of personal communication, e.g. increased email traffic or virtual meetings as was observed during the survey period.

Respondent 33 found it "more difficult to work on collaborative projects". Respondent 68 indicated that WFH makes one "Feel disconnected and isolated – also 'out of the loop' on key activities and changes currently underway at my institution", which supports the statement made by Respondent 49 in the Social Isolation theme. Respondent 67 added "... I feel isolated. The general connection is missing ... we may settle into a new pattern of engagement". Respondent 82 feels that the WFH scenario "makes relationships more 'gappy' and requires more effort to compensate for the lack of chance meetings". Evidence suggests that in-person meetings allow for more effective communication rather than emails, video conferencing or phone calls (Bohns, 2017) in being more convincing, attracting more attention or being able to observe social cues (Battiston, 2017).

Related to the themes of Social Isolation and the feeling of being Disconnected, academics felt that they were experiencing 'Decreased Collegiality' as they "struggle to maintain relationships" (Respondent 18) or "no longer have working relationships with colleagues" (Respondent 11). The theme of Stressful Meetings is highlighted by a few. Respondent 4 outlines that online meetings while WFH are often "stressful with contestation", and often result in "less and poor communication" (Respondents 4, 61 and 64). Respondent 67 highlights that "there is HIGH stress at our team TEAMS meetings". The pandemic has also resulted in "increased work uncertainty and instability in the university and sector" (Respondent 14).

7 Benefits and Sustainability Results

Whilst many challenges were raised, there were also a number of benefits of working from home identified by Australian academics such as: (i) 'new fruitful engagement patterns', (ii) increased collaboration and (iii) strengthened collegiality, see Figure 11.2.

The theme of 'New Engagement Patterns' is highlighted by a number of academics who appreciate the benefits associated with WFH by using the technology. This is supported by a number of qualitative comments: Communication with colleagues "several times a week" (Respondent 44) helps support "interaction and discussion about students" (Respondent 19). Some even indicated "meeting on teams daily, so we are still in touch and we could make calls whenever we need to discuss" (Respondent 67) which indicates the ability to interact more frequently. Others indicated that engagement is more frequent with direct team members "With a few (up to five colleagues) I have good contact". Regular interaction with colleagues ensures that "we are working well as a team ... meet for coffee every morning and keep the social aspects front and centre" (Respondent 88) thus trying to support virtual social interaction. Respondent 41 suggested that "... maybe we are even closer as we talk more and include personal chit chat about the home situation".

Academics appreciate the effort made by some leaders to connect with them on a social level during these new engagement patterns, "... the boss sent everyone brownies as a thank you for our work" added (Respondent 88). Respondent 83 highlighted that "the social side of things is very important now ..." which is why this respondent "run(s) University-wide virtual tea breaks where we have colleagues present about their hobbies ... online craft group on Teams and we talk about knitting, crocheting and needlework ... about to launch a virtual storytelling group with the expertise of one of the learning technicians".

FIGURE 11.2 Benefits in working from home

Respondent 88 presented how social media is adopted for engagement, "we use Twitter for this to some extent" as well as "weekly themed virtual Research Cafe meetings via teams". This engagement seems to need to still find its balance as indicated by Respondent 82, who states that there is "too much social interaction with colleagues".

Related to the theme above is the second theme of Increased Collaboration. Respondent 22 indicated that through regular engagement the WFH arrangements "made us closer, more connected". This was supported by Respondents 28, 30, 37, 44 and 48, who state that WFH "has brought us closer and stronger", and ensured that our collegiality is "strengthened". Respondent 32 added that WFH has "strengthened some relationships with colleagues (we are in it together)", as well as "improved communication from exec (the executive)". WFH has also facilitated collaboration amongst academics of the same level, as suggested by Respondent 39 "I have had the chance to work closely with those at my level of understanding and ignore or dismiss the ones on a different level. So, in fact very positively as it meant I was working with like-minded colleagues".

The results from a chi-square goodness of fit test showed that a significant number of respondents (n = 45, 63%) stated they considered that they were able to sustain their current WFH arrangements 'indefinitely', as illustrated in Table 11.2. The data from the benefits outlined above can be attributed to the feelings of sustainability as stated by respondents.

TABLE 11.2   Sustainability of work at home

Sustainability (time)	Percentage
Indefinitely	63
Other	11
Two months	10
A month	6
A few weeks	3
One week	1

8   Challenges Associated with WFH Communication Arrangements

The physical and social distancing of COVID-19 meant that academic staff were required to quickly adopt new ways of communicating with their students and with colleagues (Blewett, 2016). The type of Working From Home (WFH) arrangements academics were adopting for communicating overall during the

TABLE 11.3   Communication tools used (with students & staff)

Sustainability (time)	Staff %	Students %
Email	38	46
Video conference tools	99	97
Social Media	9	34
Phone call	9	3
Learning Management System (LMS)	29	87

pandemic is summarised in Table 11.3 and was categorised according to email, video conferencing tools (i.e. Zoom/Skype/WebEx), Social Media (Facebook, WhatsApp, Line, Google tools), Learning Management System (Blackboard, Moodle, Canvas) and Phone calls. Challenges for higher education academics included the immediate pedagogical uptake and adoption of technologies which have moved slowly in recent years or with no effect on student learning due to the gap in understanding the effect on student learning (Blewett, 2016). Many universities did not have online capabilities, resources or academic capacity to transition to the sudden online delivery. Few higher education institutions offered online delivery prior to COVID-19, and many were not prepared for the transition (Archibald et al., 2019; Crawford et al., 2020).

Email and Video conferencing tools were significantly adopted for communication with both students and colleagues (p < .0005 in each case). Video conferencing tools were the most used communication tool by academics with their peers and students (see Table 11.3).

Recent literature suggests that worker efficiency improves with low levels of WFH but decreases with 'excessive WFH', implying a 'sweet spot' where worker efficiency – and thus productivity – is maximised at intermediate levels of WFH. Academics fall into the category of a highly skilled occupation where (Grundke et al., 2018) working from home is most common due to the nature of the work that can be done remotely.

9   Future Proposals and Lessons from Academics' Experience in Working from Home

Strict state border controls and state and territory movement restrictions including working from home since March 2020 have meant that Australia has been relatively lucky in managing COVID-19 spread to date in comparison with other countries. The hardest hit state in Australia in 2020 so far has been Victoria which has seen a very strict lockdown from March to November, 2020. In the past, working from home has been looked down upon by many where barriers have been highlighted such as lack of social interaction, a perception that 'being seen' was necessary in order to be working or to make career progress, and inability to separate home and work. Research studies have found it to be more of a managerial decision rather than a function of work that suppressed its uptake (Hopkins & McKay, 2018).

Compared to the reported levels of WFH prior to COVID-19, it would seem that as restrictions are eased, WFH will constitute a greater proportion of working days than before (Beck et al., 2020). This move suggests that the education itself has to think about the redesign of their delivery modes from primarily face to face to more of a blended approach. Anecdotal evidence suggests international students in Australia who once opposed the online environment are getting more accustomed to the way classes run in the new era which have resulted in greater flexibility to their accessibility to higher education. Some possible strategies that can be put in place to ensure sustainability are staff support policies and mechanisms to ensure staff wellbeing. Regular communication meetings to discuss matters of concerns suggest that staff are able to communicate matters of concerns in a forum setting. One strategy may be to collect best practices from academic members and incorporate them into policy and training and support to equip staff to the new teaching and learning era of the 21st century.

10   Conclusion

Working from Home was thrust upon academics across the globe and was in many ways haphazard as COVID-19 suddenly forced itself upon all sectors of work resulting in school closures for many parts of Australia with the added stress on working parents having to manage home and work pressures. With more time to prepare for WFH and with less home-based distractions in the future, the overall experience may become more positive as we move forward. For this to happen and for any effective Working from Home system, policies must include the lessons learnt, that being as this chapter presented, communication and social interaction as key factors in the sustainability of the new way of teaching and learning. It has been a huge social and organisational experiment, although forced upon employees, every sector including higher education institutions has had to make the necessary adaptations in personal, social and technological ways. The ability to work from home does offer the higher education sector opportunities for sustaining work during the Pandemic (and beyond) and reducing commuting and physical resource costs to attend meetings, deliver curriculum and complete usual business tasks. This study provides fruit for thought that institutions will have to consider post pandemic not only changing delivery modes of instruction but to put into place approaches that make sure that both professional and personal needs of academics are taken into account to ensure sustainability in delivery of higher education courses.

References

Alon, T. M., Doepke, M., Olmstead-Rumsey, J., & Tertilt, M. (2020). The impact of COVID-19 on gender equality. *Covid Economics Vetted and Real-Time Papers, 4,* 62–85.

Archibald, M. M., Ambagtsheer, R. C., Casey, M. G., & Lawless, M. (2019). Using zoom videoconferencing for qualitative data collection: Perceptions and experiences of researchers and participants. *International Journal of Qualitative Methods, 18,* 1609406919874596. https://doi.org/10.1177/1609406919874596

Australian Government, D. O. H. (2020). *Coronavirus (COVID-10) current situation and case numbers.* https://www.health.gov.au/news/health-alerts/novel-coronavirus-2019-ncov-health-alert/coronavirus-covid-19-current-situation-and-case-numbers#covid19-summary-statistics-

Battiston, D., Blanes, J., & Kirchmaier, T. (2017). *Is distance dead? Face-to-face communication and productivity in teams.* Centre for Economic Performance, LSE. https://ideas.repec.org/p/cep/cepdps/dp1473.html

Beck, M. J., Hensher, D. A., & Wei, E. (2020). Slowly coming out of COVID-19 restrictions in Australia: Implications for working from home and commuting trips by car and public transport. *Journal of Transport Geography, 88,* 102846. https://doi.org/ https://doi.org/10.1016/j.jtrangeo.2020.102846

Bick, A., Blandin, A., & Mertens, K. (2020). *Work from home after the COVID-19 outbreak.* Working Papers. Federal Reserve Bank of Dallas. doi:10.24149/wp2017r1

Blewett, C. (2016). From traditional pedagogy to digital pedagogy: Paradoxes, affordances, and approaches. In M. A. Samuel, R. Dhurpath, & N. Amin (Eds.), *Disrupting Higher Education Curriculum* (pp. 265–287). Brill Sense.

Bohns, V. (2017). *A Face-to-Face request is 34 times more successful than an email.* Retrieved August 17, 2020, from https://hbr.org/2017/04/a-face-to-face-request-is-34-times-more-successful-than-an-email

Bolisani, E., Scarso, E., Ipsen, C., Kirchner, K., & Hansen, J. P. (2020). Working from home during COVID-19 pandemic: Lessons learned and issues. *Management &*

Marketing. Challenges for the Knowledge Society, 15(s1), 458–476. https://doi.org/ https://doi.org/10.2478/mmcks-2020-0027

Connelly, R., & Ghodsee, K. (2011). *Professor mommy: Finding work-family balance in academia.* Rowman & Littlefield Publishers. https://find.library.unisa.edu.au/primo-explore/fulldisplay?vid=UNISA&search_scope=All_Resources&docid=UNISA_ALMA51158031910001831

Crawford, J., Butler-Henderson, K., Jurgen, R., Malkawi, B. H., Glowatz, M., Burton, R., Magni, P., & Lam, S. (2020). COVID-19: 20 countries' higher education intra-period digital pedagogy responses. *Journal of Applied Learning & Teaching, 3.* https://doi.org/ 10.37074/jalt.2020.3.1.7

Doidge, S., & Doyle, J. (2020). Australian universities in the age of Covid. *Educational Philosophy and Theory,* 1–7. https://doi.org/10.1080/00131857.2020.1804343

Grundke, R., Marcolin, L., & Squicciarini, M. (2018). Which skills for the digital era?

Hopkins, J., & McKay, J. (2018). Investigating 'anywhere working' as a mechanism for alleviating traffic congestion in smart cities. *Technological Forecasting and Social Change, 142.* https://doi.org/10.1016/j.techfore.2018.07.032

Hovhannisyan, N. A. W. K. (2019). *International business travel and technology sourcing.* NBER Working Paper 5862. https://doi.org/http://dx.doi.org/10.3386/w25862.

Klapdor, M. (2020). *COVID-19 Economic response—free child care.* Parliament of Australia. Retrieved July 15, 2020, from https://www.aph.gov.au/About_Parliament/ Parliamentary_Departments/Parliamentary_Library/FlagPost/2020/April/ Coronavirus_response-Free_child_care

Nash, M., & Churchill, B. (2020). Caring during COVID-19: A gendered analysis of Australian university responses to managing remote working and caring responsibilities. *Gender, Work, and Organization, 27*(5), 833–846. https://doi.org/10.1111/ gwao.12484

Singh, U. G., Nair, C. S., & Watson, R. (2021). The transformation in Higher Education in Australia during the Covid-19 pandemic. In H. Almeida, P. Fonesca, S. Gonclaves, C. Malca, F. Neves, C. Dias, & M. Velososo (Eds.), *Pandemic and remote teaching in higher education* (Vol. 11, pp. 37–62). CINEP/IPC. https://www.cinep.ipc.pt/index.php/ simposio/78-sobre-o-cinep/eventos/271-vol-11-pandemic-and-remote-teaching-in-higher-education

Wells, A. (2020). *Stepping up for employees.* Retrieved November 2, 2020, from https://www.insurancejournal.com/magazines/mag-editorsnote/2020/11/02/ 588975.htm

CHAPTER 12

Reconnecting Teaching Discourse in Higher Education

Establishing and Remodeling Interfaces

Beatrix Kreß

Abstract

The suddenness of the pandemic situation caused an immediate implementation of digital environments. Despite some negative surprise effects, this new challenging situation has prompted new creative impulses for further development, for productive re-structuring, adapted to new needs and developmental trends, and a quick adaptive reestablishment of the functionality in internal and external interface management. The practices of an effective reconnection of the discourse are not only of great importance at the institutional level, but also at the educational micro-level. This chapter, based on a discourse analysis of communicative contexts in digital environments, outlines some aspects of adaptive teaching practices, in order to support the macro-cohesive mechanisms of reconnecting the interrupted discourse as well as improving the dynamics and interaction of supported, collaborative and autonomous learning processes.

1 Starting Point: Higher Education and Digital Environments

It is common sense by now that higher education facilities, like many other institutions, were hit by surprise by the pandemic situation, which abruptly brought an end to face-to-face teaching and a synchronic discussion culture with physical presence of all participants. On the other hand, different developments in higher education, such as e-learning, blended learning, mobile learning, MOOCs and so on, pushed forward an understanding of teaching and learning that focuses on availability of content and asynchronous learning with all its advantages and disadvantages.

Therefore, a hybrid situation was found at the beginning of the curfew, caused by the COVID-19 pandemic. Some teachers in higher education found themselves well prepared, having already produced videos or other material, which could be shared easily through digital media. Others had the impression that they had to create something out of nothing. However, "being ready" or not is only one side of the coin. Higher education is based to a significant extent on face-to-face communication, on discourse, debate and discussion as an instrument of recognition and knowledge building. The situation, caused by the pandemic, put a sudden end to that and led to a rather isolated, fragmented learning environment, which many participants of the teaching-learning discourse experienced as the opposite of fruitful and inspiring discussions (Ehlich, 2014, p. 48, speaks of the "lonely learner"), expected as an integral component of higher education. This lack of opportunities for spontaneous, instant, oral exchange – communication as a way of knowledge production and knowledge development – is felt by students and lecturers alike.

2 Teaching and Learning Discourse: Expectations

Why do university members – students and lecturers – miss direct communication, despite the fact that most universities established different videoconferencing technologies to allow this kind of exchange? For a better understanding it might be useful to clarify the expectations. *Learning outcomes* are an established term to define results of learning processes in higher education (cf. Cedefop, 2014, p. 74, 2017, p. 29): "Learning outcomes are defined as 'statements of what a learner knows, understands and is able to do on completion of a learning process, which are defined in terms of knowledge, skills and competence'". Learning outcomes are achieved through different methods, the classroom discourse being one of them, which – almost already traditionally – is enriched by high expectations. Coming from a taxonomy of skills and learning progression (cf. Anderson & Krathwohl, 2001, p. 27), *remember, understand, apply, analyse, evaluate* and finally *create*, classroom discourse is expected to foster all of them. Knowledge is shared through discourse; understanding can be ensured by communication in question-answer-schemes, and by guided debates whereby higher ordered analytical and critical competences should be facilitated. Linguists emphasize desirable side effects: Communication skills, the ability to use terminology and the scientific register appropriately, to express difficult processes and connections, but also to formulate an opinion or evaluation and be capable of arguing it. An acceleration of knowledge and the creation of new insights is expected through that (cf. Lemke, 1990, pp. 87–124; Redder, 2014, pp. 32–33; Ehlich, 2014, pp. 45–48). As the scientific debate – and hence the classroom discourse as a discussion in the scientific community "in miniature" – is shaped by controversy (in a productive way), students also acquire social skills: How is opposition stated without being too offensive, but still clear? How can a strong deviation be mitigated?

In general, social aspects should not be underestimated. Learning in a group is different from the fragmented and rather isolated learning through mediated mobile learning at home. And therefore, it is not surprising that students give us feedback that social aspects, more precisely, the lack of direct social contact and communicative exchange, are the most stressful issues in the current situation.

Before talking about the technical surrounding and actual learner behaviour and learner interaction, I would like to emphasize another aspect of classroom discourse, which seems to be present in the previous considerations rather incidentally. This is the orality of communication between peers and lecturers within the classroom. It was Ong (1982) who highlighted the shift to literacy and written language as a development away from the oral society and its way of thinking and producing knowledge. The scientific community with its specific practices of communication is a world even more dominated by writing instead of direct speech than most others. Nevertheless, direct interaction, face to face discussion, requires other skills and competencies, which are valuable as such. This is: the ability to formulate one's thoughts rather spontaneously, to react quickly to the performances of others and to do that in a communicatively and socially adequate manner. The expectations are – also due to our written bias – high and orientated to linguistic norms and elaborated formulation of thoughts.

3 Learning in the Pandemic: Technical Aspects and Observations of Learner Behavior

As stated already above, at the beginning of the pandemic, universities were mostly in a rather comfortable situation, as trends like mobile learning, blended learning and distant learning had already reached the academic world years ago, so learning platforms and other tools for distant learning have been established. To foster a direct verbal exchange and interactive learning, video conferencing platforms were set up. There, through voice and picture/microphone and camera, a face-to-face like situation is supposed to be established. Most video conferencing systems allow so called breakout rooms, where smaller groups can be created to work together separately.

The expectation was that lecturers and students alike would come to these video meetings, turn on their microphone and their camera, and a situation, quite similar to the usual classroom, would develop. However, moments like these were seldom. Students usually did not switch on their camera and when they contributed to the lecture, it was rather through the chat feature; only a few of them unmuted themselves. This usually creates a rather uncomfortable situation for the lecturer, as he/she cannot be sure, whether he/she is talking to a bunch of 'ghosts' for half an hour and of course this situation is very far away from the ideal of an interactive and discursive form of learning. The only possibility to assure presence and attention seems to be a voting tool, where a quick inquiry can be started by the lecturer. However, questions that fit into this format are not always obvious.

The reasons that can be found for this situation are various. First of all, students claim technical reasons. A lot of them moved in with their parents during the curfew and the elder generation often had a weak internet connection, a bad bandwidth. Not all of the students used a laptop computer with an integrated microphone and a camera. In surveys, however, the students also often gave psychological reasons. They stated that they felt a great barrier to opening their cameras and microphones. The sudden focus on their own voice or picture made them feel awkward and seemed to significantly increase expectations of the relevance and quality of the contribution. A rather secondary reason for the reluctance are difficulties with turn-taking and the simultaneity of multiple channels. Of course, sometimes participants used chat and the also existing possibility of shared notes concurrently or somebody was in the process of writing in the chat (which is displayed by some systems), while somebody else was also talking, but usually the communicative traffic was rather low and easy to handle by the lecturer/moderator.

4 Coping Strategies, Adaptions, Solutions: How to Encourage Participation?

The situation described above was, of course, unsatisfactory. One might as well put PowerPoint presentations provided with sound, videos or screencasts online. This functions perfectly for pure knowledge transfer, but already the previously stated second step of learning progression, remembering, thus understanding, cannot be secured by this unidirectional way of teaching and learning. When we keep in mind that the use of video conferencing systems is directed to the highest level of interactivity (cf. Haack, 2002; Grissom, McNally, & Naps, 2003), and therefore the highest steps of learning progression, this situation cannot be satisfying.

Most tools provide the possibility of creating smaller groups in breakout sessions. There, students usually are a little bit less reserved and willing to unmute. It is impossible though, or at least very hard to handle to be equally present in these sessions as a lecturer, as one can be present in only one room at a time due to technical reasons. So there have to be well defined tasks and stimuli for discussion. Just a rather open question or the pure request to discuss a certain topic will not be enough, as nobody can bridge a break by paraphrasing and elaborating the question, or "direct" the answers in the right directions. The participants also need clear instruction to secure their results and to provide a person, who is (technically and functionally) able to transfer the outcome into the virtual classroom.

Another possibility to save some of the advantages of classroom discourse, such as the linguistic examination of theoretical content in order to practice terms and scientific expression, and to promote the higher level learning outcomes, is the relocation of these aims into the written medium – which, admittedly, sounds like a contradiction to what was said above. However, the dialogue in video conferences seems to be so loaded from the technical and as well from the psychological side, especially in larger groups, that it seems only suitable for rather simple interactions, such as inquiries, questions and answers in chats etc.

So, theoretical discussions, the deepened work with theoretical texts and the practical and analytical implementation was shifted to the written medium. The tasks for writing were then modelled in a way to preserve some of the discursive benefits. This was realized by impulses that allowed personal involvement in a special way. The importance of applicability of knowledge and learning outcomes and their embedding in everyday life is commonplace, and it became even more important through the remote and somehow unreal situation of the curfew. On the other hand, the material and the task should be able to encourage a kind of interior dialogue, a discourse with oneself, so different viewpoints and their argumentation were possible. Finally, however, it was also important that the challenge did not resemble well-known exam formats such as term papers or the like. The skills that are to be developed through these types of examinations are certainly embedded to a sufficient extent in the current study programs and promote other competencies such as a critical review of the state of research, developing and arguing one's own research focus or research question and writing a longer academic text in a structured and appropriate way.

In the new established written tasks, the focal point is different. It is on multi-perspectivity, argumentation and a "dialogue" of these different point of views with each other, so that not one thread is argued through a longer text, but the skills, promoted by a fruitful debate. What has been said so far should be clarified by using an example. It comes from a seminar with the title "Language and migration". The lecture focusses on multilingualism and the linguistic research on heritage languages. Sociolinguistic considerations of migration

FIGURE 12.1
Silhouette adult, male and female
(from Krumm & Jenkins, 2001; open source http://heteroglossia.net/Home.2.0.html)

and diversity in society are also a subject of discussion. After a unit on research methods in multilingualism, students were asked to draw a language portrait of themselves. This method is often used in language biography research. The outline of a human body is used as an object, where respondents should fill in "their" languages, i.e. languages they have at disposal in their everyday life, languages they are able to speak (not necessary fluently) or languages, to which they can relate (emotionally) in correspondence with the functions in their life and places in the body which symbolizes these functions.

So, there might be a language of profession and/or of thinking placed in the head, a language for emotions in the heart, a language of fear in the stomach and so on. The drawing activity is to be commented on, in our case in the written form. The results are surprisingly differentiated; students come to very diverse solutions. This task is usually more demanding for persons with a biographically monolingual starting situation. They often only understand at second glance that they also have more than one language available and have an emotional relation to – dialects, foreign languages they acquired at school etc.

This already changes common patterns of thinking, as usually the multilinguals with the migration background are the ones in an "inferior", less comfortable situation. Yet in this situation for them, the question was clear and the "monolinguals" had to think harder. This demands a great share of thinking and self-questioning. In a second step, the students were asked to defend their now discovered multilingualism towards a monolingual institution or organization. Classically, the school is a place that stands for a monolingual habitus (Gogolin, 2008). By arguing, why schools should foster multilingualism, students had to include argumentation that might not be obvious to them. They had to convince schools (or another monolingual institution), what languages

RECONNECTING TEACHING DISCOURSE IN HIGHER EDUCATION

FIGURE 12.2 Two language portraits, one with migration background (left); one "monolingual" portrait (right) (adapted from Krumm & Jenkins, 2001)

can mean for a multilingual person, what functions they have and why these languages (of origin) should be promoted instead of hidden away in favour of the hegemonic, official language. Thus, students should not only acquire the need to change perspectives, but also learn to bring together scientific and everyday argumentation. They could use linguistic arguments from the theoretical background of the seminar, but also personal reasons and arguments in favour of multilingualism from their own considerations during the language portraits. Doing so, two different argumentation styles are merged and links and synergies can be observed. The third step of this task is a reflection about the question, if this method can be used in linguistic research and if so, how. This should provide the transfer into the theoretical and linguistic field. The written products were handed in and of course extensive feedback was given.

Of course, a task like this is not a one-to-one transfer of a classroom discourse into distance learning. It is, however, a way to come to a communicative exchange that is on the one hand scientifically substantiated without being part of the usual and typical scientific text types. Beyond that, it fosters multi-perspectivity and by that also encourages social factors, as it allows the students an unusual view on a socially and societally relevant topic. The thorough feedback afterwards was also part of some kind of dialogue, as a lot of students talked about the lecturer's comments, so some kind of meta discourse started subsequent to the task itself.

5   Advantages and Disadvantages

As stated before, the procedure described is not a substitute for face-to-face interaction in the classroom. It can adapt some important issues, but it is still totally different to the spontaneous communication we expect from direct exchange. It has, however, certain advantages. In usual seminar discourse there is always a larger number of silent or invisible participants. Some of the students are too shy, too reluctant to take part in the discourse, but there is also the phenomenon of the social loafer, who leaves the work to the rest of the group. Nobody can hide with the procedure just described. And the results are surprising. Most students, who evaluated this lecture afterwards very affirmatively, handed in very interesting, well elaborated drafts on the topic. The written approach was particularly advantageous for students, who are not able to engage in a quick and vivid discussion.

However, the written procedure is completely different from the oral approach, not only in terms of its production conditions. It is focused on different skills – cognitively and communicatively – which cannot be adapted by any other medium. Another disadvantage is the loss of peer-interactions. The students and the whole seminar are focused on the lecturer and the interaction between student and lecturer. This has different consequences: differences in knowledge come into play as well as hierarchy and concern about possible evaluations, so sometimes the freedom of spontaneous interaction in the classroom, that is possible through the ephemeral nature of oral communication, is lost.

6   Conclusion

There are two rather clear findings and implications. First of all – and that is, in principle, an ancient wisdom of e-learning – it is not enough to provide a technical surrounding that makes learning possible. The content and the methods have to fit in with the learning environment. Secondly, and this is not new either, face-to-face teaching and learning is not totally transferrable to a mobile and remote scenario. There are changes, losses, but also gains. One benefit lies in the fact that restrained students can profit from this approach. Those, who usually go by the board in a lively discussion, now have the opportunity to bring in their point of view and receive feedback. Although the spontaneity is lost, the possibility to prepare und to reflect opens new ways of arguing and fits better with the personalities of some learners.

However, classroom discourse cannot be replaced. In cultures and societies that are characterized by heterogeneity, diversity and ambiguity, the skills, promoted by this method, are of high importance. Being able to see different perspectives, understand and adapt them, bring them forward in a socially accepted way is still something, that can be practiced in classroom discourse, which makes it an indispensable part of higher education.

References

Anderson, L. W., & Krathwohl, D. R. (2001). *A taxonomy for learning, teaching and assessing: A revision of Bloom's taxonomy of educational objectives.* Longman.

Cedefop. (2014). *Terminology of European education and training policy: A selection of 130 key terms* (2nd ed.). Publications Office. http://www.cedefop.europa.eu/en/publications-and-resources/publications/4117

Cedefop. (2017). *Defining, writing and applying learning outcomes: A European handbook.* Publications Office. http://dx.doi.org/10.2801/566770

Ehlich, K. (2014). Argumentieren als sprachliche Ressource des diskursiven Lernens. In A. Hornung, G. Carrobio, & D. Sorrentino (Eds.), *Diskursive und textuelle Strukturen in der Hochschuldidaktik: Deutsch und Italienisch im Vergleich* (pp. 41–54). Waxmann.

Gogolin, I. (2008). *Der monolinguale Habitus der multilingualen Schule.* Waxmann.

Grissom, S., McNally, M. F., & Naps, T. (2003). Algorithm visualization in CS education: Comparing levels of student engagement. In S. Diehl & J. Stasko (Eds.), *Proceedings of the 2003 ACM symposium on Software Visualization (SoftVis '03)* (pp. 87–94). Association for Computing Machinery.

Haack, J. (2002). Interaktivität als Kennzeichen von multimedia und hypermedia. In L. J. Issing & P. Klimsa (Eds.), *Information und Lernen mit Multimedia und Internet. Lehrbuch für Studium und Praxis* (pp. 127–136). Beltz PVU.

Krumm, H.-J., & Jenkins, E.-M. (2001). *Kinder und ihre Sprachen – Lebendige Mehrsprachigkeit.* eviva.

Lemke, J. L. (1990). *Talking science: Language, learning, and values.* Greenwood.

Ong, W. J. (1982). *Orality and literacy.* Methuen.

Redder, A. (2014). Wissenschaftssprache – Bildungssprache – Lehr-Lerndiskurs. In A. Hornung, G. Carrobio, & D. Sorrentino (Eds.), *Diskursive und textuelle Strukturen in der Hochschuldidaktik: Deutsch und Italienisch im Vergleich* (pp. 25–40). Waxmann.

CHAPTER 13

Afterword

Suzanne Majhanovich and Allan Pitman

As this Afterword is being written, the Omicron variant of COVID-19 is becoming rampant across the world and the daily growth of new cases is an alarming indication that the pandemic is not over, will continue to disrupt all elements of society, and perhaps will become endemic, forcing permanent adjustments to everyday life. We will not be returning to life as we knew it in the near future, if ever. In the context of this volume, it is helpful to revisit the messages and suggestions provided in the various chapters for addressing the reality of the pandemic as it has affected higher education and speculate on the success of the actions taken to ensure sustainability of higher education and its mission in society in the future. As we reflect on the contributions of this volume, we contextualize our discussion in terms of the institutional issues brought to the fore at the meta, meso and micro levels

1 Institutional Issues

The various chapters have focused on particular issues that higher education institutions have had to address in coping with the situation created by the pandemic. By proposing Education in Emergencies (EiE) as an organizing principle, as introduced in Chapter 2, Leihy, Freeman, Teo & Kim, provide the opportunity to consider both the negative, perhaps traumatic effects of a crisis but, equally importantly, the ways in which such a set of conditions can act in a transformative way. As they describe ways in which both industrialized highly developed countries and developing economies have addressed the nine areas in their Education in Emergencies model, it is interesting to note how in some cases developing nations have been better able to rise to the challenges than would have been expected. It will be instructive to trace how Higher Education institutions whether in developed or developing countries can sustain the solutions they have come up with to cope with the disruptions. In this Afterward, we have found it useful to borrow some ideas from the Annales school of social historians and elaborated by Ladurie (1981, pp. 270–289), who describes the crisis to include forms of disruptions due, among other events, to pandemics and their demographic, social and economic effects. An important

© KONINKLIJKE BRILL NV, LEIDEN, 2022 | DOI:10.1163/9789004512672_013

consideration for us in the present circumstances is that a crisis need not be of short duration. How universities adapt to and adopt new conditions which may not settle to a stable "normal" for some time – even decades – is a matter for conjecture at this time

With the shift to the funding of the public universities in developed nations moving over the past several decades from models of government-funded institutions to one of government-supported bodies, the reliance on cash flow generated from the entrepreneurial selling of student places to foreign, full fee-paying customers has rendered them vulnerable to sudden changes in this source of revenue. This dependency is unevenly spread across universities and, within them, across departments and programs. This provides a degree of instability in the employment status of instructors, principally those on contract, but also for tenured and tenure track faculty in vulnerable units.

The responses of governments to the COVID-19 pandemic led to major disruptions in the operation of universities around the world, with the closure of on-campus activities for an extended period. The clearest model available to enable teaching to continue was to make as many activities as were possible available to students while excluding them from the live campuses. In this, there was a huge disparity between institutions as to their readiness and capacity to shift resources and instructors rapidly to on-line course construction and presentation. In developed countries, very frequently a mix of on-campus, on-line and mixed models of course delivery were already in place. Many had professional IT course development personnel already in place, experienced in working with faculty in the construction of these courses. As has been pointed out in several chapters, it is the hope of instructors and teachers that things will eventually return to normal; that they coped with the new modes of course delivery because they had to, but the preference is for in-person programs and the way things were before the pandemic struck. However, it seems to be accepted that in future programs will be blended in nature, delivered partially, as in the past, in person on campus, partially through digital platforms. Various authors in the volume have concluded that the blended approach is advantageous, not only from the financial benefits to the institution to offer programs digitally, but also that it has actually improved and strengthened course delivery overall. The fact that the pandemic does not show signs of abating seems to imply that the adjustments made by higher education institutions to their programs were not only absolutely necessary but will probably continue for the foreseeable future.

The changes wrought as a consequence of the pandemic cannot be assumed to have equal long-term effects on the ways in which instructors go about their work. Some innovations will become permanent, others will be seen as short-term solutions to a transient situation. Others will continue, but with further modification to sit beside a mix of teaching-learning environments. Indeed, as Kozlov, Levina and Tregubova point out (Chapter 3), pressures to transform the university were already mounting, due to the massification of post-secondary education, the increasing digitization of courses and their roles in the global economy; COVID-19 served as a catalyst to hasten needed change.

Within any one country's system of post-secondary education, much will depend on the degree to which individual university administrations take up the new technologies and provide adequate resources for instructors in the form of qualified personnel, access to on-line modalities and equipment for them to prepare and deliver course content and engage in interaction to their students. This again will vary widely, given ideologies and embedded theories about teaching and learning, as well as financial resources. There is the potential for a further widening of gaps between the rich countries and their institutions and the less economically developed countries.

2   At the Meta Level: National System, Governmental

At the national level, governments and their education systems responded to the crisis in a range of interesting ways which in some ways reflected the relationship between central organization and relative independence of institutions. In China the government has supported a network providing open access to top-quality online courses throughout the country (see Delcroix-Tang, Chapter 4). In Turkey, digital provision of school and post-secondary education was heavily digitized in central areas prior to the pandemic (see Pembecioğlu, Chapter 5). In response to the crisis the bandwidth available to the Ministry of Education was expanded to accommodate the expansion in course delivery over the internet. The government, through the Council of Higher Education and Ministry of Education, promoted the Digital Transformation Project in Higher Education which developed a Distance Education Platform, largely centred at Sakarya University but made available to 15 other universities in the network.

3   At the Meso Level: Individual Institutions; In-house Solutions

Regarding the expectations of instructors, it is noted that instructors tend to see the return to on-campus activities, including the lecture in the "new normal".

AFTERWORD

This speaks to institutional traditions and well-established practices. The lecture has been the historical essence of knowledge transmission in universities, along with the tutorial/seminar. The lecture has evolved in interaction with technologies of the time: the overhead projector, the microphone, the PowerPoint presentation, student interactive devices (voting). Woodcock (in Chapter 7), makes the point that the traditional lecture was already coming under critique in light of the possibilities offered by new technologies of communication and the outside experiences with digital materials of the newer generations of students of so-called "digital natives." It is noteworthy that Ricci and Luppi (Chapter 8) report the view of colleagues at the University of Bologna that the lecture "is not dead," but will continue enhanced by "a variety of on-line measures." The degree to which they see the lecture transformed in any significant way is moot. This view is reflected in the readjustments described at the University of Sanya in China (Delcroix-Tang, Chapter 4). Kozlov, Levina and Tregubova draw attention, however, to the potential for the loss of what they call the "upbringing potential", or something like Bildung, because the distancing could result from an over-reliance on digital approaches which lacks the human personal factor.

Some universities were, prior to the COVID-19 crisis, already well immersed in the digital models of course delivery, as illustrated by the Romanian case of West University of Timişoara. Crăciun and Oprescu (Chapter 6) provide a good example of how processes already in place were able to be adapted quickly by stepping up training support for instructors and students, given the material conditions were already in place. It is also interesting to observe the changes amplified in the teacher education programme not only in delivery modalities but also in the content as it related to the changing relation of teacher, students and technologies in the future work of the potential school teachers in the programme.

The Chinese study (Delcroix-Tang, Chapter 4) gives some insight into the short and long-term possibilities for transformation. This is possible because of the severe measures taken by the Chinese government to suppress the spread of the virus and the subsequent reopening of campuses after a relatively short period. The initial period involved a "bumpy" switch to on-line course presentation and access to materials from other institutions in their network, with high stress levels due to feelings of lack of expertise and knowledge in working on-line. This was succeeded by a mix of return to traditional on-campus work and mixed on-campus/digital activity. However, with new variants of the virus and breakouts appearing across the globe, it remains to be seen whether campuses in China, for example, will be able to remain open for instruction following a more traditional approach to program delivery. The on-line course development will no doubt have to undergo refinement as higher education institutions are forced to rely increasingly on digital formats, virtual learning and the like to sustain their programs as the pandemic continues.

4 At the Micro Level of the Faculty Member

The pandemic's effects on the wellbeing of faculty members do not occur in a vacuum. The past decades have seen significant shifts in the nature of university education and the socio-political location of universities. Increasingly, instruction is being undertaken by contract personnel without tenure, or even the expectation of long-term employment. The existence of Departments and programs is becoming more dependent on student numbers as business models of these institutions move from supply side provision to demand side operation, with the concomitant competition for students. Evaluation of instructors – and for many their continued employment – has become closely tied to student perceptions. This evaluative aspect is further complicated by universities' obsessions with international and national rankings which place strong emphasis on research productivity. A clear stressor in the pandemic crisis has been the difficulty in balancing academics' research output with the additional time and energy devoted to dealing with the forced changes in their teaching responsibilities. What appears at first to be a paradox emerges from studies of instructor wellbeing when job satisfaction and burnout are studied (Beltman, Sheffield & Hascher, Chapter 9). It was possible for instructors to express well-being with regard to success in implementation of the new digital method of course delivery while facing the precariousness of their position when the institution did not renew the contract putting an instructor out of work. On reflection, however, it is not unreasonable to see that the work itself might be rewarding and satisfying intrinsically, but the institutional and crisis pressures should interact to increase stress levels and burnout. The dual nature of a crisis is worth noting here: A time of disruption can lead to both positive as well as negative outcomes. One such example is the increased focus in some institutions on support to faculty in becoming confident in the application of the technologies available for enhancing their teaching and course presentation.

Ilardo and Cuconato (Chapter 10) also place the stresses on faculty in the context of the changing role of the university with respect to the massification of post-secondary education and introduce a further pressure: the shift in emphasis on the nature of knowledge from the acquisition of knowledge for long-term qualification to the establishment of the capacity for life-long

AFTERWORD

learning – including skills associated with digitization. It is one thing to become comfortable and adept with the new instructional technologies; it is quite another to come to terms with the new role instructors play in this form of program delivery. They suggest that the identity of instructors is changing from that of "sage on the stage" imparting knowledge to passive student recipients to learning facilitator interacting with students who in some ways guide the learning process. For some instructors the ability to undergo transformation of their identity will be a challenge and may determine whether they can play a role in the Knowledge Society. The COVID-19 pandemic has accelerated the changes.

The closure of campuses for periods of up to a year forced instructors into the need to do the work that usually occurred on-campus to be performed at home. While this might be seen as an advantage in the saving in travel and time, it came at a cost. Faculty were unable to interact directly with peers. Domestic needs and distractions such as caring for children unable to attend school but themselves being taught on-line, and finding a suitable place to work introduced a set of issues which, while not entirely new in all cases, became significant causes for concern (see Watson, Singh & Nair, Chapter 11). For some, the reliability and strength of internet access available from home was problematic. These factors presented themselves on top of dealing with personal fears about the virus and varying degrees of confidence in skills for on-line instruction. Watson, Singh & Nair report that the instructors who had no choice but to adapt to the on-line modalities despite problems inherent in working from home nevertheless felt they handled the transformation well for the time being. However, how sustainable is this approach as the pandemic does not end and the prospect of closed campuses continues? These authors caution that institutions will have to take into account the professional and personal needs of academics and put into place initiatives to support their well-being.

Various chapters in the volume have detailed innovative ways in which on-line courses have been developed to include active interaction between the instructor and the students as well as other technological features incorporating virtual learning for example, to make digital learning more like real face-to-face classes and practicum experiences. Beatrix Kreß (Chapter 12), however, reminds us that the speed with which universities had to move their programs totally to digital platforms meant that many on-line courses did in fact replicate transmission models of teaching which are not the most conducive to the learning experience. Furthermore, she notes that face-to-face experience is not directly transferrable. Overall, she reminds us that there are losses in the mobile and remote teaching environment but also the possibility for some gains. If the on-line courses have elements to allow for interaction through video-conferencing with break out rooms and chat features, timid students who might have avoided participating in vibrant classroom discussion can quietly express their opinions and receive immediate feedback from the instructor. She contends that although spontaneity is lost in the new way of teaching and that classroom discourse is not easily replaced in on-line course, nevertheless, if certain features are included in the digital class, other important features of learning such as the change to prepare and reflect on issues and present arguments in a safe environment can be beneficial for both students and instructors.

5   Concluding Comments

We do not know what will be the medium and long term aftermaths of the COVID-19 pandemic. It is only the subject of speculation whether, like the so-called Spanish Influenza of the early twentieth century, it fades away or changes its relation to us from one of pandemic to being endemic with successive variants being countered through vaccines or other measures. This is an important consideration in the speculation as to what the future holds for university teaching, the image that instructors have of themselves and their students, and the types of institutional supports which will be necessary for their wellbeing.

To return to the *Annales* School, a metaphor of societal and institutional change and stability that comes to mind is that of an ocean. Events occur as surface waves; there are currents that flow that move aspects over time, often circulating but never as identical on their cycles; below are the still waters which stay unchanged. Crisis occurs in the form of an ocean floor eruption which stirs the still waters and manifests itself as surface disruptions. In time things settle, carrying the pre-eruption past, but changed. So we may think of universities and the roles played by the instructors within them. We have yet to see how that future will unfold.

Reference

Ladurie, E. (1981). *The mind and method of the historian* (S. Reynolds & B. Reynolds, Trans.). University of Chicago Press.

Index

access to education   20, 38, 69, 86, 88, 90–92, 147, 168

case study   7, 8, 50, 55, 56, 62, 112, 115, 122
COVID-19 pandemic   VII, 1, 2, 5–11, 15, 16, 20–22, 27, 28, 31, 32, 35–37, 39, 40, 43, 46, 47, 54–56, 59, 60, 63–66, 68, 85, 86, 88, 100, 101, 104, 110, 112, 122, 131, 132, 134, 143, 144, 148, 150, 151, 153–155, 157–161, 166–168, 171, 181–183, 185, 186

digital learning   64, 77, 89, 151, 185
digitalization   5, 6, 31–36, 59, 60, 63, 66, 69, 74, 75, 77, 147
distance learning   1, 4, 8, 11, 34, 36, 37, 39, 64, 67, 72, 76, 88, 92, 107, 113, 115, 116, 120–124, 177

educational research   160
emergency remote teaching   1, 2, 4, 89, 96

facilitators   10, 152–155, 185
flexible learning   60, 61, 65, 90, 96
formative educational evaluation   113, 116, 117
future proposals and lessons   167

higher education   1–8, 10–12, 15–24, 26–28, 31–34, 36–38, 50, 43, 46–50, 53, 55, 56, 59, 60, 63, 65, 66, 68–70, 72–79, 102, 104, 124, 131, 147, 157–161, 163, 167–169, 171, 172, 178, 180–182, 184
higher education for sustainable development (HESD)   6, 46–50, 53, 55, 56
higher education in emergencies domains (HEED)   17–19
higher education policy and practice   15, 18
higher education systems   5, 15, 17, 20, 21, 26, 28, 75

innovation in learning and teaching   8, 113, 114, 116, 124
integrated approach   48, 51

knowledge society   10, 147–150, 155, 185

lockdown   1, 4, 8, 27, 55, 65, 73, 104, 106, 109, 110, 112–114, 124, 158, 168

national development   52

online education   6, 40, 63, 64, 66, 91, 96, 117
open source technologies   85

quality system   6, 46, 56

re-education of educators   31, 35
reflective practices   10, 154

student-centered   4, 6, 51–54, 56, 62, 64, 74, 149, 153
support   VIII, 3, 9–11, 16–18, 22, 23, 25, 28, 35, 37, 40, 48, 53, 54, 61, 63, 68, 74, 77, 86, 95, 102, 103, 106, 108, 109, 114, 116, 123, 132–134, 136, 137, 140–144, 148, 149, 153–155, 159, 162–165, 168, 183–186

teacher(s)   1, 3–5, 7–11, 20, 33–42, 46, 53, 54, 61–63, 66, 68, 69, 71, 72, 74, 85–96, 114, 115, 119, 121–124, 131, 132, 134, 141–143, 148–155, 162, 171, 181, 183
teacher training program   7, 35, 85–88, 94, 95
teachers' new roles   10, 33, 39
teaching and learning discourse   172
technology   VIII, 2, 4, 7, 10, 12, 17, 27, 36–39, 52, 55, 56, 61, 64, 77, 85–88, 92, 93, 95, 96, 101, 102, 104–106, 108, 110, 148, 150, 151, 153–155, 160–162, 165
transformative shift   48, 55, 56

university   VII–IX, 1, 3, 5–9, 11, 25, 26, 31, 32, 35, 37–43, 47, 50, 52, 54, 55, 60, 63, 64, 66, 67, 69–74, 76–79, 85–93, 95, 96, 100–103, 106–110, 112–116, 122, 124, 131–134, 136, 140–144, 147, 148, 150, 153, 159, 160, 164, 165, 172, 182–184, 186 video conferences in higher education 167, 175

wellbeing VII, 4, 8–10, 131, 132, 134, 135, 137–144, 168, 184–186

working from home
benefits 161, 165
challenges 161
sustainability 161, 165